There and Back:
Living & Learning Abroad

There and Back:
Living & Learning Abroad

Calvin PRESS
COLLEGE
Grand Rapids, MI • calvincollegepress.com

Published 2015 by the Calvin College Press
3201 Burton St. SE
Grand Rapids, MI 49546

Publisher's Cataloging-in-Publication data

Names: DeGraaf, Donald G., author.
Title: There and back : living and learning abroad / Donald G. DeGraaf.
Description: Grand Rapids, Michigan: The Calvin College Press, 2015. | Includes bibliographical references and index.

Identifiers: ISBN 978-1-937555-02-3 (pbk.) | LCCN 2015955800

Subjects: LCSH: Foreign study--Handbooks, manuals, etc. | American students--Foreign countries--Handbooks, manuals, etc. | Christian college students--United States. | Christian universities and colleges--United States.

Classification: LCC: LB2376 .D39 2015 | DDC 370.116--dc23

Front cover design: Scott Laumann
Interior design and typeset: Katherine Lloyd, The DESK

This book is dedicated to the memory of a dear friend and colleague, June DeBoer, who over the years was a constant encouragement as she challenged and equipped students to find their calling while pursuing their dreams. For many students, these dreams included study abroad. June helped them see their experiences as an opportunity to learn to dwell well in God's amazing world.

Contents

Part Three: Returning Home

THERE IS TREASURE EVERYWHERE

Something hidden. Go and find it.
Go and look behind the Ranges –
Something lost behind the Ranges.
Lost and waiting for you. Go!
–Rudyard Kipling

You have picked up this book because Rudyard Kipling's words ring true. You want to go and look behind the ranges. You want to find something hidden. You want to travel and study abroad. An adventure, an unknown place, new experiences — all these are waiting for you to explore. Kipling nicely describes the wonder of travel. Yet his words also lead to deeper questions about its purpose: what is the "something" that is hidden? If you go, will you find it? Will you know how to look? How should you prepare for the journey?

This book gathers up these questions and asks, what does it mean to study abroad well? How can you embrace the tensions of living and learning in a new place? How can you explore new places and also become rooted to where you are studying? How can you develop a supportive community with your fellow students and also engage the people and culture of your host community? How can you study well and also travel well? How can you learn to open your eyes and heart to God's amazing world?

As a director of off-campus programs at a small liberal arts Christian college, I think these are important questions for you and for faculty who lead study abroad experiences. When we travel, our experiences in a new environment can be so exciting and so overwhelming that at times we forget to ask how they might help us to grow spiritually. We forget to ask the questions that can transform our lives. As one colleague noted, "Will the mere experience of jumping on a plane, train, or bus provide transformative opportunities? Can some travel be better or worse than other travel? And specifically for those of us from faith-based higher education, what impact does the journey have on students' faith and worldview?"[1]

Fortunately, the experiential nature of studying abroad lends itself to deep learning when we are intentional about our objectives and open to the teachable moments that emerge as we engage new people, places, and cultures.

Recently I visited with students studying in Budapest and discovered they were in the middle of a small domestic crisis. Who was going to clean the tiny kitchen they all had to use to cook their meals? How often? How well? Living in community is hard, and the aggravation of sharing their cooking space had left the group disgruntled. The next evening we all set out on a walking tour of the eighth district of Budapest, which had been scheduled as part of their weekly class.

Our tour guide, Andy, was young and spoke excellent English. He had a wonderful sense of humor and had even served as a camp counselor in Boone, Iowa. Who would have guessed? He was passionate about Budapest and the lessons we might learn as we walked the eighth district.

We started at the National Museum where Andy introduced the tour by encouraging each of us to look deeply on our walk, for there was "treasure" everywhere in the buildings and people we would encounter, but much of this treasure was now hidden. He explained that although the eighth district was outside the original walls of the city of Pest, it had been an important and diverse neighborhood. Throughout its history, the eighth district had housed palaces and slums, battlefields and churches, rich and poor, Jews and Roma. It had been the scene of intense fighting during World War II between Russian and German troops, and it had served as the backdrop for much of the 1956 revolution against communism that was brutally crushed by the Russian army.

As dusk turned into darkness, we were exposed to the beauty and brokenness of this wonderful neighborhood. Then Andy stopped and asked us to look. On one side of the street stood a beautiful, newly renovated hotel, while on the other side we saw an old, once glamorous mansion that was now nothing more than a rundown building. "We're going to walk into this battle-scarred building," Andy said, and he asked us to remember his challenge to look for treasure everywhere.

We walked into the vestibule and began to look around. We saw crumbling walls, but we also began to find beauty. The steps were marble, the wrought iron railings artistically made, but when we looked up, we saw the real beauty above our heads. A magnificent fresco was painted on the ceiling; it was breathtaking. As Andy stood at the top of the stairs, holding his cellphone pointed at the ceiling to better illuminate the fresco, he told us the following story.

After the communists arrived, this glamorous house was confiscated and subdivided into a number of small apartments. The fresco on the ceiling was covered with cheap paint. Over the years, the once beautiful building fell apart and eventually was scheduled to be torn down. Then someone noticed the paint peeling off the ceiling and that something lay beneath this layer of paint. The cheap paint had preserved a fresco. Here was hidden beauty if only you had the eyes to search it out and find it.

As Andy pointed out the fresco, he made a passionate plea for his people and culture to find beauty not just in old buildings but also in other people — the Jew, the Roma, the person who is different. I looked around the dimly lighted corridor and realized that we were comparing the broken down building, the cheap paint, and the beautiful fresco to the dingy-kitchen squabble that had marred our day together. I saw students thinking about how hard it is to live in community, to look below the surface, to see the wonder of each person, and to move beyond petty grievances to discover the beauty God has created.

It was a lovely, serendipitous moment that often happens in off-campus study programs, where lessons come together in ways that make them real and memorable. Our hearts were softened and prepared for the rest of the evening. We met a Roma family and crowded into their living room to hear stories and listen to their music. We shared. We laughed. We sang. We saw the hidden treasures in Budapest in her people, in Andy, and in one another.

This book will help you find treasure everywhere as you study abroad, whether you are taking a short three-week intensive course in Germany or spending a semester in Honduras. We will think about how the lens of faith enables you to see what you might otherwise miss. We will consider the study abroad experience as a pilgrimage, one you take a step at a time, looking around at others and the world as you go.

Think of this book as an interactive journal for you as an individual and as part of a group. Your group may want to read it together and discuss particular questions or the broader themes presented in each chapter. Or you may wish to use the book individually as a prompt for your own journal entries. You'll find blog posts from former students in each chapter. These reflections offer wisdom as you shape your own study abroad experience and also provide the context for the questions you will find throughout the book. Use the reflections and the questions to prepare for your experience, to think deeply about the challenges you'll encounter as you study abroad, to document your own growth, and to explore, affirm, and expand your faith throughout your journey.

This book is divided into three sections. The first section asks you to think about why you want to study abroad, how you will view the overall experience, and how you can prepare for the adventures to come. The second section encourages you to explore a number of possible situations that you may encounter while studying abroad. This section is not meant to be sequential, so feel free to skip around and read chapters as appropriate to your experience. The third section examines how you can apply the lessons learned abroad once you return home. This framework and the opportunity for reflection will remind you that while your particular experiences are unique, you are also sharing a pilgrim journey with others who have been there and back.

The small seashell [🐚] you will find throughout this book is another reminder that you are joining a long tradition of pilgrimage. The scallop shell or *concha de vieira* has long been a symbol of the Camino de Santiago, the pilgrim road to the tomb of St. James the Greater, Santiago de Compostela, in Spain. The shell appears on signposts along the way and is worn by pilgrims themselves as they journey toward their destination in the company of fellow travelers.

I hope this book will be both guide and companion, offering the reassurance that your experiences will be hard, rich, and good and also challenging you to think deeply, act justly, and live wholeheartedly during your time abroad and beyond.[2]

May you find treasure everywhere. Blessings on your path!

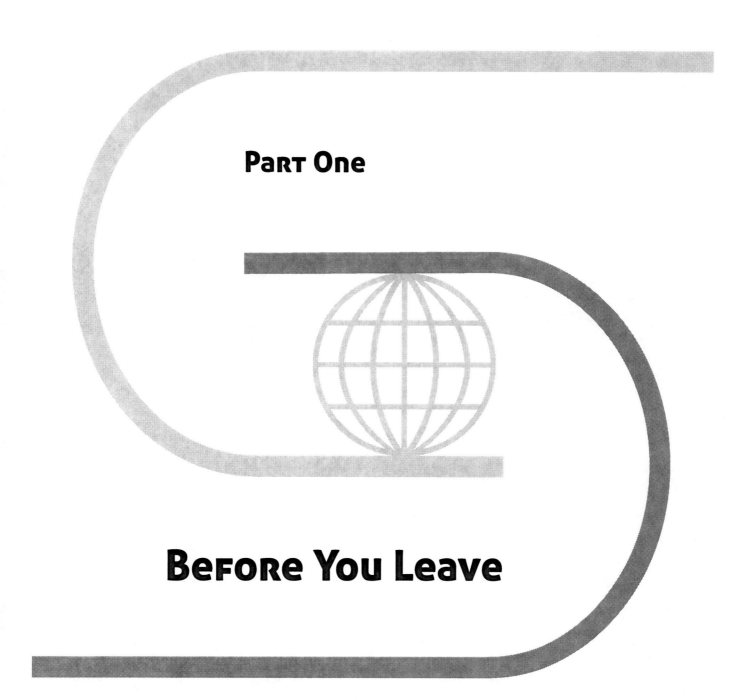

Part One

Before You Leave

Chapter One ——————

WHY STUDY ABROAD? ☉

We travel to bring what little we can, in our ignorance and knowledge,
to those parts of the globe whose riches are differently dispersed.
And we travel, in essence, to become young fools again, to slow
time down and get taken in, and fall in love once more.
–Pico Iyer

You know, it's funny what's happening to us. Our lives have become digital,
our friends now virtual. And everything you could ever want to know is just a
click away. Experiencing the world through endless secondhand information
isn't enough. If we want authenticity, we have to initiate it. We will never know
our full potential unless we push ourselves to find it.
–Curt Morgan

Life is like a box of chocolates.
You never know what you are going to get.
–Forrest Gump

John walked into the study abroad office and blurted out, "I am sick of this place. I grew up here, I am studying here, and I need to leave. Where can I go?" It was late in the semester, but there were still spaces available in the Hungary and Ghana programs. "I have friends going to Hungary," John mused, "but I don't think I should just travel with them or go to Europe. I think it would be better to take the plunge and go to Ghana with eight people I've never met."

This story is not unusual. Although you may know where you want to go or what you want to study, many students know only *that* they want to travel, not where or why. In fact, the first step in choosing a study abroad program is to answer this question: "Why do I want to study abroad?" You may want to pack your bags and leave campus to have an adventure, to study another language or a particular subject, to grow as a person, to experience a new culture, to see the wonders of the world, to meet new people, to get out of your campus bubble, or to have fun.

Whatever your initial goals, there are many resources to help you travel. Guidebooks introduce you to famous places and the cultures of more than 200 nations around the world; internet sites offer travel tips and must-do adventures. However, these resources often cater to tourists who are seeking entertainment, distraction, and escape. This book will help you plan a study abroad experience that can be so much more. It will help you form a better answer to the question, "Why do I want to study abroad?"

TRAVELING WISELY

The ease of travel today has created a paradox. The easier it becomes to travel widely, the harder it becomes to travel *wisely*. We are left with plenty of frequent flyer miles and passport stamps, but we might suspect that our travels, and even our studies abroad, lack something vital. We need to ask *why* and *how* we travel.

Many experienced travel writers, such as Michael McCarthy, are asking these big questions:

> After 30 years of traveling the planet, whether to beaches for well-deserved vacations or to new cities and countries to see the sights, I eventually came to the conclusion that a love of travel is just pointless wandering. Oh, there's nothing wrong with a well-deserved vacation — renting some sunshine after many months of hard work in some dark northern climate where the sun never shines, rejuvenating body and soul — but it seems that so much of what we call tourism is a waste of time. Worse yet, it is extremely damaging to the planet and to many of the people who depend on tourism for their livelihood. Does this mean we should all stay home to save the world from ruination by carbon pollution and exploitation? Not at all. What it means is that if we are going to spend a lot of time and money wandering the world we ought to think a little more deeply about where we go, what we do, and what impact we have upon the people we meet. If your journey has no purpose, why do it?[1]

Similarly in his article "Why We Travel," Pico Iyer suggests that traveling opens our eyes and our minds to truly "feel" the places that we so often hear about or experience virtually through the media. Although we can "travel" around the world with a click of a button, Iyer stresses the importance of physically traveling to a destination, of "leaving all my beliefs and certainties at home, and seeing everything I thought I knew in a different light, and from a crooked angle."[2] At the same time, Iyer acknowledges that we take ourselves with us on our travels. We never enter a new cultural experience without carrying along our own preconceived notions.

For example, Maddie noted in her blog that

I am aware that upon arriving in Ghana, I will envision my own stories about the people that I meet and the places that I visit based on what I have already learned about the history and the socio-economic standing of Ghanaian society. It will be a challenge to act as a complete stranger and remove any assumptions I have about Ghana; however, I will aim to let the people and the places I visit tell the narrative of my new cultural experience rather than let my mind and pre-conceived notions tell a fictional story of Ghanaian life.

Why do you want to study abroad? Why did you pick the program you did? Read Laura's blog post below, written prior to her leaving for a semester in Hungary. Can you relate to her inability to pinpoint why she decided to study abroad?

"Why are you going to Hungary?" If you've talked to me about my trip, you probably asked me that question. And I probably mumbled a generic answer: It's a good program. I've always wanted to go to Europe. It's open to students of any major. It just sounds really, really cool.

In reality, I don't have a definite answer for why I'm going. But here I am, about to embark on this grand, mysterious adventure on another continent, to live in a country where only 20 percent of people speak my language. My general thoughts about the trip haven't gone much past, "This is going to be awesome."...

I've spent so much time looking forward to the fun things that I've forgotten to realize that I won't be the same Laura when I come back. In a small way or a big way, I will be changed. There are new passions, new perspectives, new ways of life to discover here. Perhaps I will fall in love with this place [Budapest] in ways I never thought possible. Perhaps I really will move there someday. How do I know what the future holds?

This is all pretty vague because I still don't know why I'm really going to Hungary or what's in store for me there. But God knows, and I believe he will be working in me through everything. If there's one thing I know, it's that the great Potter's wheel can spin anywhere, and it will most certainly be spinning in Budapest, Hungary.

What role did your faith play in your desire to study abroad? Was there a direct link, as presented by the student reflection below, or was it more of an underlying factor? How would you like to see your faith affected by your experience?

The reasons behind my study abroad experience usually elicit confused faces and awkward silences as people struggle to find words to respond. I went because God

Do you agree with Iyer that we should leave behind our beliefs and certainties? How might you respond to the question, why do people need to travel?

As you reflect on your upcoming study abroad experience, how do you think it will be similar to traveling as a tourist? In what ways will it be different?

Take a moment and search online using the key words *why we travel*. Read some of the top responses and summarize them. Which responses resonate with you and why?

told me to. I am aware of how strange that sounds – especially for people who have different beliefs than I do. It is okay to think it is weird. . . . I thought it was strange, too, but through my relationship with God I knew it was what I had to do. Even though it made no sense to me at the time, I knew I had to trust God's wisdom over mine. I had to be inner-directed at this point; I could not let others or even cultural norms make the decision for me.[3]

Answering these questions can lead you to understand some of your motives for studying abroad and also encourage you to consider how your faith will affect your overall experience. Although you might not use the phrase, "God told me to study abroad," the idea of being "called" by God to study abroad is an important concept to explore. How might a sense of calling affect your overall experience? How might it cause you to think about the experience in a different light?

METAPHORS WE LIVE BY

Another way to think about studying abroad is to consider what metaphor or image might describe your experience. George Lakoff and Mark Johnson in *Metaphors We Live By* claim that metaphors are so pervasive in our everyday lives that they actually organize how we think and how we act. Metaphors give us ways to understand our experiences. But Lakoff and Johnson also suggest that changing a metaphor can drastically change our overall experience. Take for instance the common metaphor "argument is war." Do these expressions sound familiar?

> "Your claims are *indefensible*.
> He *attacked every weak point* in my argument.
> His criticisms were *right on target*.
> You disagree? Okay, *shoot!*
> He *shot down* all my arguments."[4]

You may be shocked to realize how easily and how often you fall into war-like behavior when you are arguing. Lakoff and Johnson claim that not only do we structure our arguments around the "argument is war" metaphor but also the ways in which we act:

> We can actually win or lose arguments. We see the person we are arguing with as an opponent. . . . Though there is no physical battle, there is a verbal battle, and the structure of an argument — attack, defense, counterattack, etc. — reflects

this. It is in this sense that the ARGUMENT IS WAR metaphor is one that we live by in this culture; it structures the actions we perform in arguing.[5]

Once we begin to understand how metaphors shape our language *and* our interactions, we realize that if we change a metaphor, we can also change our behavior. So instead of seeing argument as war, we can perhaps see it as dance. With that metaphor we no longer feel compelled to win or lose since we see that it takes two people working together to frame an argument as a dance. One person responds to the lead of a partner, following his or her points and answering the moves made by the other. There is an element of compromise, of working together to inform and learn from each other.

In the process of imagining a different point of view, of creating a new metaphor, we can open ourselves up to new possibilities, to see things the way they really are, or to imagine the way they could and should be. Citing Etienne Wenger, David Smith and Susan Felch point out that

> even when our outward behaviors appear similar, what is in our imagination may change our sense of what we are doing, and so our experience of doing it. [Wenger] asks us to imagine encountering two stonecutters at work, and asking them what they are doing. One of them replies, "I am cutting this stone in perfectly square shape." The other, apparently carrying out the same action, says, "I am building a cathedral." In terms of chisel-holding skills, there may be little difference between the two of them. They are, however, experiencing what they are doing differently. As a result they may well be learning quite dissimilar things from the activity, even growing into different people.[6]

This process of changing our mental metaphors in order to change our behavior is supported in psychological literature, where some have theorized that we all have a schema through which we see the world and ourselves.[7] Within this schema we tend to look for evidence that confirms our assumptions. If we see our work simply as cutting stones, we may see ourselves treading an endless wheel, doing what others tell us, and having little control over our lives. We find confirming evidence of this schema as we focus on what our boss says, and we may blame our job for health concerns, stress, and lack of fulfillment. However, if we change our schema and see our work as building cathedrals, that work takes on new meaning. We are part of something larger than ourselves, and work becomes a place of fulfillment and pleasure.

Metaphors, in other words, can serve as a frame or schema for your study abroad program. Being intentional about the metaphors you use can change the ways you see and the ways you actually experience the months you spend in another country. For instance, how might you exchange the metaphor of the "grand tour" to faraway lands or the metaphor of being a tourist for a richer metaphor? How might you look for new frameworks that will lead to new thoughts and behaviors?

To get you started, here are three different metaphors for the study abroad experience. As you explore each metaphor, think about the ways each one unleashes your imagination to view the study abroad experience in a new light.

STUDY ABROAD IS A JOURNEY

The journey metaphor is similar to thinking about your time abroad as a tourist or traveller, but it adds nuance and depth to those images. The journey theme is already a familiar part of our lives:

> They remembered the *departed* in their prayers.
> His life *took an unexpected direction*.
> I've tried being reasonable, and I don't want to *go down that road* again.
> I'd like to *return* to what David was saying earlier.
> He always says things in a *roundabout* way.
> This term, we will be *exploring* the psychology of sport.
> It is an excellent *guide* to English vocabulary.
> For more information, *visit* our website.

Although it is familiar, we can also see how the journey metaphor can help us better understand our lives. Journeys are all about movement, departures, and arrivals. They are about the process as well as the end result. In their book *Teaching and Christian Imagination*, David Smith and Susan Felch remind us of some possible implications of thinking about study abroad experiences in terms of journey. The journey metaphor, they write,

> encourages us to imagine learning as taking us away from our origins into new lands, requiring us to let go of some cherished attachments and embrace the new experiences and the new sense of self that arise along the way. . . . Plans for learning become maps and progress reports; we find ourselves looking forward to crossing thresholds and reaching milestones and destinations.

Journey-talk raises questions of where we begin, what direction we choose, which maps we will trust, and what wonders, dangers, and distractions might lie along the way. It may also nudge us to think in terms of traveling companions and needed encouragement.[8]

If you think of study abroad as a journey, your role as student requires active participation as you interact with people and places along the journey. The role of your professor or teacher becomes that of a guide, and together you gain an appreciation of the journey itself rather than thinking merely about its ultimate destination. You can also travel hopefully with a sense of purpose and belonging while acknowledging that learning never stops and the journey continues. In the words of Robert Louis Stevenson, "To travel hopefully is a better thing than to arrive."[9]

STUDY ABROAD IS A HEMP ROPE

Hemp rope is made from the long fibrous threads of the hemp plant that are twisted together with thousands of other threads to create a strong cord. If each of these threads represents an individual student's life story, we can see how when you study abroad your life story is twisted together with others to tell the collective story of your group. Additional threads are added as the group interacts with others in the host country. As these threads accumulate, the rope grows thicker to include stories of the community where your home college or university is located, stories of the university and community abroad where you will be studying, stories of people you meet as you travel. If you look closely, you will be able to see God's bigger story of what is going on in the world and how each of our lives intertwines with this story.

In *A Million Miles in a Thousand Years: What I Learned While Editing My Life*, Donald Miller makes the case that God wants us to live great stories. But he also reminds us that

> The point of a story is never about the ending. . . . It's about your character getting molded in the hard work of the middle. . . . It's as though God is saying, *Write a good story, take somebody with you, and let me help.*[10]

Seeing study abroad as a tightly twisted hemp rope composed of many stories can help you understand the importance of learning from others and seeing how their lives are intricately connected through the larger telling of God's story in this world. Students, professors, and everyone you come into contact with become actors in God's unfolding story. You begin to see how you can build a great story that joins with the bigger story of your program, college, local community, the universal church, and ultimately God's work in his world. Emily, who grasps this metaphor, writes:

> We thrive in our relationships with each other, with our wonderful Peruvian families and friends, with professors, and even with strangers that we encounter when we wander through the city. . . . We thrive in the everyday challenges, the chances to change and grow in Arequipa. Every day we are presented with opportunities to observe and learn new things, and all at a level I have never before experienced in my life.
>
> Author David Smith phrased this idea beautifully in his book, Learning from the Stranger.
>
>> If we find ourselves among the privileged, members of a dominant language and culture, used to thinking of ourselves as the center and "foreigners" as oddities at the margins, then Jesus' call to "go and do likewise" has a different ring. Its undertones whisper: humble yourself. Realize your own need of mercy. Realize that God does not choose to live tamely within the circles of belonging that you draw. Learn from those who are of other cultures; God may be at work in them in ways that you desperately need.[11]
>
> I have discovered so many ways in which I desperately need to "learn from the stranger" here in Peru. God has thrown these opportunities in front of us at the most surprising moments.
>
> One of these moments occurred during mass in a Catholic cathedral, of all places. A Peruvian friend had brought me to the cathedral to observe the mass with her. As I sat beneath the intricately decorated cathedral ceiling, I noticed long lines of people, whole families, gathering in the side aisles. They were waiting silently to confess their sins to the priests. I knew this Catholic practice but had never seen it. I was equally intrigued and humbled. How many of us take the time every week to actively humble ourselves before God and confess specific sins before him as these Peruvians were doing? Do we actively concentrate on his mercy to forgive and his power to restore our souls every day? I am not always so dedicated, not like these Peruvian Catholics. This was a crucial lesson that I needed to learn in that cathedral.
>
> There are many moments like these for us, moments in which we learn something from the Peruvians that we might not have otherwise learned back at home. Every day, among the craziness, the frustrations, and the triumphs, we are presented with these opportunities to grow mentally and spiritually. We are oh so very blessed by our gracious God! He is "directing our paths" in astonishing ways.

STUDY ABROAD IS A BLANK CANVAS

The image of a blank canvas simultaneously stirs excitement and dread. On the one hand, a blank canvas is an opportunity to mold an experience into your own masterpiece. As Ross Morley writes, "Travel is like a giant blank canvas, and the painting on the canvas is only limited by one's imagination."[12] On the other hand, the endless possibilities of a blank canvas can also bring anxiety as you wonder where to start, what to include, and what to exclude.

Just as perspective is important for the artist, you must work to understand the angles from which you see your experience. As you think about study abroad as a blank canvas, you become the inventor, the artist, the person in control. Your professor might be seen as either a mentor or an art critic waiting to see how the canvas will be filled. And what about God's role? In what ways does God enter the picture or direct the process?

MOVING FORWARD

Think about your own life story in light of the following excerpt from David James Duncan's book *River Teeth*. Duncan is talking about the way a tree decomposes in a river, releasing its nutrients back to the river and soil in a natural cycle of life and death. Then he notes,

> There are, however, parts of every drowned tree that refuse to become part of the cycle. There is, in every log, a series of cross-grained, pitch-hardened masses where long-lost branches once joined the tree's trunk. "Knots," they're called, in a piece of lumber. But in a bed of a river, after the parent log has broken down and vanished, these stubborn masses take on a very different appearance, and so perhaps deserve a different name. "River teeth" is what we called them as kids, because that's what they look like. . . .
>
> Our memory of experience, our individual pasts, are like trees fallen in a river. . . . And a story — a good shared story — is a transfusion of nutrients from the old river log of memory into the eternal now of life. But as the current of time keeps flowing, the aging log begins to break down. Once-vivid impressions begin to rot. Years run together. . . . Chunks of the log begin to vanish, completely. . . .
>
> There are, however, small parts of every human past that resist this natural cycle: there are hard, cross-grained whorls of memory that remain

Which of the metaphors described in this chapter appeals to you the most? Why? How does each help you to view the study abroad experience differently?

How would you finish this statement: "For me, study abroad is . . ."? Once you have completed the statement, explain why this metaphor appeals to you. What insights does it provide as you think about studying abroad? How might this metaphor help you to see the study abroad experience in a new way? How might your metaphor inspire you in positive directions that enable this experience to help you become the kind of person God wants you to be?

inexplicably lodged in us long after the straight grained narrative material that housed them has washed away. . . . These are our "river teeth" — the time defying knots of experience that remain in us after most of our autobiographies are gone.[13]

🐚 What are the river teeth of your life? What are the river teeth of your faith journey? These are the stories you will bring with you as you travel abroad.

🐚 Think about your own life story and which river teeth you might be willing to share with your classmates and those you meet during your study abroad. Your story should communicate, "This is why I am who I am." The story could be about a person, a place, an event, or a time that has been formative in your own development.

🐚 Think about returning to these questions after you have been abroad for a month. What new metaphors (if any) have emerged for you? Have any new river teeth become a part of your life story?

Chapter Two

Seeing Study Abroad as Pilgrimage

*Pilgrimage is . . . a physical, emotional and spiritual journey
that goes inward, upward and outward. . . .
Pilgrimage is a spiritual practice that reminds us
of our sacred purpose – to grow closer to God.*
–Christian George

*Travel is about attitude and aspiration as much as about geography.
What is at stake is not discovering distant countries and exotic habits,
but making the move out of ordinary space and time.*
–Leonard Biallas

The impulse to move and to travel is age-old, and the practice of pilgrimage lies deep in the heart of many cultures and nearly every major religion of the world. In any given year, as Sheryl Kujawa-Holbrook notes, "millions of Hindus and Buddhists will journey to the banks of the river Ganges at Varanasi, India, in the hope of healing and spiritual rebirth. In the West, five million Christians will go to the shrine dedicated to the Virgin Mary in Lourdes, France, also hoping for healing and spiritual renewal. In Europe alone, more than six thousand sacred sites will receive between seventy and one hundred million pilgrims. Each year two million Muslims will make the journey to Mecca, the most holy city of the faith, to fulfill their religious obligations to visit once in their lifetime. Furthermore every year over four million people will travel to the National September 11 Memorial and Museum in New York City to remember the tragedy that occurred there in 2001."[1]

In chapter one, we explored three metaphors for study abroad. In this chapter, we will take our time to consider pilgrimage as a metaphor that can both deepen and enrich your overall experience. Indeed, the metaphor of pilgrimage will structure the rest of this book. While you may not anticipate visiting shrines, going to bathe in holy rivers, or traveling to Jerusalem or Mecca, seeing your study abroad experience as a pilgrimage offers you the opportunity to explore what God wants to teach you through your upcoming journey, to move inward, upward, and outward as the epigram from Christian George reminds us.

MOVING FROM TOURISTS TO PILGRIMS

The mindset of a pilgrim is very different from that of a tourist. A tourist seeks to escape from his or her life situation and circumstances in a search for entertainment and the exotic. Sociologists portray tourists as bringing their homes with them wherever they go. Even though tourists want to empty themselves of their routine activities or imposed timetables, they remain separate from the culture they visit and like moviegoers observe rather than participate. As a result, tourists return home unchanged. Tourists depend entirely on guidebooks, looking for predictability, dependability, and security; they ultimately consume the experience by taking pictures, buying souvenirs, going on walking tours, and purchasing postcards to share their adventures with their friends and family back home.[2]

In contrast, a pilgrim seeks to engage the culture he or she is encountering. The word *pilgrimage* derives from the Latin word *peregrinus*, meaning stranger or foreigner. Pilgrims recognize that they are strangers who must leave their homes behind. They wish to participate, to be changed, to respond. Instead of trying to consume experiences, pilgrims become part of the unfolding story around them, letting the story shape them as they learn to see the world in a different way. Leonard Biallas reminds us that

> When we travel as pilgrims, our motivation goes beyond that of tourists and travelers. We go not for recreation, but for "re-creation." We go to make changes happen, rather than merely waiting for them to occur. We leave home not so much to see holy sites, but rather to be transformed. . . . Our goal is not mileage on the odometer, but lived experience consistent with becoming more fully alive human beings and sharing that experience with others. Every step along the way is as important as reaching the destination. Indeed, the final destination is not found on a map, for the journey never ends; it only deepens.[3]

Such a deepening, transformative journey has been promoted by the United States National Park Service as a way to deal with the park system's deteriorating natural resource base. Developed by Joseph Sax, the "intensive experience" seeks to replace consumption with contemplation: "The more knowledgeable and engaged the visitor, the less he [or she] wants or needs to pass through the parks quickly or at high speed. The quantity of resources the visitor needs to consume shrinks as he discovers the secret of intensiveness of experience, and his capacity for intense satisfaction depends on what is in his own head."[4] The intensive experience, like the pilgrim experience, encourages visitors to know, search, and understand. If you decide to have an intensive, pilgrim experience while you study abroad, you will commit yourself to intentional learning about the people, culture, and places with which you will interact.

Still, no matter how much we learn about a new place or culture, no matter how much we try to engage, there will always be, even for the most intent pilgrim, an element of being an outsider or tourist. When asked about a pilgrimage he once undertook to southeastern Cuba, Thomas Merton acknowledged that his travels were 90 percent tourism and 10 percent pilgrimage. And perhaps "this is as much pilgrimage as most of us can stand."[5] It is wise to be realistic about the difficulty of being a pilgrim, but it is important also to strive to make pilgrimage our way of life.

The following reflection from Ellie, who studied in Budapest, demonstrates the difference between being a tourist and being a pilgrim. At the end, she lists some ideas for becoming more respectful in her travels.

> *Something else that has been on my mind this week has been the idea of tourism. While sitting by the Danube this week, a bus pulled up and out flooded a swarm of tourists. They eagerly ran up to the bank of the river, and without pausing to take the view in, whipped out their cameras and snapped the sunset away. Watching this take place just made me sad, and it convicted me of my own tendencies to document the experience instead of live it. It's so easy to get greedy and solely seek to check a new country off the list, post a selfie, and move on. Although I often fall into that trap too, I find it to be an extremely selfish way to approach travel and an abuse of our privilege as travelers. Instead, we should ask ourselves, how do we treat the places we go with respect? How would I want myself, and my home, treated by visitors? I think a few ways to show respect is by being present, observant, self-aware, and doing everything in our power to understand a place's unique culture, language, history, and people — instead of simply popping in and out and "using" it for our own agenda.*

LEARNING TO BE A PILGRIM

Pilgrimage is an ancient practice of the Christian church. To be sure, not all pilgrims set out with the same motivations. While some traveled to draw closer to God and to bring him glory, others left for the thrill and adventure, "punctuating their journeys with carousing, drinking and sexual adventures," treating their pilgrimage as nothing more than a holiday. Some traveled out of a sense of duty to church or family, or in response to serious illness (their own or a loved one's), seeking to obtain the favor

What can you do to make your upcoming study abroad trip an intensive pilgrim experience rather than simply using the experience for your own purposes?

of God. Others seemed to have left to deny the parish priest his monopoly over their spiritual welfare. Still others traveled out of fear of the judgment of God, believing their hope of eternal life rested in earning their salvation through acts of devotion.[6]

Despite these potential pitfalls, seeing study abroad as a pilgrimage helps us anticipate the ways in which it can and should be a transformative experience. As Phyllis Tickle notes,

> Pilgrimage is the one of the ancient practices that most threatens what is familiar and what has been . . . with the almost absolute certainty that nothing will ever be the same again. The old verities will either die on pilgrimage or else they will rejuvenate and morph into sinewy understandings and holy affections that change every part of the life being lived. Either way, with pilgrimage, nothing is as it once was. Beware.[7]

This challenging vision of pilgrimage is rooted in the Bible. The stories in the Old and New Testaments present a picture of a people always on the move — physically, mentally, and spiritually. Charles Foster in *The Sacred Journey* helps us see that the nomadic, pilgrim life embodies much of what God values.

- *Living on the edges*. Edges are exciting places. It is at the edges that things collide and new syntheses occur. It is from the edges that God speaks to us. It is when we are on the edges that we are more inclined to listen.

- *Discerning the cost of hospitality*. The practice of hospitality involves both offering and accepting hospitality from others we meet along the way. This may involve risks, yet practicing hospitality lets us give and receive lessons that we need to learn. Giving hospitality allows us to challenge society when it is inhospitable, respond to social injustice, and break down the barriers of the world. Receiving hospitality helps us remember that we are not in control and that we often need to rely on the generosity of strangers to survive.

- *Walking in solidarity with the marginalized*. There is a potent and important connection between the necessary, self-imposed marginalization of the pilgrim and Jesus' own bias toward marginalized people.

- *Building intimate relationships with humans and the environment*. God calls us to build relationships with him, with other people, and with the environment. Pilgrims walk lightly along paths; they take the time to develop relationships and to learn about the people and places where they travel.

- *Seeing the world with new eyes.* On a pilgrimage there is a new view every step as God teaches us to see the world and those around us with new eyes.

- *Packing lightly.* Nomads and pilgrims have the loosest possible hold on their possessions as they trust God to provide for their needs.

- *Overcoming challenges.* Physical pilgrimages involve overcoming such challenges as aching bodies, blisters, hunger, and diarrhea, and make us more conscious of the obstacles we need to overcome in our spiritual lives as we strive to connect more fully with God.

- *Getting a taste of Christian radicalism.* Foster writes, "Nothing that is not radical is Christian. That takes some grasping. The road can help us grasp it. A stockbroker on pilgrimage for a week will be able to imagine better what it means to leave everything and follow Jesus. He'll be on the fringes of places and the fringes of society, and hence in the heart of the kingdom and the company of its elite. . . . Those little tastes of the kingdom can become addictive." Herein lies the power of pilgrimage and the reason why we are warned to beware, because after a pilgrimage there is the real possibility that nothing will be the same again. "Salvation is by grace, not by pilgrimage. But pilgrimage can help to create the conditions in which grace can work best."[8]

> What aspects of the nomadic, pilgrim life appeal to you as you think about your upcoming study abroad experience? How might these challenges help you think about study abroad differently?

> How might your upcoming study abroad experience help you draw closer to God and his calling for your life?

MOVING FORWARD INTO PILGRIMAGE

As you prepare to be a pilgrim, the model developed by practitioners of experiential education may be helpful. Experiential education is defined as a process through which students construct knowledge, acquire skills, and enhance values from direct experiences, resulting in individual change, whether in thought or deed.[9] Experiential education instills a sense of ownership for you, as a student, over what you learn. "The ultimate result is that individuals accept responsibility for their own learning and behavior, rather than assigning that responsibility to someone else."[10]

In experiential education, the four phases of the learning cycle are experience, reflection, processing, and application.[11] These can be mapped onto the movement of pilgrimage itself: the call, the departure, the journey, and the homecoming. When we think about study abroad as both pilgrimage and an intensive form of experiential education, we can expand our model to include the following stages:

- **Preparing the Way:** All travelers must prepare for their upcoming journeys, and preparing for a pilgrimage is no exception. Preparations include both organizing the logistics of your journey and ensuring that your heart is open to what God has in store for you. We will consider this stage more carefully in chapter three.

- **Crossing the Threshold:** You must be intentional as you move into a new place. It is wise to craft, perhaps with your family and with your study abroad group, some rituals that will prepare your heart and soul to be a pilgrim on a sacred journey. We will return to the concept of threshold in chapter four.

- **Experiencing the Journey:** Engaging fully in all aspects of your study abroad demands time for reflection both individually and with others. It also demands that you intentionally apply lessons learned while you are abroad and as you return home. Chapters five through eighteen will help you engage fully in your study abroad pilgrimage.

- **Returning Home:** Just as you cross a threshold to begin your pilgrimage, so you must re-cross it to re-enter daily life upon your return. You will find ways to share your experiences with others and to begin to understand what the experience will mean as you move forward. Chapters nineteen and twenty will help you think about ending well and returning home.

- **Integrating Lessons Learned:** As you return home, it is important to figure out how to live with the knowledge of what you've learned while away. For some this is more difficult than for others; however, the ultimate aim is to put one's learning in perspective, understanding what it means and what it will continue to mean to be a pilgrim in God's world. Chapter twenty-one will give you some tools for translating your study abroad experience into the rest of your life.

Stages of Pilgrimage

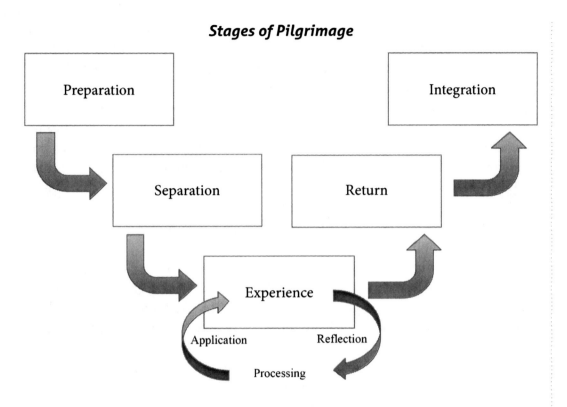

UNDERSTANDING YOUR GOALS

The epigram from Christian George that began this chapter summarizes what it means to be on a pilgrimage: "Pilgrimage is . . . a physical, emotional and spiritual journey that goes inward, upward and outward. . . . Pilgrimage is a spiritual practice that reminds us of our sacred purpose — to grow closer to God."[12] As you prepare to study abroad, pilgrimage offers a powerful metaphor to help shape your experience. Pilgrims wish to move toward the center, toward a deeper understanding of themselves, a deeper relationship with God, and deeper interactions with others. In this process, pilgrims hope to be transformed and open to the lessons that God wants to teach. Because pilgrimage is a practice, it requires intentional thought and action not only as you engage with those you meet on your journey, but also as you set goals that will keep your mind and heart focused.

Pilgrimage is a reminder that there are all kinds of hardships that you might encounter throughout your time away, but instead of resisting these hardships, it

As you prepare to be a pilgrim, write out some goals that will help you move on an inward, upward, and outward journey.

is best to embrace and learn from them. Each inconvenience and disturbance can teach you something sacred about your faith, your God, and yourself. In the book *Dangerous Wonder*, Michael Yaconelli writes, "I'm ready for a Christianity that 'ruins' my life, that captures my heart and makes me uncomfortable."[13] Brian Orme echoes this sentiment when he writes: "Following Jesus was never meant to be the safe alternative to an unpredictable life; following Jesus is inherently life-altering, deconstructive and always evolving."[14] Seeing your study abroad as an ongoing, not always predictable, pilgrimage can help you better handle the unexpected events that will certainly occur.

Being on a pilgrimage also reminds us how important other people are to our journey. Pilgrims often rely on the hospitality and graciousness of those they meet along the way. As pilgrims, we have the opportunity to engage those we meet with humility and genuine curiosity as we walk and grow together.

Pilgrimages help each of us see how much we need to depend on God as we explore and learn about new places. We get to learn that God is alive and at work in every corner of the world. Pilgrimages can also invigorate us to strive to be more like our Lord in thought, word, deed, and devotion. As Jim Forest writes, "Whether the journey is within your own backyard or takes you to the other side of the world, the potential is there for the greatest of adventures: a journey not only toward Christ but with him."[15]

While Emily was in Peru, she reflected on this journey toward and with Christ:

We are made in the image of an unimaginable God. This comes with much responsibility. I thought of Mary Oliver's inspiring question, "Tell me, what is it you plan to do with your one wild and precious life?"[16] Created with purpose and passion: What is it that I will do with this one wild and precious life? What is it that I am meant to do today, this week, and in the next three and a half months as I study here in Peru?

Academically, how do you plan to foster your intellectual curiosity? Individually, how do you want to grow as a person? Relationally, how do you plan to engage with others in your group and in the host country? Spiritually, how do you hope you will grow in your relationship with God? What do you plan to do with your one wild and precious life?

Chapter Three ──────────
PREPARING THE WAY

Integral to the art of travel is the longing to break away from the stultifying habits of our lives at home, and to break away for however long it takes to once again truly see the world around us. This is why "imagination is more important than knowledge," as Albert Einstein noted, and why the art of pilgrimage is the art of reimaging how we walk, talk, listen, see, hear, write, and draw as we ready for the journey of our soul's deep desire.
—Phil Cousineau

The day on which one starts out is not the time to start one's preparations.
—Nigerian Folk Saying

Preparation no more spoils the chance for spontaneity and serendipity than discipline ruins the opportunity for genuine self-expression in sports, acting, or the tea ceremony.
—Phil Cousineau

Your path to studying abroad started with a call to go, a desire to venture forth and to expand your education beyond your home campus. This chapter asks you to reflect on your initial calling to study abroad as well as to explore what you need to do to plan for your upcoming experience. In the Middle Ages, Christian pilgrims weighed many practical and spiritual considerations before they set forth on their journeys. Travel was dangerous, and plans to respond to these dangers had to be made. Those who go on pilgrimage today benefit as much from careful preparation and planning as did travelers in the past. As Sheryl Kujawa-Holbrook reminds us, "Although modern travel is in many ways less arduous than in ages past . . . the sacred art of pilgrimage is still demanding. The work of transformation [which is the heart of pilgrimage], calls for a great deal of physical, mental, and spiritual stamina."[1]

HEEDING THE CALL

Think about the questions that have
defined your life up to now. How have
these questions led you to decide to
study abroad?

We tend to prefer answers to questions. Answers are meant to reassure. Questions usually disturb. Yet nothing is as significant as the power of questions in our quest for wholeness and meaningful participation in the world. Questions ruffle the smooth front of what we already know and open us up to new possibilities. In many ways, our questions define who we are and how we live. As Jim Wallis suggests, "Every new direction in one's life journey begins with some new questions."[2]

Henri Nouwen says that questions "have to be lived rather than developed intellectually." To which Charles Rigma adds,

> In other words, we need to cease taking our world for granted and begin taking our questions into the arena of life by living them out practically. True questioning can only lead to a new doing. Searching can only lead to shattering some of our securities. And risk-taking, when born of a desire to live more truly and authentically, can only lead to new life.[3]

This search for a way to live more authentically can be seen in the decision to study abroad.

Thinking about your study abroad experience as a pilgrimage can be one way to further this search. The call to pilgrimage is an urge to venture forth; it is a longing for deeper experiences than those available immediately at hand. As you prepare to be a pilgrim, you might ask yourself these questions:

- How do I learn about other cultures in the most appropriate ways?
- How do I learn to love the stranger and let the stranger love me?
- How do I respond to the many types of injustice in this world?
- How do I learn to be a radical disciple of Jesus Christ?
- How do I interact with others from different faith traditions?

These are difficult questions to answer, yet they can provide insight into your calling to study abroad and direction as you seek to live a faithful life. We will look more carefully at these questions in later chapters.

For some people, a call is many years in the forming, and when the move to begin one's journey is made, it is done from clear motivation, high purpose, and ideals. Others answer a call on short notice and without great clarity about inner or outer destinations. Consider one student's reflection on her lifelong dream to study in Spain:

Ever since I was a little girl, the word wonder has been etched into the lines of my journal. Throughout my life, this wonder-hunt has led me to the world of teaching as a vocation as well as to the doors of our off-campus programs office to study abroad. I want to study in Espana, from the mountain landscapes to the architecture of Gaudi; Espana provides the perfect environment for what I deem "holy wonder." As a future Spanish and social studies teacher, the language, history, and culture of Espana only heightens this sense of "holy wonder". . . . Ultimately, I hope to let go of my cultural naivety and step out of my personal comfort zone. . . . In the end this God given gift of "wonder" has placed a holy calling on my life to go to Spain, and with His strength and for His glory, I will follow God's plan to reach beyond — to let go and to become a part [of God's unfolding story.[4]

On the other hand, some decisions to travel are made very quickly. In his auto-biography, *The Big Sea*, Langston Hughes recounts his first trip to Africa, working as a crewmember on the *S. S. Malone*. The night they sailed, Hughes met a fellow shipmate, George, who had come aboard a few hours earlier. The ship's Filipino steward had seen George hanging around the docks and yelled, "Hey, colored boy! You, there! You want a job?" And right on the spot, George, who was months behind on his rent, decided he did want a job and swung himself up on the ship. "He walked on board with nothing but a shirt and a pair of overalls to his back," Hughes recalled, "and lay there in his bunk, laughing about his landlady. He said she intended to put him out if he didn't find a job. And now that he had found a job, he wouldn't be able to tell her for six months."[5]

PILGRIMAGE PRACTICES

Once you have heard the call and settled on a study abroad opportunity, it is time to prepare for departure. Yet in our busy lives, preparations are often short changed, put off until a few days before leaving. As you frantically begin to pack and try to remember what you learned from orientation, you realize there is just not enough time to do everything you want to do before departing. Usually you worry about all the physical tasks that need to be completed. It is easy to forget altogether the mental and spiritual preparations that should be made before leaving home for a study abroad experience.

This focus on the physical is unfortunate, as preparing yourself mentally and spiritually can contribute a great deal to the overall success of your experience. In order to avoid this common trap, think about how you can be intentional about

Can you trace a long path from your early longings to your decision to study abroad, or did your call come quickly, when an opportunity arose?

Are you, like George, leaving anything unfinished as you prepare to travel abroad?

Why did you choose the particular location for your study abroad? What was appealing about the specific program you decided to join?

preparing for your studies abroad, investing the time needed to make your preparation worthwhile. Historically, pilgrims tried to develop practices or virtues that would assist them in their journeys. Much as a runner develops training practices to run a marathon, so too must you as a student pilgrim develop practices to make your study abroad experience a pilgrimage rather than a tourist trip. Five practices, inspired by a fifth-century conversation between Zi Zhang and Confucius about travelers on a sacred journey, offer one place to begin.[6]

PRACTICE THE ARTS OF ATTENTION AND LISTENING

As you prepare for your upcoming adventures, begin to strengthen your powers of observation. Begin to see the small, everyday things that point toward wonder. Recently I was in Bergen, Norway, eating breakfast at a cafe that overlooked the drop-off location for an outdoor pre-school. As I watched families arrive by foot, car, and bike, I was hit by the realization that we all share so many core values. Sending a child off to school was a wonderful example of the love we share for our families, regardless of other cultural differences we might see. The moment came to me quietly as I watched and listened to the world around me. So in the weeks and months ahead, take time to develop your powers of observation, create time to let the world come to you, and begin to see new things on familiar paths. Practice the art of paying attention to how God is working in this world.

PRACTICE THE ART OF RENEWING YOURSELF EVERY DAY

Practice the art of creating space to think, to reflect, to wonder, and to get to know yourself. Prepare yourself physically, mentally, and spiritually for the opportunities that lie ahead. Take the time to walk and exercise so that you will be physically fit to explore the places where you will travel.

Prepare yourself mentally and spiritually for the highs and lows you will undoubtedly experience. Take time to prayerfully set some goals for your upcoming experience related to your physical, mental, and spiritual health. Practice the art of spending time with yourself — and enjoying it!

As you leave for your experience abroad, remember this: There is a critical need for you to develop practices that create health and balance in your heart, mind, body, and spirit. Focus on what you need to be successful, what you need from others, and what you can give to the group and others to make them successful along the way.

PRACTICE THE ART OF MEANDERING TOWARD THE CENTER OF EVERY PLACE

The way of the pilgrim is the way of the seeker. The seeker embarks with sacred intent, taking an inner and outer journey toward discovery, service, and love. As you prepare yourself for your upcoming travels, begin to read literature, study the visual arts, or listen to music that comes from the place where you are going. Begin to feed your curiosity. Take some time to identify specific places you want to visit as part of your time away.

In addition, practice the art of meandering. As opposed to hiking, meandering implies that the walker has no predetermined destination, allowing for unexpected surprises such as fortuitous encounters with someone or some place. Phil Cousineau suggests that you "Take your soul for a stroll. Long walks, short walks, morning walks, evening walks — whatever form or length it takes. Walking is the best way to get out of your head. Recall the invocation of the philosopher Søren Kierkegaard, who said, 'Above all, do not lose your desire to walk: Every day I walk myself into a state of well-being and walk away from every illness. I have walked myself into my best thoughts.'"[7]

PRACTICE THE RITUAL OF READING SACRED TEXTS

Reading the Bible and other spiritual writings can help prepare you for the inner journey of your outward travels. Reading stories and other pieces of history from the places you will be living and visiting can also create a rich connection across generations of practitioners and pilgrims. This literature can help us recognize that we share so much of our human experience with others.

An important aspect of this reading practice is grounding your own faith. Students who study off-campus can feel adrift at times. Staying true to your faith and nurturing it while you are away can be difficult, so begin to ensure a strong foundation for your faith before you leave. Talk with trusted friends and mentors about what you believe, and create some goals for how you want to grow spiritually while you study abroad. The more grounded you are, the more prepared you are to share and engage with others of different faith traditions, opening yourself to listen to the faith journeys of others while also being willing to humbly share your own journey.

PRACTICE THE ART OF GRATITUDE

When my family and I lived in Hong Kong for a year, I was able to work briefly with an organization called I Will Not Complain. Its mission was to

As you read through the practices of pilgrimage, what practice will be hardest for you? Easiest? Why?

How might you begin to incorporate these pilgrimage practices into your life both here and now (before you leave) and also while you are studying abroad?

inspire people to take responsibility, to fulfill their potential, and to work together to overcome challenges and achieve success for themselves and their organizations. I always liked the mission of this organization, and I encourage you to think about how you might incorporate I Will Not Complain into your own off-campus experience.

Yet the art of gratitude goes beyond simply saying, "I Will Not Complain." Gratitude asks us to see God working in and through every aspect of our lives and to turn all our joys and concerns over to him. As you prepare to leave, work to keep things in perspective and to develop a sense of joy, living in the moment, and not sweating the small stuff. Cultivating this mindset can only enhance your time away and your life overall.

TRAVELING LIGHTLY

The scene is familiar: Students are at the airport ready to leave for their study abroad experience, but there is a problem. One student's luggage is overweight. Rather than pay the cost of the overweight bag, the student has opened the suitcase, trying to find things to remove or repack. The process is frantic and usually ends with parents or friends taking some items back home. In the moment, the student is able to see that some items are not necessary. This scene is often the result of not planning carefully or packing with the intention of bringing along all the comforts of home.

In the weeks prior to leaving on a study abroad experience, you will probably ask plenty of packing-related questions like, What should I take? What should I leave behind? Is there a packing list? The answer to all of these questions is "Pack less than you think you need." After you have collected all the things you plan to bring with you, ask of each item, do I really need this? Remember that what you bring will tell a story, your story, of where you are going, and what you are hoping will happen. What do you want your story to be?

Rick Steves, a renowned travel guide, says, "You'll never meet a traveler who, after five trips, brags: 'every year I pack heavier.' The measure of a good traveler is how light he or she travels."[8] Simplifying is part of the challenge of a pilgrimage, but the difficulty of packing light is that you have to plan for something you can't yet possibly understand.

Packing light, then, is not simply a matter of taking fewer things in your suitcase; it is also a philosophy of pilgrimage. One student, after his semester in Spain, encouraged others to pack their bags half-full and also to arrive in their host country half-full. "You come to another country," he wrote, "to 'fill up.'" If you pack half-full, you'll have room for new experiences, memories, thoughts, and challenges. In your study-abroad experience, he noted, "the only way to return full is to bring things that you don't mind throwing away and to leave extra space inside to put new things. You will throw off old habits and mindsets, discover new talents and interests, and meet unforgettable people, but you will need room to put it all, both inside yourself and inside your bag."[9]

🐚 Do you agree that you should pack half-full? Although the author doesn't mention the Christian faith as a reason to travel light, what connections can you make between traveling light and being a Christian? How might your faith affect your packing process?

🐚 How might you prepare yourself to be half-full as you leave on your study abroad experience? What expectations can you let go so that you can remain open to what God wants to teach you "in the moment?"

🐚 What do others recommend you pack for your experience? What is your packing list for your upcoming pilgrimage? As you compare these lists, what is essential for you, and what might you be able to leave behind?

🐚 Imagine your whole life as a pilgrimage, not just your study abroad experience. Imagine you can only pack so much. Allison Vesterfelt asks us to consider these questions: "What would you bring? What would you be willing to leave behind? Are there things, thoughts, and ideas you are so attached to that they're preventing you from getting anywhere? What are they? What would happen if you released your tight grip on those things for just a minute? Maybe, just maybe, you would get to see what is *out there*."[10]

FURTHER PREPARATIONS

Besides thinking about your calling to study abroad, or why you want to go abroad, or what you should pack, there are a multitude of other important tasks you should attend to prior to your departure. The list below is not comprehensive, but it should help you formulate some good questions during your orientation and your subsequent planning to study abroad. Try to use the questions to learn as much as you can about the people and places where you will be studying, as well as other important health and safety concerns prior to your departure.

Background information on the country and region where you will be studying

- What is a historical overview of the country/region where you will be studying? Are there any good novels or books that might help you better understand the culture and history of the region?

- How has the United States interacted in this region of the world historically? How are Americans viewed?

- What are the key historical events for the country/region?

- What is the current political structure of the country?
  - » Who is the current president? Who are key opposition party members?
  - » What type of government structure is in place?
  - » Are politics a sensitive subject within the country/region? Why or why not?

- What are the largest exports and imports of the country?

- What are the current challenges and issues facing the country/region?

Background information on the cultural heritage of the country or region where you will be studying

- What type of music is popular? What is the national anthem? Is the region known for any specific type of music?

- What does the native cuisine include? Is the country/region famous for any specific kind of food?

- What are the cultural expectations for dress for males and females? What type of clothing should you bring?

- Are there any unique holidays that the country/region celebrates? Will you be there for any major holidays?

- What is the national sport? What are some common pastimes for students or families of different socio-economic levels?

- What is the national religion? Are there taboos that you should know about?

- What are the cultural norms for alcohol consumption? Remember that the drinking age for most countries is 18 years of age, so you will likely be of legal drinking age while abroad. This makes it even more important to understand the cultural expectations regarding alcohol.

- What important landmarks or national treasures will be near to where you will be studying?

Background on world events

- What is currently happening in the world that you should know more about? Specifically, what is happening in the region of the world where you will be studying?
- What are the current events happening in the country where you will be studying?

Logistical concerns

- What is the name of the local currency? What is the exchange rate of this currency with the U.S. dollar?
- How do you plan to access funds while you are abroad?
- How can you begin to gain some survival language skills for the area where you will be studying? Is there a good phrase book that you can purchase to help you with basic communication?

Health and safety concerns

- Are there any specific health concerns present in the country or region where you will be studying? What immunizations are recommended by the U. S. Center for Disease Control (CDC) for the country or region?
- What are the alcohol policies of your program? How do you personally want to handle decisions related to alcohol?
- What are the norms surrounding gender roles and interactions between men and women, women and women, men and men? Gender roles and expectations vary from one culture to another. Think about what this means for you during your off-campus experience, including what steps you can take to reduce vulnerability or offense in your interactions.
- What are some of the local laws in the host country that you should be aware of?

- How can you begin to cultivate a sense of situational awareness while you are studying off-campus? Situational awareness is the skill of monitoring what is going on around you so you see potential threats before — and as — they develop. Situational awareness will allow you to avoid potential dangers before they happen. For example, as you enter a crowded marketplace you might move your wallet to your front pocket or carry your backpack in front of you. Likewise, if you begin to see something that might distract you from being aware, you might look for ways to exit the situation as quickly as possible.

- How can you keep a healthy balance between being paranoid and scared versus being naïve (e.g., thinking "Nothing will happen to me") while you are off-campus?

As Richard Slimbach reminds us, "Certainly, no pre-departure orientation process can prepare you for *every* experience you will encounter during your time abroad. Travelers experience and react to situations in vastly different ways. But whoever you are and whenever you go, you are more likely to minimize your frustration and maximize your learning if you treat 'getting ready' as an integral part of your total experience — a type of journey of its own."[11]

Chapter Four ——————————
CROSSING
THE THRESHOLD

Be Safe and Well — Peace, Love.
–Traditional farewell among Egyptians leaving on a pilgrimage

Have patience with everything unresolved in your heart and . . .
try to love the questions themselves as if they were locked rooms
or books written in a very foreign language. Don't search for the answers,
which could not be given to you now, because you would not be able to live them.
And the point is, to live everything. Live the questions now. Perhaps, then, someday far
in the future, you will gradually, without even noticing it, live your way into the answer.
–Rainer Maria Rilke

L isten. Your life is happening. You are happening. . . . A journey, years long, has brought each of you through thick and thin to this moment in time as mine has also brought me."[1] These words of Frederick Buechner are a fitting introduction to your departure day. Think about it: This day is a miracle. God has been preparing you and each of your classmates for this trip for a long time. The packing is done, the good-byes said, and now it is time to get on a plane and depart. But before you leave, the question remains, what will you do with this gift, this miracle?

As you begin your pilgrimage, you need a proper sending forth. Sacred journeys often start with crossing a threshold. The threshold of a house marks not only a physical marker, inside to outside, but also a transition from one world of experience to another — from the familiar to the unfamiliar, from the known to the unknown. As you go through security at the airport you are crossing a threshold for your own sacred journey, going from the familiar to the unfamiliar, opening yourself to a world of possibilities.

FIVE QUESTIONS FOR CROSSING THE THRESHOLD

As you take this step through airport security, recognize the significance of this simple act and reflect on how you want your study abroad experience to shape you. Read again the Rilke epigram, printed at the beginning of this chapter. Rilke asks us to love and live the big questions, and it is these questions, Parker Palmer suggests, that we should embrace as we step across a threshold. Thresholds are opportunities, and as Palmer reflects on these opportunities, he quotes a poem by Anne Hillman, "We Look with Uncertainty" in which she meditates on the old "clear-cut answers" we leave behind as we look through a "new doorway awaiting . . . daring . . . vulnerable . . . learning to love."[2]

This poem evokes for Palmer questions that he wants to love and live into:

"How can I let go of my need for fixed answers in favor of aliveness?"
"What is my next challenge in daring to be human?"
"How can I open myself to the beauty of nature and human nature?"
"Who or what do I need to learn to love next? And next? And next?"
"What is the new creation that wants to be born in and through me?"[3]

These are big questions, but they are also life-giving questions that allow us to build a better world, a world we want and need to come into being.

CROSSING THRESHOLDS TO STUDY ABROAD

What are the thresholds you will be crossing as you depart to study abroad? Consider the following two perspectives — the first from a student and the second from a professor — about preparing for their off-campus experiences.

> **Reflection One (from Katie)**

We stood in a circle for a moment before deciding that those leaving for Hungary ought to stand in the center, where we might lay our hands on them in blessing. Prayers were offered spontaneously and sweetly, characteristic of the gentle affirmations I have come to cherish from these friends. We asked for strength for long, homesick days, openness to the presence of God in a new place and a new culture, joy and patience and hope in the face of challenge and change. We thanked God for them. We asked him to cradle them. We asked him to carry them safely home. We meant every word.

And I thought, for a moment, that this was beautiful, and a bit absurd. Should we not each take the center in turn? Each student there prepares in these weeks for a fresh chapter of life, for an academically delineated period during which one would hope each would grow and change, during which both joy and challenge will be found. I hope each of those friends faces trials with hope and fortitude. I pray each twists wildly toward the light of Christ.

As you look with uncertainty to the months ahead, what life-giving questions would you like to wrap your life around – living your way into their answers a bit more every day as you cross the threshold into your study abroad experience?

But there is something sacred about a sending out, a commissioning — a semester abroad can be understood as a pilgrimage, and perhaps should be widely recognized as such. Each journey upon which we embark presents an opportunity to act out the metaphor of journeying toward Christ. And prayers of blessing set a tone for the trip, reminding us of the immortal weight of our lives, the holiness we so often glimpse, so often display, only accidentally.

As you read Katie's reflection, what do you think it means to "twist wildly toward the light of Christ"? How do you hope to draw closer to God over the next few months?

Reflection Two (from Amy)

As some of you know, I went to Ghana with seventeen students, my husband, and our two daughters (aged 3 and 6). While my husband and I had served in the Peace Corps in rural Senegal, some friends and family reacted negatively to our plans to take our children to Africa. By society's standards, it did not seem very rational to rent one's house, take one's children from school and go to Africa! But I believed that God wanted me to help my students and children learn about the richness of his world, by eating fufu, seeing the bright kente cloth, studying about the continent, and worshiping with Africans. I believed God wanted me to guide others as they lived and worked in a different culture. However, I had to trust that God would bring such outcomes. And to be honest, on some days — when some of you students were ill, travel plans fell apart, and no one wanted to eat fufu yet again — it was hard to see God's plan for the Ghana semester.[4]

One aspect of crossing a threshold is looking forward to what is coming, but the other aspect is looking backward to what you are leaving, the separation that you will experience as you leave home. In this short reflection from a professor (remember, your faculty director crosses thresholds to lead study abroad experiences, too!), we see that not everyone is supportive of decisions to teach or study abroad. As you cross your own threshold, did others express doubts about your leaving? If so, what were these doubts? How did you respond to these questions?

Many of you will be starting your pilgrimage with other students whom you know and are excited to journey with. For others who may be doing a partnership program from a third-party provider, you may be meeting your group in country and thus starting your journey alone. Whether you are traveling alone or with trusted companions, your journey is ultimately a solitary one. You must discover your own lessons and chart your own course. How do you feel about starting alone? Excited, eager, anxious, sad, fearful?

● What core beliefs (or worldviews) are you taking with you? How has your faith informed these core beliefs? Which beliefs have you thought about carefully, and which have you assumed simply because they are currently and locally accepted by those close to you (family, friends, teachers, etc.)?

● What are you intentionally bringing with you from home as a way to remember your home culture? What are you intentionally leaving behind?

As Joseph Dispenza notes, "No one departs on a journey without some anxiety. Fear of the unknown is an essential part of our human program. If we were perfectly fearless, we could find ourselves in trouble at every turn. Rational fear is appropriate and can even be a gift. It encourages us to be circumspect — surely one of the qualities that leads us to true awareness. We must not allow irrational fear to take over, however. Fear of that sort can overwhelm us and severely limit the progress of our journey, preventing vitally important lessons from reaching us."[5]

The following is an excerpt from a female student's travel journal as she traveled from the United States to Morocco, where she was to meet her instructor and study abroad group. As she was in transit, connecting through Paris, she shared these thoughts on her apprehensions and fears about going forward, despite all her preparations and her sense of calling to participate in the program.

I'm at the airport in Paris waiting in line to check in. I'm the only person at the terminal with a fair complexion. Mothers with children, men with business partners, I seem to be the only person traveling alone. Not for long. A man taps me on the shoulder. Surprised by this foreign touch, I turn around. "Bonjour Madame" — that is all I can understand. I'm not flattered. I'm afraid. I don't know what's going on. He obviously wants to help me to the gate and sit next to me. I turn away, looking in vain for someone who can understand my plight.

Before I precede any farther towards Morocco, I find a bathroom and don my head covering. Although women in the bathroom stare at me, I feel a sense of security and seclusion with the scarf. Tightly drawn around my face, I seek anonymity amidst the crowd. I want to blend in and escape the stares and "Bonjour Madams." If I feel this insecure in a Paris airport, how will I ever make it off the plane in Morocco? . . .

Cigarette smoke fills the airport despite the "No Smoking" signs. Everyone seems to be smoking. . . . A wave of nausea comes over me. I suddenly don't want to go to this country that I have longed and dreamed of for so many years. My tense body doesn't want to board the plane. I hesitate as they call all passengers to board. I sit

Smooth transitions and worry-free pilgrimages are rarities. As you cross your threshold into your own pilgrimage, how can you prepare emotionally for the trials that will come your way?

frozen with fear of the unknown. What is wrong with me? Slowly I make my way towards the boarding ramp. I am the last person to board the plane.

I am the last person off the plane. My light backpack suddenly becomes unbearably heavy. For the first time I notice the intense heat and the perspiration dripping off my brow. I cannot go any further. I sit down in silence, hands shaking, knees trembling, tears silently streaming down my face. No friend to talk to. No guide to direct me. I am alone in a strange country.[6]

MARKERS FOR CROSSING THE THRESHOLD

Most organized pilgrimages begin with an opening ritual. This ritual formally marks the moment when pilgrims pass from secular to sacred time. A Roman Catholic pilgrimage may begin with High Mass; a family pilgrimage may begin with a special prayer time; and a college service-learning trip might begin with worship or a prayer. These markers are important acts of noticing God's involvement in the journey.

In the Middle Ages, Phil Cousineau reminds us, "departing pilgrims first sought out the special pilgrimage blessing of a local priest. In those days, [a pilgrimage] was considered so dangerous that it was uncertain whether you would even return. Leaving on pilgrimage without a blessing was inconceivable, as was leaving without your affairs in order. . . . The departing pilgrims were celebrated with a Mass in which they took confession and communion, then the rites of the blessing of their walking staffs, satchels, and drinking gourds. Psalms were sung to 'infuse courage into the hearts' of the pilgrims, then they put on their long cloaks and hats, recited the prayers of the *Pilgrim's Itinerarium,* and set out with their fellow marchers down the long road."[7]

As you depart, what markers would you like to put in place to signal your leaving? Consider a ceremony to bless, or at least mark, the start of the pilgrimage. A ceremony doesn't need to be fancy or complicated, but it should mark the moment. Consider some of the following markers:

VERSES

Do you have a verse, reading, or poem that speaks to you about your upcoming journey? Think about the following two stories; they are not unlike your own. You, too, are beginning a journey whose outcomes are unknown, and your journeys will not be without testing and rewards. But even on the difficult days, you can be assured that you are not alone, and that God is with you, sustaining and strengthening you.

As you cross your threshold, what are your fears? Which of these fears are rational and help lead you to new insights? Which of these fears are irrational and should be left at home?

In Genesis 12, God calls to Abraham: "Go from your country and your kindred and your father's house to the land that I will show you. I will make of you a great nation, and I will bless you, and make your name great, so that you will be a blessing" (Gen. 12:1–2). God's promise to make Abraham a blessing is one that comes to all of Abraham's children, including those of us who are traveling to a study abroad program.

Right before his own death, Moses speaks to Joshua and encourages him that God will be present, even as the Israelites walk across the Jordan into a new land. "Be strong and bold. . . . It is the LORD who goes before you. He will be with you; he will not fail you or forsake you. Do not fear or be dismayed." (Deut. 31:6–8).

PRAYER

As you venture forth, consider how the following ancient prayer, taken from the pilgrim mass said along the Camino de Santiago, could be a blessing to you:

> God, who brought your servant Abraham out of the land of the Chaldeans, protecting him in his wanderings, who guided the Hebrew people across the desert, we ask that you watch over us, your servants, as we walk in the love of your name. . . .
> Be for us our companion on the walk,
> Our guide at the crossroads,
> Our breath in our weariness,
> Our protection in danger,
> Our home along the way,
> Our shade in the heat,
> Our light in the darkness,
> Our consolation in our discouragements,
> And our strength in our intentions.
> So that with your guidance we may arrive safe and sound at the end of our journey, and, enriched with grace and virtue, we may return safely to our homes filled with joy.
> We make this prayer in faith.[8]

As you read through these verses and prayers, do you have a verse or a story or prayer that you want to be a marker for your upcoming study abroad experience?

As you cross the threshold today, how might you use markers in your upcoming journey?

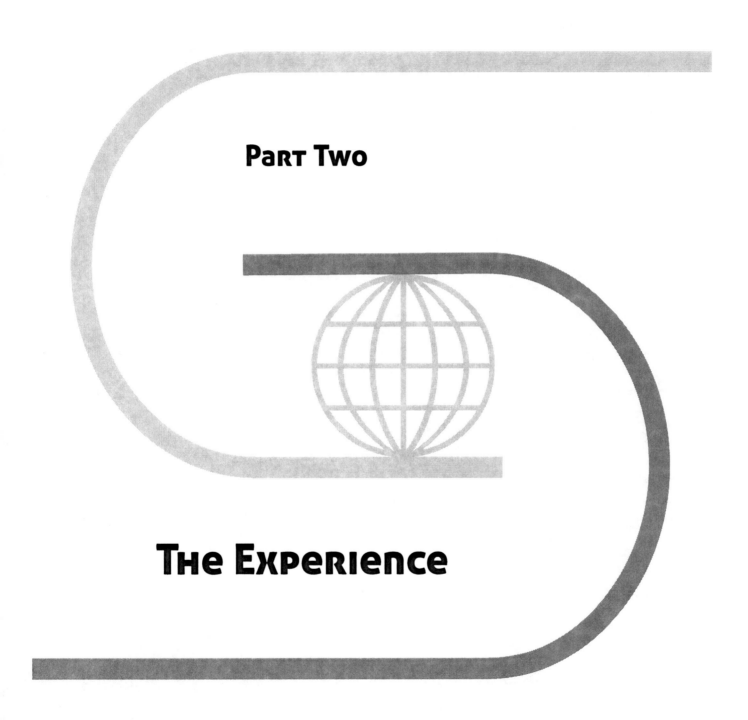

Part Two

The Experience

Chapter Five

EMBRACING THE JOURNEY

Adventure is not in the guidebook,
Beauty is not on the map,
Seek and you shall find . . .
Life beckons.
—Painted over the door at the Hong Kong Outward Bound School

If I have a hope, it's that God sat over the dark nothing and wrote you and me,
specifically, into the story, and put us in with the sunset and the rainstorm as
though to say, Enjoy your place in my story. The beauty of it means you matter,
and you can create within it even as I have created you.
—Donald Miller

You have prepared for your experience, crossed the threshold, and arrived at your site. The "official experience" has finally begun. But what's next? In his book *The Sacred Journey*, Frederick Buechner writes, "We search, on our journeys, for a self to be, for other selves to love, and for work to do."[1] Let's think about each of these statements briefly:

- *"We search, on our journeys, for a self to be."* This experience is going to stretch you to think differently about who you want to be and how you want to relate to this world. Be intentional in reflecting on who you are becoming during your time away.

- *"We search, on our journeys . . . for other selves to love."* During your time studying abroad, you will find these other selves in a variety of places — in the host nationals you meet as well as in the group of students studying with you. As you embrace your journey, how are you going to care for one another, to live, learn, laugh, and even cry together as you become a part of one another's lives?

- *"We search, on our journeys . . . for work to do."* What is your work while you study off-campus? To do well in school, to make new friends, to get involved in your new community — all of these are great goals, but if you see your experience as a pilgrimage, then the overarching goal is to draw closer to God. As you pursue this goal, an integral part of your work is to stop, reflect, and discover the meaning in this experience for you.

In your life abroad, I hope you will see God's faithfulness as you learn to be intentional, learn the importance of being known in community, and learn to make reflection a part of your work. As you settle into your new surroundings, one way to begin the process of being intentional is to think about what habits you want to cultivate during your time away. This chapter presents three habits that flow out of the practices of pilgrimage described in chapter three: the art of looking, the art of being, and the art of journaling.

The use of the word *art* here is intentional. There is no set path or prescribed set of steps to achieve as you learn to embrace your journey; rather you need to develop a mindset and skills that enable you to creatively accomplish your specific goals. These goals may be different from those of your classmates, but together you can help one another look, be, and journal better.

THE ART OF LOOKING

Earlier in chapter three, you were encouraged to practice the art of attention and listening by noticing the small everyday things that point to wonder. The art of looking builds on this practice of attention. In *On Looking*, Alexandra Horowitz argues that we miss so much in our lives simply because we don't take the time to look. We have not developed the art of seeing.[2]

How do we develop this art? We begin by realizing that our expectations shape what we see. We see what we expect to see. Horowitz learned to counteract her expectations of her own neighborhood by walking around her block with eleven different experts ranging from an artist to a geologist to a dog. These experts helped her emerge with fresh eyes, mesmerized by the previously unseen fascinations of a familiar world.

Horowitz also found that half of looking is knowing where to look. A small bit of knowledge goes a long way in directing your gaze. Once you have an eye for certain things, even when you are not looking for them, they will jump out at you. But how do we learn where to look? Horowitz suggests taking these steps: 1) Get out and explore your new surroundings (walking is best), follow your curiosity, and learn more about the areas where you live and plan to visit. 2) Take trusted mentors, invite new friends, learn from them, ask questions, challenge expectations. 3) Constantly remind yourself to pay attention. As we gain experience in looking well, we become more expert. We pay better attention in our everyday lives because not only do we know *where* to look but we also know *how* to look.

When you first arrive in a new place, you are often more open to your surroundings. The challenge is to maintain this openness and continue to see the familiar with new eyes. A good example of developing the art of looking can be seen in Kate's blog post from Honduras.

> *How do you explain a new way of seeing God? See, here at Calvin or at our homes, we know where to experience God. He's in the grace before dinner, in our quiet devotion time, or in the church that we've built for him, somewhere between the fancy sound system and the padded pews. Not only do we know where to find God, but we also know what to expect from Him.*
>
> *When you go abroad, those times and places don't always come with you. It's hard to have that quiet time with a rooster crowing under your window. It's hard to get a lot out of church when you can't even understand what the pastor is saying. See, it's hard when we're comfortable, to always tell the difference between experiencing God, and all the habits we've built up around experiencing him. In Honduras, those habits were gone, and we were forced to see God in different, unexpected ways.*
>
> *In Honduras, with my group, we met God together. And sometimes that was in places that we didn't expect. We met God when we talked to and prayed with the Honduran workers who make some of our clothes for less than minimum wage — and then the same day talked to and prayed with one of the company's executives from Kentucky. I met God in a tiny rural village in the mountains where people came together every night to pray together. I saw God working in the faith of people who planted coffee every season not knowing whether or not it would grow, but trusting that God would provide either way. And this picture of God I saw, that we saw, got just a little bit bigger.*

As you continue to settle into your new home, take time to cultivate the art of looking. Challenge yourself to see from different perspectives; slow down and invest in your new surroundings. Look for new ways to see God. You will be surprised in so many ways.

In a college commencement address, philosopher Nicholas Wolterstorff challenged graduates to develop two eyes: the eye of the mind and the eye of the heart. He asked them to develop knowledge, discernment, and critical engagement, and also to develop empathy, compassion, and care. "Do not be so focused on knowledge

How have you seen God in the first week of your time abroad?

How do you hope to develop the art of looking during your time abroad? What do you hope to look for? What more would you like to know about your neighborhood and city?

As you start your study abroad experience, what do you need to look for to develop the eyes of both your mind and your heart?

that you neglect compassion," he said; "do not be so overcome by compassion that you neglect knowledge. The eye of the mind without the eye of the heart is heartless competence. The eye of the heart without the eye of the mind is mindless empathy. You need both eyes, both the eye of the mind and the eye of the heart, both the eye of discernment and the eye of empathy . . . to weep with those who weep and rejoice with those who rejoice."[3] In his own way, Wolterstorff was encouraging graduates to develop the art of looking to develop both the mind and the heart.

THE ART OF BEING

The art of being can be thought of in terms of two distinct commitments, one related to the individual and the other related to community. In terms of the individual, the art of being builds on the art of renewing yourself presented in chapter three. As a part of this practice, you were encouraged to develop the art of spending time with yourself — and enjoying it! This is difficult. A recent study asked participants to turn off all their electronic devices and sit with their own thoughts for somewhere between six and fifteen minutes. The majority of participants rated the task as difficult and unpleasant.[4]

Do you enjoy being alone with own thoughts? What strategies might work for you to create space to slow down and be more reflective?

Studying abroad often provides a lot of time for you to be alone, which, in turn, offers you a choice. Either you can embrace the solitude, or you can scurry around, filling up your time as best you can. The art of being challenges you to accept this time alone, turn off your devices, and enjoy getting to know yourself. Find ways to quiet yourself and to think deeply about what you are observing, feeling, and experiencing while studying in a new place. As Pico Iyer points out, spending time alone and just being "isn't about turning your back on the world; it's about stepping away now and then so that you can see the world more clearly and love it more deeply."[5] This takes courage, but the study abroad experience offers you a gift, the gift of practicing the art of being in solitude.

While it is good to withdraw and spend time with yourself, it is also important to connect with others in meaningful ways. The art of being in community requires that you develop a sense of faithful presence within the various communities where you find yourself. As John Taylor, a missionary in Africa, wrote in the early 1960s, "Africans believe that presence is the debt they owe to one another. . . . The Christian, whoever he may be, who stands in that world in the name of Christ, has nothing to offer unless he offers to be present, really and totally present, really and totally *in* the present."[6]

This idea of faithful presence has found new attention through the writing of James Hunter, whose book *To Change the World: The Irony, Tragedy, and Possibility of Christianity in the Late Modern World* encourages Christians to be faithfully present within their work, within their spheres of influence, and within all aspects of their lives.[7] Faithful presence allows us to use our gifts for the flourishing of others wherever they are and to let others step into our own lives to help us flourish as well. One student, reflecting on her service-learning placement in Hungary, shows us how faithful presence might look in an international setting:

> *Not all young couples move to Budapest to teach English. I was curious what made them different than other young couples I know. As the semester has progressed, Paul and Erin have become signposts for me. Harding speaks to the importance of signposts in his book* Hope and History *as people who guide the next generation by walking with young people for a season.[8] It has truly been a gift walking with Erin and Paul and watching the way they live out their faith at their school. . . . They do their best as teachers and as people to live out their faith in everyday life. I would not say they are the best teachers at their school, but they come each day and have invested into this community, these students, and this country. . . . Erin and Paul have lived out Hunter's theology of faithful presence beautifully. They have faced the fact that they will not drastically change the world by being English teachers, while at the same time they understand that being English teachers here in Hungary means something. My dream used to be one that included traveling to foreign countries in Africa so that I could save the world. After walking with Erin and Paul for a semester and reading Hunter, it is clear my idealized, selfish dream is impossible, yet I have learned to be grateful for the opportunity to be where I am and invest in that specific place with my life thanks to this semester in Hungary.[9]*

Who has been a faithful presence in your life? What can you learn from their example? Do you think the idea of being faithfully present will be difficult or easy for you? Why or why not?

THE ART OF JOURNALING

Keeping a journal while on the road is a time-honored tradition because it helps the traveler reflect on his or her experiences. Although you will naturally organize, assimilate, and integrate new experiences into your view of the world, this process is often short changed in our hurry to be somewhere else mentally. So as you begin to move forward toward your own pilgrimage of discovery, consider keeping a written record of your experiences in the form of a journal or blog. Writing invites the needed reflection to facilitate growth and learning.

As you think about how to write in a way that invites change, try to move beyond "today I did this, tomorrow I will see that" to think in terms of drafting a journal that records your feelings and your observations. These kinds of journals are both descriptive and interpretative.

Good description records concrete details of an experience. It may be a scene, an event, a conversation, a discussion, or something from the media. Your role is to use vivid words to recreate scenes on paper that can be clearly visualized. Descriptive writing also lets you identify your feelings as things happen to you. Joseph Dispenza notes that "emotions come swiftly when you are away from home and exploring new worlds. Without a way of describing them clearly, gathering them together, and fixing them, they will be lost to the winds. . . . A journal of feelings elevates your trip from a mere sight-seeing excursion to a . . . journey. Keeping a chronicle of your feelings gives you the opportunity to trace the movements of your heart as you make your way. It transforms a trip of discovery into a journey of self-discovery."[10]

Interpretation starts from description but goes beyond it. Interpretation takes a particular happening — for example, wandering alone through your new city, meeting a new friend, getting lost in a good book, hanging out at a park, or talking with a classmate or host family member — and seeks to place that experience in context. In reflecting on this specific experience in the light of your readings and discussions, past experiences, or the cumulative study abroad experience of which you are a part, you take a slice of life and try to make sense of it in terms of a larger framework.

The most valuable writing is clear and detailed in its description of events, places, and people. Putting words to your observations and feelings helps to interpret the meaning of these events, relationships, new learning, and experiences. Tell a story in your journal, describe sensory images, introduce an interesting character, or focus your writing on a specific image or event. As you read Kate's blog, note her descriptions of the people and their interactions with each other. These descriptions draw us into the story as she transitions into the insights the story provides in that moment.

> *People are tethered to technology, and they have forgotten how to see things. I went on a sunset tour of the Grand Canyon with a bus full of tourists, and at every overlook they swarmed out, fanny-packed and sun burnt, and snapped pictures on their iPads.*
>
> *"Every person in America should see this," a woman drawled while digging through her purse for lip-gloss. She retreated to the bus after her picture was snapped.*
>
> *"Honey, faster," another women said. "We have more pictures to take."*
>
> *"What's the best place to get a sunset photo?" a man asked the driver.*
>
> *And suddenly it isn't about standing and breathing in the spectacular sight.*

Have you ever kept a journal? Why or why not? How would you like to reflect on and record your experiences during your time away?

What will be more difficult for you, describing people and places or sharing the insights gained from these experiences?

It isn't about being still and witnessing something bigger than yourself. It's about taking a picture where you look good so you can post it to Facebook and prove you had a great time on your vacation. Does it even matter anymore if you have fun on vacation if you don't have evidence that you did?

If journaling is difficult for you, try this exercise, suggested by Shawn Wong:

When you're out and about each day, take a postcard-like picture (or buy a postcard) of something that you're actually looking at. In your journal write down the things that aren't in the picture — sounds, smells, things outside the border of the picture you're holding — anything that strikes you as interesting to note. This exercise captures a precise experience at a precise moment. Do not buy a postcard and then write on the back later when you're not on location — that defeats the purpose. Number the postcards or date them. Do this each time you want to preserve a moment or location. At the end of your study abroad program, you will have an impressive record of your overall experience.[11]

Chapter Six

Cultivating Your Intellectual Curiosity

I have no special talents.
I am only passionately curious.
–Albert Einstein

The Jewish philosopher Abraham Heschel maintained
that there are three ways to react to the universe:
"exploit it, enjoy it, or accept it with awe."
Exploitation is the way of the tourist,
enjoyment is the way of the traveler,
awe is the way of the travel pilgrim.
–Leonard Biallas

n chapter one, we asked, "Why study abroad?" and saw that there are lots of answers to this question. As we return to the question in this chapter, however, we want to emphasize the second word: "Why *study* abroad?" As a study abroad professional, I believe that off-campus experiences must be connected to academic goals — after all, we do call it *study* abroad. I also want to connect study abroad with my Christian faith and with my love of travel. Am I asking too much? Maybe, but I recently came across this quote from Thomas Aquinas College in California about the purpose of a college education: A liberal arts education "begins in wonder and aims at wisdom."[1]

Travel brings me to wonder, and when I am caught up in the wonder of it all, I find myself humbled, grateful, and curious. I am open to the small beauties that surround me and to the marvel of being part of something much larger than myself. This sense of wonder leads to my seeking new knowledge, which in turn can bring me to wisdom. The essence of wisdom is discernment — discernment of right from wrong, helpful from harmful, and truth from delusion.

When we wonder about all the beauty and injustice that abounds in our world, it brings us to want to know more about God who holds this world in his hands. And gaining knowledge about God can lead to wisdom, as Proverbs 4:5–7 encourages: "Get wisdom; get insight: do not forget, nor turn away from the words of my mouth. Do not forsake her, and she will keep you; love her, and she will guard you. The beginning of wisdom is this: Get wisdom, and whatever else you get, get insight."

Wonder that leads to knowledge that leads to wisdom — this is what can make studying abroad so special. Are you currently experiencing the wonder of your study abroad experience? Where is your intellectual curiosity taking you? Are you beginning to see how it might lead to wisdom?

INTELLECTUAL CURIOSITY

Wonder can be evoked by rituals or by spiritual practices, by natural beauty, by scientific inquiry, or, if we are attentive, by day-to-day living. Yet for wonder to be evoked, we need time and space. In today's fast-paced world, we tend to do everything in a hurry. One of the results of our frantic lives is that we have developed shorter attention spans, settling for the quick answers we can find on the Internet. One of the potential benefits of your study abroad experience is the gift of time, which creates space to dig deeper, to fan the flame of your curiosity, to ask hard questions, to embrace the interesting class even if it doesn't fulfill a requirement, to join a student club, to develop a new hobby or interest, to ask questions of the locals whom you meet, to be open to new ways of engaging and feeding your curiosity.

Having time also creates space to be amazed, to think deeply, and to look for connections in this complex world. On your home campus, learning is often compartmentalized by major fields of study, so it is easy to become myopic and see the world only through the eyes of your discipline. In contrast, your off-campus experience allows you to see how history is connected to contemporary culture, business is connected to politics, philosophy is connected to justice, and language is connected to worship. As one student noted about his short-term, off-campus experience:

> One of the most impressive things about my off-campus experience was how many things our learning experience encompassed. It was not just an interim on environmentalism, sociology, outdoor recreation, or new urbanism. It was all these and more because it transcended the traditional teaching framework and showed how each of these subjects work and interact together to affect our world in both positive and negative ways. The strength of this learning experience was not in how many different subjects it presented, but in how we learned the connections between the subjects at hand.[2]

Albert Einstein reminds us that "the important thing is not to stop questioning. . . . Never lose a holy curiosity."[3] Curiosity is vital because it makes your mind active instead of passive as you become more observant of new ideas and connections. Curiosity can infuse excitement into the life of the mind as you study abroad.

Read the following blog excerpt from Anneke, who studied in Budapest, and note how her own inner curiosity is developing and how she is living into her questions.

> *I'm near the end of a memoir called* Castles Burning, *which we are reading for our culture class. It's a true story about the life of a young Jewish Hungarian girl living through the Nazi occupation of Budapest in 1944. Holocaust literature always gets me, but reading it here is an experience entirely different. It's strange, to say the least, that I could hop on a tram and ride past where Magda (the narrator) and her family hid, or where her brother was shot into the river. . . .*
>
> *This place is giving me new perspective. It's helping me see and understand things that my American history classes have chosen to leave out. It's helping me realize how much else, how many other burning castles, if you will, I'm probably missing in this world.*

LANGUAGE LEARNING

One way to exercise your intellectual curiosity while abroad is through language acquisition, and there is no better way to learn a language than to be immersed in it. Learning a language also provides an important window into a new culture. Imagine all the nuances that are conveyed through your own native language. So even if you are not planning on studying language formally while abroad, make the effort to immerse yourself in the language that is spoken in your host country. Learn as much as you can before you go and seek out ways to learn the language while you are there. Commit to engaging with others in as many ways as possible, remembering that if you only see and speak to people who look and sound like you, you are not experiencing the true beautiful diversity in this world. So go boldly, be open to all, and be fearless as you work to improve your language skills and learn from your mistakes.

When you invest in language learning, the opportunities to be amazed are multiplied, as Hannah's blog post illustrates:

> *Today was a day that I realized . . . I speak Spanish. This was an awesome realization! How did I realize this? Well, at lunch, as I was talking with Andrea and Tita, I realized that I was having a real conversation. I was understanding everything, and I was able to express myself. And I realized that I've been doing that for a while*

What are two to three questions that you hope to "live into" while you are studying abroad?

In the time you have been off-campus, what has captured your imagination and fanned the flames of your curiosity?

How has language contributed to Hannah's feeling at home in her host country? How do you think language has helped her foster her own intellectual curiosity?

now. And I realized that I actually TAUGHT in Spanish. Really! This means think-ing on the fly — there's no way to practice everything that I am going to say during teaching. I understand what people are saying, and I can talk back. I realized that I am confident to talk to anyone in Spanish at any time. I didn't feel like this at the beginning of this semester.

How are you investing in learning the language of your host country? If your language options are limited, brainstorm some strategies for engaging those whose language you do not speak. For example, can you purposefully invite a local friend who is bi-lingual to join you as you attempt to meet and make friends with others who don't speak your language?

CULTURAL EXPLORATIONS

Another way to exercise your intellectual curiosity is to explore the culture of the places you visit. Although study abroad provides a wealth of opportunities for you to grow emotionally and spiritually in your own personal life, learning about other people and places can be more difficult. As one study abroad administrator laments:

Do you feel that you are meeting local people and learning deeply about the local culture? Were the suggestions presented in chapter five about developing the art of seeing, the art of being, and the art of journaling helpful?

> Having read countless student journals of their travel-abroad experiences, I have been struck by how often the focus is on not what they have learned about the people and places visited, but what they have learned about them-selves. . . . Of course they are learning, but not about the other; rather, they are learning about the self. After my initial disquiet, I realized that what I was dealing with was also a manifestation of a wider phenomenon, now termed "Generation Me" or "Generation Look at Me." This is the generation largely raised by baby-boom parents who believed in instilling self-esteem. It is part of a wider phenomenon: simply observe how news media stories have increasingly replaced words like "us," "we," and "humanity" with self-refer-encing words like "I," "me," and "myself."[4]

Anthropologists, who study the cultures of the world, can help us further develop skills for interacting with people who are different from ourselves. Anthropology is the study of humans and their culture, past and present. To understand the full sweep and complexity of cultures across all of human history, anthropology draws from and builds upon knowledge of the social and biological sciences as well as the humanities and physical sciences. One tool used by anthropologists is participant observation.

Participant observation is a type of data collection method that recognizes the role researchers often play in situations they are studying. It relies on the cultivation of personal relationships with local "informants" as a way of learning about a culture and involves both observing and participating in the social life of a group. By actually living within the culture they are studying, researchers are able to develop first-hand accounts and gain insights into the inner workings of that culture.

As a student studying abroad, you are not a researcher formally studying a culture, but you are trying to develop your own intercultural competence; thus, many of the techniques used in participant observation can be useful as you try to understand your current cultural context.

Research techniques used by the participant observer include direct observation, interviews, and analysis of other cultural material such as written documents (e.g., newspapers) and media outlets such as television, music, and movies. All of these sources help anthropologists learn how better to read social cues and thus how better to participate in the culture they are observing. The art of direct observation is particularly relevant for you as a student, and knowing the kind of information to collect will help you become a more skilled participant observer. Here are some questions you might ask:[5]

Settings

- How does culture affect the physical spaces of your host country?
- As you observe interactions, how does the setting shape these interactions?
- How do settings encourage or discourage interaction between individuals?
- As you move through different settings in a culture, what is the overall atmosphere or feeling of various places? Where do you feel welcome? Where do you not feel welcome?
- How are places and spaces organized? How are decorations and symbols used?

People

- Whom do you seem to interact with? How do you meet people? How do people greet each other?
- How do people treat each other? How do men and women relate to each other?

- How do people treat people who are different from them (e.g., socio-economic differences, ethnic differences, etc.)?

- What type of person are you drawn to? Who seems drawn to you? Why?

- What are your initial impressions of people you meet? On what basis do you find yourself forming these impressions?

Activities and Interactions

- How are activities structured and scheduled?

- What type of activities are valued?

- Who tends to organize activities? Who attends? Who does not attend?

Developing a mindset that fosters participant observation can facilitate not only knowledge of your host country, but can also lead to a better understanding of your own culture and value system, as will be explored in the next chapter.

LET'S PRACTICE

As you learn to become a more skilled participant observer, you will discover general insights into the culture in which you are living. But you can also develop the art of seeing in specific contexts. Here, being a participant observer means examining a particular setting or event or topic in hopes of developing detailed strategies for operating well within that specific area of culture. The following exercise encourages a better understanding of the cultural norms between men and women. This is an especially important topic as you work toward developing positive and culturally appropriate relationships between men and women and avoiding situations where misinterpreted signals could lead to awkward situations or even sexual harassment or assault.

Get into groups with two or three other people. If possible, each group should have at least one male and one female. Then through interviews and observations in your host community, try to answer as many of the following questions as you can. Remember to be sensitive about who should do what. Some interviews might be best done between females or between males. Some suggestions for where to observe and whom to interview are listed below, along with sample questions to guide your inquiries.

Remember that before you start your observations or interviews, it is important to review your own feelings and convictions on dating and female/male relationships, as well as same-sex relationships. Discuss these feelings and thoughts with your group before you start your observations and interviews.

- **Where and when to observe:** Vary the time and the places where you observe people and their interactions with one another. Possible places to observe include the following:
  - » Various spots on your college or university campus
  - » Restaurants, cafes, and other public gathering places like malls, parks, clubs, and churches
- **Whom to interview (if possible):** Again try to interview a variety of people, both males and females.
  - » Fellow students and peers
  - » Professors, pastors, and others in positions of authority
  - » International student advisors
  - » Other expats who have lived in the country for several years
- **Potential questions to address:**

Dress:
  - » Is there a traditional or indigenous style of dress for women and for men? Can you describe it? When and where is it worn?
  - » What is appropriate dress for a foreigner like you?
  - » Are there some special dress customs to be aware of (e.g., taking off shoes in certain places or keeping certain parts of the body covered)?

Romantic Relationships:
  - » What are the rules for romantic relationships in this country? Do unmarried men and women date? If so, do they date in groups or by themselves? Do they need a chaperone?
  - » Is PDA appropriate for married couples? Dating couples? Anyone at all?
  - » How does a man show he is interested in a woman?
  - » How does a woman show she is interested in a man?
  - » How should a woman show she is not interested in a man who is interested in her or vice versa?
  - » How do you know when a relationship is becoming something more than just a friendship?
  - » How do men/women signal they want to pull back or cool down a relationship?

» In what types of social activities do young women and men participate together?

Behaviors:

» Are catcalls a frequent occurrence on the street? If yes, how do women respond? How do men respond?

» How do local women respond to unacceptable touching by men and vice versa? What is considered unacceptable touching?

» Are sexual assaults common in the culture? How do local authorities deal with these behaviors?

» What are the local laws with respect to sexual harassment or sexual assault?

» Are there marked differences between what behaviors are accepted or not accepted in each of the following settings: city streets, college campus, local club, restaurant, and mall?

Integration questions for the group as they prepare their report:

» How might this exercise and interacting with host country nationals on this issue help you to develop culturally appropriate responses to dealing with sexual advances of the opposite gender?

» Given your research, what behaviors relating to male/female interactions can you embrace, accept, or outright reject? How can you give yourself permission to be "rude" when cultural norms contradict your own strongly held viewpoints?

» Brainstorm some strategies to avoid putting yourself and others in potentially difficult situations related to sexual norms that might or might not be considered sexual harassment in the United States.

Once you have completed your observations and interviews, put together your group report and be ready to share with your peers as you discuss what you learned and the insights you want to incorporate into your study abroad experience as you move forward.

Chapter Seven

BUILDING CULTURAL COMPETENCE

*The greatest impact on my experience was the people I went with.
We were all very different from each other; yet, when you are
abroad that doesn't seem to matter as much,
and we just all really got along well.*

–Student reflection, France

*Slowly, through ceaseless struggle and effort, I learned to overcome
the day-to-day barriers that had previously seemed like indomitable walls.
I became an accepted part of my rural community and mastered Spanish.
I learned the simple truism that trust must precede change, and focused on
making friends with the hill farmers rather than on counting the number
of trees that got planted. And, sure enough, the less I focused
on the work, the more work seemed to get done.*

–Peace Corps Volunteer, Guatemala

*We don't see things as they are;
we see them as we are.*

–Anais Nin

n a recent study exploring the long-term personal impact of studying abroad, participants were asked what factors affected the overall quality of their experience. The themes that emerged included the internal dynamics of the group (friendships with peers), the professor/director of the program, the culture/community where the program was located, independent travel, and the friendships made with host-country nationals.[1]

These themes highlight a tension that is often evident in the study abroad experience: the importance of both internal group dynamics as well as external interactions with the people and culture of the area where the program is offered. As one respondent noted, "In Honduras the internal group dynamic was fantastic, we had an excellent group, and we just all meshed and got close to each other, so that was a real highlight." Contrast this to another respondent (in the same group) who noted that his "highlights were always with his host family . . . I became part of the family." The tension between investing in the internal group or in relationships with local community was a consistent theme throughout the study and serves as an important reminder that both of these components need to be balanced in your study abroad experience.

You do need a supportive internal community. As you study off-campus, you need a community that pushes you and holds you accountable — academically, physically, emotionally, and spiritually. But strong relationships with your fellow students should also encourage you to venture out, to engage the people and the culture of your host communities. This is critically important if studying abroad is to achieve its goal of building cultural competence.

CULTURAL COMPETENCE

Before we talk about cultural competence, we must understand what is meant by culture. For our purposes, the term *culture* refers to "the patterns of being, doing, and thinking that human communities share and to which they assign meaning."[2] Perhaps the most important part of culture are the patterns that are hidden and internal, yet that shape our behaviors and interactions with others. As has been pointed out, when you participate in a shared culture, "where people are mostly acting from a similar set of ideas and beliefs about how the world works, communication and understanding is often easier."[3] As you study abroad, you will be in situations where people operate with different patterns and from differing core beliefs. As a result, your study abroad experience enables you to develop the knowledge, skills, and values needed to develop cultural competence.

While there is no single definition of cultural competence, it is generally seen as an ability to interact effectively with people of different cultures and socio-economic backgrounds. Definitions of cultural competence also include some variation of the following four components: 1) awareness of one's own cultural worldview; 2) a positive attitude towards cultural differences; 3) knowledge of different cultural practices and worldviews as well as awareness of the dynamics inherent when cultures interact; and 4) cross-cultural skills. Developing cultural competence results in an ability to understand, communicate with, and effectively interact with people across cultures.[4]

The importance of developing cultural competence can be seen in the following fable. Imagine, if you will, that in your country everyone is born with a pair of

Prior to your departure and in the first few weeks of settling into your host community, how has your group come together? What things have you done to build this internal community? In what ways have members of this group supported you?

In what ways have your fellow students challenged you and held you accountable? How are you beginning, as a group, to reach out to your host community?

sunglasses. The color of these glasses is yellow. No one has ever thought the sunglasses were weird because they have always been there and are a part of everyone's make-up. These sunglasses represent the values, attitudes, ideas, beliefs, and assumptions that all people in your country have in common.

Many miles away in another country, people are also born with a pair of sunglasses. The color of these glasses is blue, and they represent the values, attitudes, ideas, beliefs, and assumptions that all people in that country have in common. Everything that they have seen, learned, and experienced has been filtered through these blue lenses.

A traveler from the land of yellow sunglasses who moves to this far away land may have enough sense to realize that to learn about this country and its people requires a pair of blue sunglasses, which she gladly wears. The blue sunglasses make her feel that she understands this new country. Yet upon returning home this traveler explains to everyone that the culture of this far off land is green!

The moral of the fable is clear. As we learn about another culture and try on their sunglasses, we must be aware of the colored lenses that we already wear. Although we can never remove our own biases, by better understanding the values, attitudes, ideas, beliefs, and assumptions that our own culture holds, we can minimize the strength of the yellow color through which we peer. The lighter the yellow sunglasses become, the truer the shade of the blue sunglasses. We cannot totally remove our own sunglasses, but we can become aware of their existence.[5]

So developing cultural competence requires learning about your own culture and about the culture of your hosts and being willing to invest the time and energy to develop the necessary skills (e.g., listening, flexibility, and acceptance) and virtues (e.g., humility, perseverance, and courage) such competence requires. Reflect on Bethany's blog as it relates to the ways in which culture and experience can shape your perception of the world:

Every morning, we ride the bus from where we live in Santa Lucia down to our classes in Tegucigalpa. . . . We chatter in English, try to finish our homework, and stare out the window at the mountains and pulperias and police checkpoints. This landscape, full of images that would seem strange to people back in the United States, is comfortably familiar.

Yesterday morning, I took a break from looking out the window and looked around inside the bus instead. And I saw everything I expected to see: the stickers that decorate the front of the bus, proclaiming "Jesús te ama," an aisle packed full of Hondurans chatting in Spanish, the bus seats covered with greenish fabric that

How do your culture and your host community culture differ? How do these differences manifest themselves in your interactions with people from your host community? How have you tried to interpret your own culture to your hosts?

In what ways is your faith shaping how you perceive your host community? Your overall study abroad experience?

reminds me of a forest. Ahead of me, I saw some of my fellow students who are kind of strangely becoming like family, all staring out the same window. I turned to look out the window and saw a fence in front of a hill covered in purple flowers. And we were all gazing out the same window, but I suddenly wondered if we were all seeing the same thing.

So much is about our perspective. I looked out the bus window and saw the small purple flowers and thought about how I think too much. And I wondered if the other students were simply seeing the hillside, or a memory, or thinking of family in the U.S., or just passing the time. If I could see through someone else's eyes, would I understand Honduras differently?

I know the answer is yes. Because sometimes, what we look at and what we see are two completely different things. If I could whisk one of my best friends or one of my sisters down to Honduras, we would see things totally differently. I know this because when I first came to Honduras, I saw things differently. I stepped out of the airport and was overwhelmed by the crazy traffic and the dust and so much Spanish and the clash of cultures so evident in American fast food next to pupuserias.

But now? We drive through Tegucigalpa, and my eye is caught by murals that are painted by "Accion Poetica Hondureña" (or something like that). As we pass by, I crane my neck and read bits of poetry painted on a whitewashed wall. "Que tus sueños sean mas grandes que tus miedos." And my brain is automatically translating this into English — may your dreams be bigger than your fears — and I silently agree.

And I don't know if the others in the van notice or not, or if they would care about some cliché Spanish phrase on a wall. But from my perspective, it's the purple flowers and the poetry and the things that seem little that make up life in Honduras. I think that sometimes we choose what to see, and it's easy to forget that maybe the other people gazing out the window don't see what I do.

This reflection notes that perspective shapes how you see things. Even students from the same culture are going to perceive events differently as a result of their own personal history, personality, faith, ethnic background, and culture. Within your study abroad group, what are some of the different ways you and your fellow students see the world? Your host community? How do these various perspectives enrich the overall group experience? How might some of the assumptions from your home culture be limiting your ability to understand your new host culture?

CULTURAL HUMILITY

Although we have been discussing ways to develop cultural competence, some scholars doubt whether this is even possible. Consider the following perspective:

> The concept of multicultural competence is flawed. I believe it to be a myth that is typically American and located in the metaphor of American "know-how." It is consistent with the belief that knowledge brings control and effectiveness, and that this is an ideal to be achieved above all else. I question the notion that one could become "competent" at the culture of another. I would instead propose a model in which maintaining an awareness of one's lack of competence is the goal rather than the establishment of competence. . . . There is no thought of competence — instead one thinks of gaining understanding (always partial) of a phenomenon that is evolving and changing.[6]

So if multicultural competence is not fully attainable, what does it mean to become *more* culturally aware and competent in cross-cultural situations? Researchers have identified two additional factors that are necessary to develop cultural competence: 1) awareness that cultures are dynamic and ever changing; and 2) the practice of cultural humility.

It has been noted that "culture does not determine behavior, but rather affords group members a repertoire of ideas and possible actions, providing the framework through which they understand themselves, their environments and their experiences. . . . Culture is ever changing and always being revised within the dynamic context of its enactment."[7] Cultural patterns also interact with individual frameworks, creating personal histories that affect a person's thoughts and actions. The intersection of culture, individual history, and personality draws us to the idea of cultural humility.

What is cultural humility? Humility has traditionally meant a kind of meekness, but it can also denote a willingness to accurately assess oneself and one's limitations, to acknowledge gaps in one's knowledge, and to be open to new ideas, contradictory information, and advice. "To practice cultural humility is to maintain a willingness to suspend what you know, or what you think you know, about a person based on generalizations about their culture. Rather, what you learn about [someone's] culture stems from being open to *what they themselves have determined is their personal expression of their heritage and culture.*"[8]

Studying abroad creates time for reflection and introspection, which often leads to new insights. As you see the impact of culture on how you and others think, what delusions do you recognize in yourself, your host cultures, and your home culture that may need to be dispelled?

We can (and should) study the history and culture of a particular place, but we need to realize that we should also learn each individual's history and story, and learn from those we encounter on our journeys: "When it comes to understanding the unique experience of any given individual, cultural competence is *theory*, cultural humility is *practice*."[9]

As we learn cultural humility, we need to become comfortable with not knowing everything, a lesson Leesha, who studied in Peru, recognized:

> I continue to realize that this semester has taught me to take interest in other cultures, not just in observing as one does in tourism, but in understanding and learning how a society works. However, more importantly, I have learned how not to know everything, how to ask for help. . . . One of the most important things I learned in Peru was to not pretend to have it all figured out, being alright with not having complete control. Our journey through life will be much more beautiful if it includes the special touches of the people who walked with us.

Striving to be more culturally competent by developing attitudes of cultural humility demands constant work. It implies balancing the big picture with the individual relationships we foster while abroad. Read the following blog post from Katie, who studied in Ghana, as she describes her time spent in *trotros*, Ghana's version of mass transit.

In what ways is Katie developing the knowledge, skills, and values to thrive in a cross-cultural setting? In what ways could she expand on her knowledge, skills, and values to continue to develop cultural humility?

> My first few trotro experiences were nauseating. The traffic made me nervous. Paying my fare was an ordeal. The accented English names of locations I didn't know confused me. And there was the fear that I might die on the roads of Ghana where lane changes are constant and turn signals are obsolete. But now, as I flag down at least four trotros a day, our relationship is no longer based around fear. It's based around love. Yes, I love trotros. And I'm learning from them, too.
>
> I meet the most interesting people on my trotro commute. Women with kind eyes who greet me with, "Akwaaba, sistah. You are welcome." Men with low voices who ensure that I never get ripped off and pay too much. Little babies who stare at me with almond eyes, entranced by my peachy skin and golden hair. We all share the ride, touching thighs, shoulders, and for a little while, lives. In the midst of all the hubbub of traffic in Accra, I find immense peace on the trotros, sharing in the journey with my Ghanaian brothers and sisters. I feel the presence of the Lord within those vans. My pulse calms, my eyes open, and my heart dances. Jesus provides me with His peace, which is so much greater than what the world can give. In those hours on the trotro every day, my prejudices begin to melt. My frustration

from the day dissolves. And I enjoy the journey with people whose lives have coincided with mine, if only for a few minutes.

One challenge we all face is to learn how to focus on others rather than simply on ourselves. Studying abroad offers a unique opportunity to "make us realize how insignificant and irrelevant we are, what small cogs in the massive workings of social order."[10] Read the following blog post by Hannah, studying in Peru.

By coming here, my world has gotten so much bigger. And at the same time, I am realizing how very small I am. For the past twenty-two years of my life, things have been going on here in Arequipa. My [host[family and professors and classmates and friends have been living and doing things, and I never knew about any of it! To me, my reality was in Lansing, Illinois. That's all I thought about. But . . . there's so much more than Lansing! There are people all over the world! Sure, I knew that. But now that I see that, it makes me see things a bit differently. Suddenly, I am beginning to realize how little and limited my reality is.

Google tells me that the population of the world is about 6,973,738,433 people. I make up 1.43 x 10^-7 percent of the population of the world. And a very, very large percentage of my thoughts are about me, even though I make up a very, very small percentage of the people on this planet. The more I realize how small I am, the more I realize how enormous God is. . . .

I am really little. And I am loved by a God who is really big.

> How does Hannah's faith seem to help her be humbled by the study abroad experience? How can your faith keep things in perspective for you?

CULTURE AS CALLING

Committing to cultural competence is an important piece of every study abroad experience, but for Christians it also becomes an opportunity to better understand how God calls us to love and learn from one another. Did you feel a sense of calling by God to study abroad? Now that you are living in your host community, do you feel God calling you to a particular task or ministry? When we think of ministry, we often think about serving others or working to spread the gospel, but the idea of faithful presence (introduced in chapter five) helps us to see our calling to a new place in a different light.

Connecting to others, learning about their history and culture, and sharing our lives can be a form of ministry. The Bible is full of stories that encourage us to learn from the stranger. Abraham was blessed by Melchizedek; Mary and Joseph received the gifts of the Magi; Jesus himself appeared as a stranger to the travelers on the road to Emmaus. There the risen Christ humbly walked alongside his sad followers before revealing himself as they sat together at a meal.

In your current living situation, whom are you trying to get to know better? Who might be trying to get to know you? What are you intentionally doing to learn about the history and culture of your host community?

This image of Jesus walking with others along the Emmaus road reminds us of pilgrimage and the need to venture out in humility and curiosity. Walking allows for, even encourages, fellowship, conversations, intimacy with the surroundings, and the ability to see a place in its true form. Walking allows us to go at a pace that encourages us to notice God's creation, to foster meaningful conversation, and, most importantly, to meet, fellowship, and walk in stride with those along the way.

Learning and practicing how to be with those who are different than us can also lead to new behaviors when we return home. A world in which foreigners live in distant lands reachable only by leaving home has long since disappeared. Cultural difference is all around us, and when we return home we can continue to engage in intercultural learning with humility and grace. "Today, more than ever, loving the stranger is not a specialist career. It is a matter of Christian discipleship."[11]

Although differences in languages and cultures can be obstacles, they can be overcome as we humbly and sincerely seek to meet others wherever they may be.

The opportunity (and privilege) to meet and learn from others who are different from you is a gift of studying abroad. As Lydia studying in Beijing notes,

> *I think one reason I find studying Chinese so attractive is the people I have met. . . . It is one thing to read about Chinese culture and another thing to have hours of conversation with my conversation partners about how they view marriage, government reforms and methods of teaching English. However much information I can glean from reading, I find I care about something so much more when a friend is telling me about it.*

What is your calling (or ministry) while you study abroad? How might connecting and building relationships with strangers be a part of this calling?

Chapter Eight ———————
BEING FREE

People go to admire lofty mountains, and huge breakers at sea,
and crashing waterfalls, and vast stretches of ocean, and the dance
of the stars, but they leave themselves behind out of sight.
—Augustine of Hippo

My child, do not let these escape from your sight;
keep sound wisdom and prudence,
and they will be life for your soul
and adornment for your neck.
—Proverbs 3:21–22

What happens in Vegas stays in Vegas." We have all heard this catchy phrase as marketers try to entice people to visit what is viewed by some as one of the world's most decadent locations. In essence, this saying means that you can do whatever you want to do since you are out of the watchful eye of your home community, unconstrained from the usual forms of acceptable behavior, especially related to sexual activity and drinking.

The phrase can be attributed to a tourist mentality where individuals seek to escape the norms of everyday life to be free — to do what they want, when they want to do it. When tourists explore, they expect others to adapt to their expectations and accommodate their needs. Even Christian pilgrims in the Middle Ages were not exempt from this mentality: some saw their pilgrimage as an opportunity to carouse, drink, and step out of the sexual norms of the day. These temptations are certainly still present for travelers today.

You will have many choices to make while you are away. You may be faced with decisions you've not had to face before. But the truth is, God always knows the choices you are making, and those choices can affect the rest of your life. Some of the people in your host community may take drugs as a way to relax. Some may drink alcohol casually or to excess. Some may use sex as a way to connect with others. Some may see worship as optional. As you think about how to spend your time, energy, and money, remember that God has invited you to bear witness to his grace in your life everywhere you go.[1]

Spend some time considering the question posed by Ben in the following blog post:

Who are you becoming when no one is looking? Are you embracing the mantra "what happens abroad, stays abroad" and going a bit wild?

I leave you today with the same question offered to me: Who are you when no one is looking? I challenge you to explore those facets of our character that reveal themselves in such times. During this age of constant contact and communication . . . it's clear that we often put overwhelming effort into how our facades are perceived by others. A decisive amount of our character is formed in the spotlight of others. What do you see when it's only your own spotlight shining on yourself? I pray for clarity in this introspection, that we are confidently encouraged by what we find, and that we have the strength and audacity to make meaningful, slow-working commitments to ourselves to realize any necessary changes to our inscape.

RESPONSIBLE FREEDOM

At the college where I teach, the term *responsible freedom* is one of those phrases that students tire of hearing as they are continually challenged to think about how to use their newfound freedom in responsible ways. Although they may grow weary of the repeated emphasis on making good decisions throughout their college career, they do come to understand the importance of living from an embedded inner compass that gives direction when no one else is looking. Such a compass enables them to act in ways that are consistent with their faith, their core beliefs, and the responsibilities of living in a larger community.

Are you striving to make your pilgrimage a way to challenge yourself with new behaviors like committing to more personal devotional time? Are you trying on other new behaviors, such as being more outgoing if you are an introvert or being more inwardly thoughtful if you are an extrovert?

In today's society, we often champion the freedom of individuals to pursue their own well-being and happiness. Your study abroad experience, however, raises many issues and questions connected both to individual freedom and to social responsibility. There must be a balance between the freedom you have to pursue your own goals and the responsibility you have as a member of a host family, a community of students, a part of a new culture, or even as a citizen of the world.

The term *responsible freedom* means that when we make decisions, we understand not only that we possess the freedom of individual choice, but also that we must think about how our choices relate to the larger community. Americans have traditionally understood the need to balance individual freedom and the common good.

In making the film *Thomas Jefferson*, filmmaker Ken Burns interviewed historians and philosophers, asking them to explain what Thomas Jefferson meant by the words "pursuit of happiness" in the famous phrase "life, liberty, and the pursuit of happiness." His interviewees agreed that Jefferson had in mind both individual happiness and societal happiness, and that these two were linked together. As writer Timothy Ferris explained, "It seems to me that the purpose of education is to answer the question of what the pursuit of happiness is for you. The reason we go to school ought to be not to learn some skills to get a job to make a better salary, but to find out enough of who I am so that I know how to pursue my own happiness. And that happiness is necessarily involved with that of the wider society for reasons that Jefferson saw so clearly."[2]

If individuals just pursue their own happiness and don't care about anyone else, ultimately communities begin to fall apart. One person's happiness is bound up with everyone else's happiness. Philosopher Stephen Mitchell highlighted the duty of seeking the common good: "As [Jefferson] meant it, I think it had nothing to do with hedonistic pleasure. It had to do with deep satisfaction — including the satisfactions of doing your duty to your country, of doing the right thing by your friends and by your enemies, even."[3]

Christians should also be drawn toward the common good, building God's kingdom in small ways here on earth. In this process, God is concerned with the whole world and calls us to "seek the welfare of the city . . . for in its welfare you will find your welfare" (Jer. 29:7).

How do you define responsible freedom in your own life?

One advantage of moving into a new community is the opportunity it affords to shed your past. You are living with people who know nothing of your previous successes or failures. Is there congruence between the reputation you have with friends, family, and professors at home and the reputation you are developing in your host community? As the following students note, studying abroad can offer a powerful opportunity to reshape your life or to see yourself differently. What do you want this reshaping to look like? How did the following students exercise responsible freedom in both positive and negative ways?

Reflection One

During my time in London, I grew exponentially more social. I became a little social butterfly. I didn't have a problem talking to random strangers in a pub or going anywhere by myself. . . . I learned to stop caring about what people think about me by what clothes I wear or what I look like. I loved having the freedom to wear whatever I felt like wearing on that day. . . . My previous (American) looking-glass self was shattered. I perceived my own self as an individual and

In what areas are you tempted to make bad choices? How can you seek wisdom as you think about the temptations you face?

cool for being independent. I didn't feel judged and I didn't judge in return. I loved the person I became in London. I was positive, outgoing, opinionated and fun. I finally became the person I thought I was going to become freshman year of college [4]

Reflection Two

I chose to study abroad in Ghana because I figured going to a country where the Diaspora occurred, I would surely find my culture [I am of African descent], but Ghana gave me a rude awakening. I was not seen as Ghanaian because my skin was also black. I was seen as an American by my accent and clothes. I didn't relate to the Ghanaian customs and didn't find acceptance from looking the same as most others. In my frustration I abandoned my "black identity." As far as I was concerned, it would never be an accurate depiction of who I am. . . . It took some time but eventually I got over feeling like an idiot wearing mid-calf socks and a sun hat everyday and sticking out because my appearance didn't match the norm. In abandoning outer-directed identity, I found an inner-directed identity that formed from what gave me joy. This is how I found out that I had a new master status; being a child of God. In Christ I found a spiritual identity and no longer worried about my physical/racial identity. [5]

As you study abroad, you will be presented with choices and opportunities that are new to you. Making wise decisions is important to your own growth and development. What follows are three areas where the issue of responsible freedom often plays out. As you reflect on each of them, start to define what responsible freedom means for you in the context of your study abroad experience.

ALCOHOL

What is your responsibility when you see a fellow student making a poor choice?

The use of alcohol can present unique challenges to you during your study abroad experience. You will probably be living in a country where the drinking age is 18 years old or lower. Therefore, you can legally drink alcohol if you choose. Although some study abroad programs might have specific rules about the use of alcohol, at some point you will need to make a personal decision about whether to drink. And if you decide to drink, how will you do so responsibly?

Part of this decision should be influenced by the cultural norms about drinking in your host culture. Who, when, where, and how to drink may be different than it is at home.

Another part of this decision about alcohol should be informed by understanding the context of student drinking while studying abroad. Research suggests that students generally increase their drinking while abroad and that the most serious problems that students encounter overseas — including theft, sexual assault, sickness, and physical injury — can be attributed to excessive use of alcohol.[6] As the student below notes, drinking can lead to variety of negative outcomes:

> I'd say college-age students can usually handle their alcohol, but there are always a few students who forget that there are extra risks to account for in foreign countries and cities larger than their own. Each of the times I studied in Mexico, a classmate from my home university (in a small city in Nebraska) was raped in a taxi coming home from a club at night. One was sober, but she and her friends decided to chance it and let her ride home alone after the taxi dropped off the first two girls at a house they shared. Her attack would have been prevented if she had been dropped off first. . . . The other classmate who was raped on my second trip was drunk, and her friends sent her home in a taxi because they were trying to avoid a man at the club taking her home. If someone had gone with her in the taxi, things probably would have been fine.[7]

Think carefully about how you want to handle alcohol, talk to others about your decision, discuss how your community can be supportive of your decision, and then be true to yourself. Don't let others talk you into things you do not want to do. If you decide to drink, do so moderately. Avoid hard liquors, as drinks may be mixed more strongly than you are used to. Get your own drinks, and if possible watch them being made. Don't accept drinks from strangers, and use a buddy system to take care of one another.

- What have you decided about your use of alcohol while you are abroad? What was helpful to you in making these decisions?
- Have you seen any negative consequences of excessive drinking while you have been abroad?
- In terms of behaviors such as drinking, how can you hold others in your group accountable and help one another practice responsible freedom?

SEX AND SEXUALITY

College is a time when students are exploring their ideas about sex and sexuality, though this does not mean that all college students are sexually active. It does

What customs have you already seen related to drinking in your host community? Do these customs differ from your home community? If so, how? How do local customs around drinking differ between your community and the university culture in the community where you are studying?

What are some of the general stereotypes of North Americans (taken as a whole) within your host country? What are some of the stereotypes about college students from the United Sates? About women students in particular? How might these stereotypes affect your relationships with others in your host country?

What support do you need from others to make wise decisions related to social behavior?

mean that students studying abroad need to think about a variety of issues related to dating, dress, gender roles, and even sexual harassment and assaults. Topics related to sex and sexuality are often best explored privately or with close friends, family, or mentors, but the following questions may help you think through certain issues.

Sexuality here refers both to your own concepts of sexuality as well as the cultural, societal, legal, and religious aspects of sex and sexual behaviors. Your sexuality is a part of you, informed by your own culture and values, yet you are now living in a place with different cultural values and norms related to gender roles and expectations.

One way to understand these differences was presented in chapter six, where you were asked to explore the cultural norms between men and women. What did you learn from this exercise regarding dress, romantic relationships, and sexual behaviors in your host country?

Another way to understand these differences is to explore the stereotypes we have of others as well as the stereotypes that others likely have about you.

While you likely understand the importance of examining issues such as dating, dress, gender roles, and sexuality during your study abroad experience, you might not understand the ways in which issues of sexuality relate to the concept of responsible freedom. Consider the following:

- You might be free to walk down the beach alone at 2:00 am, but if you do, are you putting yourself in a vulnerable position?
- You may have the right to wear any kind of clothes you want, but are you being respectful of local customs?
- You are free to date anyone you please, but do you understand the cultural norms of dating and relationships in your host community?
- You may want to go out drinking and have some fun, but if you drink excessively, are you allowing individuals you don't know to take control of your life?

In each of these situations, is it fair that you can't do what you want? Maybe not. But it's important that you make wise decisions — decisions that may limit your freedom but also allow you to be more responsible for yourself and more responsive to the cultural norms of your host community.

There is one important caveat to remember related to issues of sexuality and gender roles. As Nancy Newport notes, "We all want to be culturally sensitive, to get along, to be respectful, to fit in, to not offend." In this book, throughout your orientation, and as you arrive in your host country, cultural sensitivity is appropriately emphasized and encouraged. Newport continues: "[Cultural sensitivity] can be the doorway through which [you gain] entry to and acceptance with the community abroad. [But] it is very important that the cultural sensitivity training provided never requires that you to submit to behaviors that invade your personal boundaries and that feel unsafe or even uncomfortable to you. If it feels inappropriate or makes you uneasy, get yourself out of the situation. Never sacrifice yourself or your sense of safety for the sake of cultural sensitivity."[8]

Being the target of catcalls can be difficult anywhere but especially in a new culture. Catcalls also raise questions about how to respond. Should the target of catcalls try to ignore them, accept them as part of the culture, or try to change this behavior by speaking out? Perhaps the best way to learn to respond is to watch the response of locals.

Women who travel abroad often face more challenges than their male friends. In addition to dealing with catcalls, women worry that friendly greetings may be perceived wrongly, and they think twice about accepting offers of hospitality. Women have often been socialized to consider safety rather than adventure as their top priority. Travel writer Tara Isabella Burton acknowledges and chafes against these restrictions, but she also notes that male adventurers have often been inconsiderate of their host countries, assuming privilege and exercising power in ways that are not always appropriate. In contrast, she recognizes that "the tools I, as a woman, use to preserve my own safety . . . become the tools of my trade as a writer. My silence, my care, my hyper-awareness, allow me to recede into the background, to allow the people I observe to become the true subjects of the stories I tell. . . . My limitations, as a female travel writer, are also my strengths."[9]

> How does Burton deal with some of the special challenges that face women as they travel or study abroad?
>> For women in your time abroad, have you witnessed or experienced any challenges relating to your gender? How have you personally dealt with these challenges?
>> For men in your time abroad, have you experienced or witnessed any of these challenges first hand? As bystanders, how might you respond in positive and constructive ways?

Have catcalls been a part of your study abroad experience to this point? If yes, have catcalls been a challenge for you? How might the challenge of catcalls be different for men or women? How do people in your local community respond to catcalls?

WORSHIP

Worship is the heart of the Christian church. In worship we celebrate together God's gracious gifts, and we are strengthened to live in response to God's grace. Worship is also uniquely connected to culture. On the one hand, worship crosses cultures and has common elements for everyone, everywhere. We celebrate this fact when we recite the Apostles' Creed and declare that we believe in one holy catholic church. Through the power of the Holy Spirit, all Christians worship the Triune God, who transcends every culture.

On the other hand, worship is very contextual. A given culture's values and practices affect how people worship. The sharing of music and art and other elements of worship is an opportunity to gain insight into a culture and also helps enrich the whole church, strengthening the sense of connection we share across cultures through Jesus Christ. However, differences in worship practices, along with language barriers, may make it difficult for you to worship regularly.

Are you attending worship services in your host community? Have you found ways to nurture your faith while you are abroad? Studies have shown that study abroad experiences can significantly enhance the spirituality of college students from the United States.[10] However, students often report many barriers to worship within their host communities. Consider the following excerpt from Sara's blog:

> I have attended church only a few times in Spain because I have found it difficult to focus on figuring out what they are saying and also on meditating on what they are saying if I pick any of it up at all. Also the first time I went to church was at the Cathedral, and that was just completely new because I am not Catholic and couldn't figure out what I needed to do at certain times in the mass. But I was shocked by how few people there were attending the mass on a Sunday morning. Spain's documented religion is Catholic, but most of them do not attend mass or even say they practice Catholicism. My host family does not practice, and they say they only go on special occasions such as for a wedding or funeral.
>
> However, I have been attending a Wednesday evening campus Bible study with a handful of students from the University of Oviedo. These meeting are very uplifting and inspiring as the Spanish students in the Bible study are all committed to sharing their faith with others, which is difficult for me. . . . It has really opened my eyes to how lucky I am to have the opportunity to attend a Christian college and live in a community that supports me. The students here don't necessarily have that, and yet they challenge me in so many ways.

🐚 As you can see from this blog, going to formal church services was difficult for this student, but she was still able to find a way to grow within an alternative faith community. Besides formal church services, what other opportunities currently exist for you to grow spiritually with others?

🐚 What are some of the barriers that have kept you from getting involved with faith communities within your host community?

🐚 How will your life be affected if you do not worship for a long period of time? As one student states, "For me, I think there's a correlation between my health (physical, mental, emotional, and spiritual) and my time spent in church. This semester I rarely went to church, and I had a tough time with everything else in my life."[11] Are you seeing this connection in your own life?

🐚 How can you commit to be an encouragement to local communities of faith, demonstrating your solidarity with brothers and sisters in Christ and serving as a reminder of God's worldwide church?

🐚 How can you challenge your view of what worship looks like? How can you be open to God's working in your life?

Read Emily's blog post and think about how God might be whispering to you during your time abroad.

Have you ever sat down and thought about love? I mean really thought about it? Lately, I have been pondering love. Love manifests itself in many ways, but my favorites are the love whispers.

Last week in Arequipa and this weekend in Puno, I began to intentionally listen for love whispers. Listening for the voice of the Spirit and folding up my jumbled thoughts of Spanglish proved to be quite difficult, but I found that love whispers sometimes come in unexpected ways. God heard my frustration, and a friend showed me a new route to school. Then I truly began to notice love whispers in Arequipa:

The whimsical, wooden chimes strung from a high terrace.
Sweet bird song, rather than screeching.
Springtime flowers in hues of fuchsia, tangerine, and violet.
Grinning babies on the combi.
Invariable azure skies and warm sunshine.
Sharing giddy God-love with a dear friend.
Fluid conversations with new Peruvian friends.

A cake festival with my lovely host family. . . .
Soft morning light.
Listening to live Peruvian music with cheerful pan flute, writing love letters to
God with a few friends as we basked in the beauty of silence.
The moment after I helped a crippled old woman down the stairs. (She grabbed
my wrist tight, stared soul deep, and told me, "Eres hermosa.") . . .
I am still working on learning to listen, but encountering a new side of God in
Peru leaves me thrilled to wake each morning. After consistently being filled, I hope
I am learning to properly love across cultural boundaries and pour some back out.

While the above blog showed how Emily connected to God through love whispers, the following student reflection reminds us that we have much to learn from our brothers and sisters in the organized church in the global South. What can you learn about the global church and your shared faith from your host community?

In 1898 Abraham Kuyper came to America to give his famous Stone Lectures on
Calvinism at Princeton Theological Seminary. Coming from the "old European
Continent," he noted the fresh currents of Christianity that distinguished the new
nation he had traveled to.. . . Traveling to Africa for the first time as part of my
college's semester-in-Ghana program, I came to know a bit how Kuyper felt. The
global South has rapidly become the new world of Christianity. . . . What has sprung
up in Africa is amazing, and on the surface this fresh Christian expression looks
quite different from that of the old Western waters. The power of spiritual forces in
Africa, and especially the emphasis on the Holy Spirit there, are aspects of Christi-
anity that have to some extent been lost in the currents of Western Christianity.[12]

We started this chapter thinking about how, during your time abroad, your individual freedom must be balanced with a responsibility to your host community. We conclude with this prayer for pilgrims:

A journey once taken alone, we now choose to take together. Moving forward as one body into a future filled with possibility, we walk without maps, but we walk confidently, and we walk with hope, because we have chosen to be lights for each other, while on the way. We travel forward along a way we have not gone before; we travel as one who is led, arms outstretched, as one who is called forth to life. We travel in need, dependent on the Lord for strength, for assurance; dependent on each other, God's instruments, for love. Leaving known paths behind us, we choose to journey in faith and service. As the journey brought us here, so now we begin it anew, in company.[13]

Chapter Nine

Taking Risks

Only those who risk going too far
can possibly find out how far one can go.
–T. S. Eliot

Be strong and bold; have no fear or dread of them, because it is
the Lord your God who goes with you; he will not fail you or forsake you.
–Deuteronomy 31:6

The notion, then, that we human beings have a "right to risk" is misleading.
We have no choice in the matter. There is nothing but risk.
What we do have a choice about is the way we deal with life's risks.
We can delude ourselves, hide behind our fears, and pretend it isn't so.
Or we can confront the risks, announce our fears, and give it a go.
–Daniel Dustin

n the Middle Ages, pilgrimages were seen as risky experiences, considered so dangerous that it was uncertain whether the pilgrim would even return, and pilgrims were encouraged to have all their affairs in order before they left. Of course, not everyone in the Middle Ages left on a pilgrimage, and today not all students decide to study abroad. This is the mystery of risk: What makes some humans willing to take risks that others won't consider? Consider your own decision to study abroad. Did some of your family and friends question your decision to leave home and explore the unknown?

Study abroad often encourages students to take significant risks. Even leaving home in the first place is an act of courage; no one departs without some anxiety. Responding to fear can be a learning experience. Rational fear is appropriate and can even be a gift, encouraging caution and thoughtfulness. However, the challenge is to prevent irrational fear from taking over. Fear of that sort can overwhelm and limit the progress of your journey, preventing you from learning the vitally important lessons that are waiting for you.

In order to gain knowledge and understanding of your host community, to make real connections, or to converse in a new language, you must put yourself on the line in ways you have rarely done at home. The challenge as you live, study, and travel abroad is to assess risks and make good decisions. The following two blog excerpts describe how two different students met this challenge. As you read these two approaches, consider the benefits and challenges of taking such an approach.

Reflection One (from Jennifer)

Live fearlessly: For such a simple phrase, "Live fearlessly" seems like a pretty challenging goal to live up to. Yet at 5:30 a.m., after I had prayed to God for wisdom regarding my upcoming journey, these are the words that flashed above me on a billboard that was just waiting to grab my attention. Usually I love adventure-traveling, meeting new people, challenging myself. These are the things I live for! But as I headed to Michigan — a quick pit stop on the way to Spain — I felt a strong rush of nervousness that felt out of place. That's when I realized that, in all the challenges I've faced and gone up against, I've still been in comfortable territory. This is the first time I will truly be pushing my limits — going to a country where I don't know the language, the customs, and the cities. I truly have to rely on God for guidance. This time, I'm not in control.

But I guess that's what it's about, isn't it? That's what makes it exciting! I don't think living fearlessly necessarily means never being scared, but rather that we face these uncertainties with enthusiasm and joy. Realizing that God isn't limited to my world at home is so comforting and humbling, and now I know I'm ready for this adventure. I know that an amazing experience is ahead of me. And best of all, I know Who will be guiding me the entire way. I will live fearlessly.

Reflection Two (from Ben)

Say yes! as our travels have been positively and often serendipitously altered by opening up to situations [as they present themselves]. With an open and positive demeanor, we've shed the defensive skin of taught distrust and fear toward the stranger. Saying "yes" has unfolded a contiguous blessing of connections and accommodations during the incessant storms and rainfall. It's been a lesson that we've taken to heart, not only in practice. Thus, the redirections and delays have indeed slowed our mileage, but it hasn't delayed our journey. This expedition cannot be measured by miles traveled; it's a journey counted one day at a time, colored by the exchanging rotation of sun and moon. . . . Our goal is to keep pedaling west with the daily freedom to discern forks in the road and doorways that present themselves.

Now that you are living abroad, what fears did you have prior to leaving that you see were unfounded? What new fears (if any) have appeared since you have arrived in your host community?

🐚 In the two blog posts above, what appeals to you about how each of these individuals is viewing risk? Is each approach realistic? What are some variables (e.g., personality type, gender, location, etc.) that might affect how you view risk?

🐚 What is your underlying default mode when it comes to responding to risk? Are you overly cautious, or are you more of a risk-taker?

🐚 The acronym YOLO (you only live once) is often used by individuals today to imply that one should enjoy life, even if it entails taking risks. Are you embracing this approach to your study abroad experience? If so, in what ways has this philosophy had a positive or negative impact on your experience?

SITUATIONAL AWARENESS

Although no one can guarantee your safety or eliminate all risks from your off-campus study experience, programs do try to minimize risk and provide training to help you create a safe off-campus experience. Prior to departing for your study abroad experience, what type of safety orientation did you receive? These orientations often include long checklists and specific tips to develop your situational awareness and help you become attentive to personal safety issues.

While it is not the purpose of this chapter to add to these safety tips and checklists, further development of your situational awareness skills is important. *Situational awareness* means that you continuously monitor what is happening around you. When done well, situational awareness will allow you to see potential threats before — and as — they develop. It is more of a mindset than a hard skill and as a result can be practiced by anyone. It also involves learning to trust your intuition. Many times, your subconscious can notice subtle signs of danger that your conscious mind has difficulty articulating.

Situational awareness does not mean being paranoid or obsessively concerned about your security; rather, it means developing a sense of relaxed awareness whereby you are aware of what is going on around you and can act quickly if something troubling occurs. It includes being constantly aware of your surroundings and the people or events that could distract you. If something makes you uneasy, get out of the situation into a more secure environment.

🐚 If possible, review any handouts or materials from your orientation. What tips have been helpful to you up to this point? What tips have not been

What does situational awareness mean to you? In what ways have you practiced a sense of situational awareness since you have been abroad?

Do you feel that you have a good sense of situational awareness? What areas of situational awareness do you need to develop?

helpful? Have there been any times when you have not felt safe? Have you shared these concerns with other students or your professor?

How can you keep a healthy balance between being paranoid and scared versus being naïve, thinking that nothing will happen to you while studying abroad? What role does your faith have in helping you answer this question?

Research tells us that "when activities become routine and familiar, we let our guard down, especially when nothing bad happens for quite some time."[1] We can become accustomed to risk and manage the fear that arises in that particular situation. This can be good and bad, as it allows us to deal with risk in a positive way, but it can also allow us to become too complacent. In the time you have been abroad, have there been any risks that you have become complacent about that might make you more vulnerable to the potential negative consequences of the risk?

TAKING RISKS

Sometimes we take risks because we have to; other times we take risks because we want to. The following story, about my time as a Peace Corps volunteer, provides a then-and-now perspective on risks while traveling or studying abroad.

Thirty plus years after it happened, I can still remember the experience as if it were yesterday. I was a young, twenty-three-year-old male serving as a United States Peace Corps volunteer in the Philippines. I had been visiting another Peace Corps friend and was going to island hop over several additional islands to meet a group of volunteers for a few days of rest and relaxation at a beautiful, unspoiled beach paradise. I left my friend and went down to the docks to catch an overnight ferry to a neighboring island where I was to take another bus and then another ferry to my destination. When I arrived at the docks, I was told that the ferry had had been cancelled this week (for no apparent reason), but they did suggest that if I could get to a remote fishing village on the north west tip of the island, there was a smaller boat that went once a week to my next stop. Without delay I jumped in a jeepney (similar to a small bus) for a three hour journey, and at the end of the road, I got in a small banca with outriggers on both sides for another three hours to arrive in the remote village where the ferry crossing was to depart the next morning. The only problem was the boat had left earlier that morning, and the next crossing would not happen for a week.

Just as I turned away, devastated and not looking forward to retracing my journey back, someone in the village suggested an alternative. There was a fishing boat anchored off the beach that was having engine trouble, and this evening another fishing boat was coming to pull the boat back to port, the very city where I was headed. They contacted the captain and received permission for me to tag along. I quickly hired a small boat to bring me out to the disabled fishing craft, a large wooden boat with bamboo outriggers and a crew of six.

As I made my way between the two boats, I remember thinking how crazy this was. Here I was alone with a group of strangers, and no one had any idea where I was. How easy it would be to rob me and dump me in the ocean and no one would be the wiser. But at this point I was committed. As we were towed throughout the night, I sat up with the crew playing cards and learning a bit more about their lives. I did pass on the awful gin they were drinking.

In the morning, we arrived at port. I said my goodbyes, bought a few bottles of beer for the crew to say thank you, and I was on my way, richer for the experience and thankful to continue my journey without further interruption. Over the years I have reflected on this trip. Would I make the same decisions today? Probably not. Would I encourage students today to make the same decisions? Definitely not. In some ways this is unfortunate, but it is a reality of traveling or studying abroad today. Students must constantly balance the desire to take risks to say yes with making wise decisions about their safety.[2]

🐚 What risks were evident in this story? How were risks mitigated (or not)?

🐚 What would you do in a situation where you felt you had to take a risk? Are there ways that you can protect yourself? Do you see ways, perhaps as illustrated in this story, that would allow you to be open to an experience but still be aware of what you need to do to be safe?

🐚 Research on wilderness mishaps indicates that no one big decision causes a catastrophe; rather, a series of smaller bad decisions culminate in a disaster. What series of decisions could have contributed to a not-so-happy ending to this story?

Many people, especially women, are afraid to travel independently because they fear being unsafe or lonely. Consider the words of this female traveler:

> At first traveling alone made me nervous, but I quickly realized it actually made me become a safer, more cautious traveler. When I traveled with other people in the past, I often became inattentive and expected

Do you agree or disagree with this perspective? How might you respond if this woman were a female friend of yours who was thinking about traveling around the world by herself?

them to be my eyes and ears. Being on my own heightened my awareness of my surroundings, which not only kept me safe but led me to absorb more of the experience. Today I feel fearless and empowered to travel independently anywhere in the world. Sometimes what we are afraid of is exactly what we need to do in order to grow.[3]

Chapter Ten

Using Technology Wisely

Technology, it seems to me, is neither friend nor foe. It is both. Technology is not either/or. It is this and that. Technology is not value-neutral. Each technology brings with it a program for social change, however subtle. Technology has made our lives easier, cleaner, and longer, to be sure. But it has also cost us. In our exuberance over what technology does, we are frequently oblivious to what technology undoes. To be ignorant of this, to be uninformed is to be the tool of technology, not the toolmaker.

–Daniel Dustin

Those who part with $2,285 a night to stay in a cliff-top room at the Post Ranch Inn in Big Sur pay partly for the privilege of not having a TV in their rooms; the future of travel, I'm reliably told, lies in "black-hole resorts," which charge high prices precisely because you can't get online in their rooms.

–Pico Iyer

We now rarely give each other our full attention, but every once in a while, we do. We forget how unusual this has become, that many young people are growing up without ever having experienced unbroken conversations.

–Sherry Turkle

You have now likely been abroad for at least a few weeks. And as the newness of everything wears off, it is easy to lose the wonder that you had a few weeks ago. As a result, you might worry how you can sustain the learning that happens in new places. Emily, a young woman in Thornton Wilder's play *Our Town*, gives words to that worry. After she dies, Emily asks to spend just one more day with her family. She hopes to capture all the sweetness and intensity of life as she now remembers it, but to her disappointment, everyone goes through their ordinary routines, carelessly ignoring the love and beauty around them. As she says farewell and returns to her grave, Emily cries, "Do any human beings ever realize life while they live it — every, every minute?"[1]

Emily's observation challenges us to live with awareness, reminding us to appreciate all that is going on around us and inside of us. As you continue to adjust to living in your host community, how can you find a rhythm of feeling at home in your new place while also maintaining the ability to live every moment fully? How do you not lose the wonder of constantly seeing God's awesome world with fresh eyes?

As you think about finding this rhythm, continuing to be amazed by your time abroad and creating wonderful memories, it is important to reflect on the role of technology. Technology is a blessing in so many ways, providing a vehicle to document your memories and stay connected with friends and family. But it can also create tensions as you struggle with the right balance between being physically and mentally present in your host community and being virtually present on social media. Let's explore both the beauty and challenges of technology in making the most of your time abroad.

A recent research study examined the impact of social media on the experience of students studying abroad. Researchers found that 47 percent of respondents felt that social media had a positive impact on their study abroad experience, 38 percent felt that it had a negative impact, and 7 percent felt that it had both positive and negative impacts.[2]

Of those who felt that social media positively affected their experiences, they noted that it

- Connected students to loved ones at home and friends abroad in a quick and easy fashion;

- Met travel needs, such as utilizing maps, finding directions, and getting recommendations on restaurants and sights to see;

- Provided assurances of safety for the student and also up-to-date whereabouts of the student to his or her family;

- Provided a means to share the experience through pictures, videos, and blogs;

- Facilitated adjustment to a new culture.

Of those who felt technology and social media negatively affected their experiences, they noted that it

- Hindered students' ability to fully immerse themselves into the culture;

- Encouraged students to latch on to home and stay in their comfort zone, thereby discouraging spontaneous exploration and taking away from the adventure.

How are you currently using technology during your study abroad experience? What gadgets (iPods, smart phones, cameras, computers, etc.) are you currently using?

THE BEAUTY OF TECHNOLOGY

In the 1990s, the great debate among educators was whether to allow students to use email on their study abroad programs, as many feared that email would decrease immersion in the host culture. Next came cell phones, causing educators again to worry about the impact of allowing phones for students. In the years since these early worries, we have seen cell phones transform study abroad by helping students interact with host communities and providing a safety net in case of emergencies.[3]

Today, technology and social media can help you prepare for your study abroad experiences, stay connected to family and friends at home, and keep in touch with new friends from your host communities when you return home.

Technology and social media can also aid reflection. Not only can you share your own experiences through pictures, videos, and blog posts, but you can also read about the experiences of others at the same time. This sharing allows friends and family to live vicariously through your experiences and can help everyone gain better understanding of the larger world.

How much time are you currently spending online? Is this more or less time than you spent online at home?

THE CHALLENGE OF TECHNOLOGY

The question related to technology and social media is not whether we should eliminate them from our lives when studying abroad, but rather what is the right balance between staying connected online and engaging the world. Recent studies show that study abroad participants may have crossed the threshold of spending too much time alone and online. For example, one study found that United States students abroad spend more than four hours per night communicating back home through social media. A similar study found that one group of students averaged 4.5 hours per day online, and that 83 percent of their contacts were with other North Americans, either at home or in their host communities.[4]

So what are the negative impacts of all of this time online? Sherry Turkle examines how technology is changing our lives. Although she recognizes the many benefits that technology provides, she argues that we might have too much of a good thing and that our relentless connection to technology can actually lead to a new solitude. As technology ramps up, our emotional lives ramp down.[5]

While technology can help us connect to others, it can also cause us to miss out on the richness and messiness that face-to-face interactions demand. When we spend excessive time online, we sacrifice conversation for mere connection. As Turkle reminds us,

How has your online time enhanced your study abroad experience? In what ways has your time online taken away from your study abroad experience?

Do you agree with Turkle's concerns about the dangers of being overly connected to social media and technology? Why or why not?

Connecting in sips may work for gathering discreet bits of information, they may work for saying, "I'm thinking about you," or even for saying, "I love you," . . . but they don't really work for learning about each other, for really coming to know and understand each other. And we use conversations with each other to learn how to have conversations with ourselves. So a flight from conversation can really matter because it can compromise our capacity for self-reflection.[6]

Recently while in Beijing, I was riding on the subway, and as I looked up and down the aisle, all I could see were people glued to their phones or online devices. No one was interacting with anyone else. It struck me then that Turkle's concern is real: we have become accustomed to spending time alone together. When you study abroad, this can have both positive and negative consequences. Spending time alone provides space to think and reflect, but you must be careful not to withdraw into an online cocoon of music, games, and conversation with faraway friends.

You need to unplug from electronic gadgets and find ways to engage with others. Again, Turkle challenges us to think about how our connectivity affects our connection to place:

When Thoreau considered "where I live and what I live for," he tied together location and values. Where we live doesn't just change how we live; it informs who we become. Most recently, technology promises us lives on the screen. What values, Thoreau would ask, follow from this new location? Immersed in simulation, where do we live, and what do we live for?[7]

Do you think a technology fast might be a good thing for your group? If yes, at what point of the experience and for how long?

One director of a study abroad experience encourages students to take a technology fast during the early stages of their travels together and invest this time in the group and in the people and culture of their host communities. This director tells the story of a group in Guatemala huddled under shelters during a rainstorm at a forestation project. "Normally, students with time to kill would turn habitually to their smart phones. Without that option, one noticed a column of unusual ants, and soon the whole group was on hands and knees examining the ground."[8]

Some study abroad professionals feel that students are not to blame for all the connections. Rather, it is parents who want to hear from their son or daughter every day. Is this true in your case? Did you talk with friends and family before you left about how frequently you would contact them while you are away?

The challenge of technology doesn't simply mean online technology. Cameras, videos, and other means of documenting your experiences can serve as extra filters that obstruct rather than enhance your experiences. Consider Johnson's blog post as he recalls his memories of a concert in Budapest:

Last week, my study abroad troupe and I were thrust into a concert during dinner. The group played a violin, a music box, and bagpipes, and they invited us to come dance with them. Although part of me wishes I'd joined in, viewing the scene from the back of the room held its own reward. . . . For a short while, no one had a monopoly on his or her own narrative because everyone was being written into a single story.

That's what I like about concerts. They invite a group of humans to be utterly and sometimes begrudgingly present in something like a community for a few hours. For a short while, the veil of social media is pulled away and everyone is actually being social. Well, mostly. There's still a shaky video being taken, a twitter account being updated (seven hash tags), and a host of other documenting taking place.

I get it — you want to remember this stuff. You want the Facebook albums and scrapbooks (maybe). But in all honesty, would you really forget a scene like that? If you were really present, actually present, would you still need a camera? Because cameras only document one-fifth of your senses.

It's a ridiculous thing to say, but my point is that our desire to remember sometimes impairs our ability to make the memory itself. Like missing the coolest part while trying to focus the stupid camera, or closing the aperture right as the lights glint perfectly, etc.

I understand that cameras serve a purpose — it's just that I've noticed that pictures always look differently than the way I remember them. I guess it's because pictures only contain visual data, whereas memories include every kind of stimuli. I wish that memories wouldn't fade, because they're the best pictures you could ever take. I doubt we'll ever be able to store memories like we do pictures, but I have one suggestion for preserving your memories: live in them. Put down your camera and drink in the world, knowing that you are eminently part of every moment and embracing the fact that this particular moment will never come again. It's almost like forcing your brain to cram before an exam, except it's cramming and remembering instantaneously (and it's less stressful). These are Polaroids of the mind. Give them a shot. I bet you'll take some pictures you won't forget.

In a TED Talk, Daniele Quercia talks about his research in using mapping applications not only to promote the quickest way from point A to point B but also to seek alternative routes that provide beauty and happiness. One summer, he remembers,

What are some of the "Polaroids of the mind" that you are taking of your study abroad experience? Are you documenting your experiences in ways that may actually keep you from living them?

In what ways are you letting yourself be trapped in routines of technology and other habits that make you miss beauty only a block away?

I lived in Boston and worked in Cambridge. I bought a racing bicycle that summer, and I bicycled every day to work. To find my way, I used my phone. . . . I took a different route one day. I'm not entirely sure why I took a different route that day, a detour. I just remember a feeling of surprise; surprise at finding a street with no cars, . . . surprise at finding a street draped by leaves and surrounded by trees. But after the feeling of surprise, I felt shame. How could I have been so blind? For an entire month, I was so trapped in my mobile app that a journey to work became one thing only: the shortest path. In this single journey, there was no thought of enjoying the road, no pleasure in connecting with nature, no possibility of looking people in the eyes. And why? Because I was saving a minute out of my commute.[9]

REMEMBERING THE JOURNEY

One particular challenge for technology arises when we visit sacred sites, places of mass destruction (such as concentration camps), graveyards, and other sensitive areas. Photography may be banned or restricted, but even if it is not, questions arise as to the appropriateness of selfies, smiling group portraits, tweets, and other media displays on sacred and hallowed ground. A related question is whether we can be fully present in the moment if we spend too much time taking pictures to remember (and show others) where we have been. Creating a "Polaroid of the mind" can be more respectful and more long-lasting than snapping yet another digital photo.

How could you do a better job living into your memories while studying abroad? What is the best way for you to document these memories, remembering the lessons learned along the way?

One study-abroad professor noted that he and his students came to appreciate places where cameras were prohibited: "Our eyes, ears and spirits were far more sensitized. . .where we were freed from 'getting the shot.'" He also reflected that selfies too often distract us from pilgrimage: "The selfie could provide a sacred pausing if it didn't involve so much posing. . . . [It] involves a level of performance that often pulls us out of the place itself. . . . We cast ourselves as the star and think about how to entertain our followers. Tours of revered spaces become an opportunity to post a photo. . . . to have something to share on social media."[10]

🐚 Do you take selfies? For you are there any unwritten rules about when and where you take selfies? If you needed to develop two or three guidelines about when and where to take selfies, what would they be?

🐚 Have you ever taken a picture in a place where it was not allowed? In the moment, did you decide that your desire for that perfect picture was more important than respecting a request from a local host or place where you were visiting? Photography can be a powerful tool for understanding and sharing, but it can also widen the gap between the host and the traveler. How can you be intentional about how you use photography in a respectful way, to build bridges or enhance engagement?[11]

Technology will continue to play a large role in your study abroad experience. This chapter has asked you to step back and think about how you can intentionally use technology and social media in appropriate and responsible ways. No doubt the answer to these questions will vary from individual to individual. Travel writer Pico Iyer provides this answer:

> So what to do? The central paradox of the machines that have made our lives so much brighter, quicker, longer, and healthier is that they cannot teach us how to make the best of them; the information revolution came without an instruction manual. All the data in the world cannot teach us how to sift through data; images don't show us how to process images. The only way to do justice to our onscreen lives is by summoning exactly the emotional and moral clarity that can't be found on any screen.[12]

So be intentional about asking yourself the hard questions about technology, and then try to live into the answers. Continue to create space to think deeply and engage fully. In addition, challenge your peers to do the same. It takes courage to confront these difficult questions, but if we have any hope of realizing life while we live it — every minute — we don't have a choice but to continue to challenge ourselves daily.

Chapter Eleven

Practicing Hospitality

Tourism is about consumption, but pilgrimage is about hospitality because hospitality desires vulnerability and learning.
–Student reflection, Honduras

Hospitality is offered in many ways – sometimes by a simple gesture of acknowledgement, a warm smile, a cup of coffee, listening patiently without interrupting, offering information, a word of encouragement, or simply by being present with the other person in silence. Hospitality requires time, patience, and kindly persistence. It cannot be rushed. It sees the bigger picture rather than seeking the quick fix.
–Ken Kraybill

Hospitality is the skill of making someone feel genuinely at home, welcoming people with warmth and joy. To be hospitable is to create a physical and spiritual space that is safe and comfortable, where the stranger is respected and accepted. Many cultures value hospitality, but in the Christian tradition, hospitality is linked directly to our relationship with Christ. When St. Benedict wrote in his rule for monastic communities, "Let all guests who arrive be received as Christ," he was reminding his fellow monks of Jesus' words to his own disciples in Matthew 25:34–40:[1]

> Then the king will say to those at his right hand, "Come, you that are blessed by my Father, inherit the kingdom prepared for you from the foundation of the world; for I was hungry and you gave me food, I was thirsty and you gave me something to drink, I was a stranger and you welcomed me, I was naked and you gave me clothing, I was sick and you took care of me, I was in prison and you visited me." Then the righteous will answer him, "Lord, when was it that we saw you hungry and gave you food, or thirsty and gave you something to drink? And when was it that we saw you a stranger and welcomed you, or naked and gave you clothing? And when was it that we saw you sick or in prison and visited you?" And the king will answer them, "Truly I tell you, just as you did it to one of the least of these who are members of my family, you did it to me."

Such hospitality is radical and potentially life-changing for both the host and the guest, and it is a fundamental practice for Christians. We are to be kind, gracious, and compassionate to others, and particularly to strangers, because in welcoming them we are welcoming Christ himself.

When we think of hospitality, we often think about how we can extend hospitality to others, but another aspect of hospitality is learning to accept it graciously. Radical hospitality depends on this give-and-take relationship. During your experience abroad you are likely to be the recipient of the hospitality of others. Through this process, you are learning to let go and to rely on the generosity of others. Even the simple act of getting into a taxi late at night in an unfamiliar place and trusting the driver to take you home is a reminder of our own vulnerability and our need for others. Hospitality then becomes, as Leonard Biallas reminds us, an "unsought grace":

> Desmond Tutu explains it this way: "In Africa they say that a person is a person through other persons. We can only be human in fellowship. The law of our being is that we have been created for togetherness, for communion." . . . Hospitality is not about abundance or totality, but just sharing, real sharing. We become one with the stranger as we allow the other to stand before us as a unique person. We rejoice in our mutual interdependence. Self-imposed barriers tumble down, as well as our tendency to deny them recognition. This mutual "making present," as Martin Buber calls it, confirms the stranger even though there are differences in structures, visions, and practices. The stranger is an unsought grace, an unexpected source of life.[2]

Hospitality is also integrally woven into the practice of pilgrimage. Pilgrims throughout history have had to rely on the hospitality of others to survive. They have also learned to practice hospitality toward one another as they journey together toward their destination.

The idea that hospitality encompasses both giving and receiving is illustrated in Luke 10:25–37, where Jesus is asked, "Who is my neighbor?" Jesus responds not with a list of neighbors and non-neighbors but with a story — the story of the good Samaritan.

The question posed to Jesus is similar to the question we might ask today about hospitality: *Who is my neighbor*? Whom must I treat in a neighborly way? What sorts of persons fall inside or outside the boundaries of neighborly obligation? Of course, we recognize on some level that everyone — black, white, rich, poor, educated, and uneducated — is our neighbor.

Yet Jesus ends his story with a different and more profound question: *Who was a neighbor to the man who was hurt?* Consider how Hannah's time abroad led her to think about hospitality differently:

Last week in one of our classes, we talked about the Parable of the Good Samaritan. I think that most of the time when I think about that parable, I identify myself with the Samaritan. I want to be a good neighbor to the people around me and to help and serve them unconditionally. However, in class we talked about this parable from the point of view of the scribe whom Jesus is talking to. The scribe would definitely want to identify himself with the priest or the Levite, but since they do nothing to help the beaten man, the scribe cannot identify himself with either of those people who receive so much respect in his culture. Furthermore, because of the terrible reputation of Samaritans, the scribe CANNOT identify himself with the Samaritan. Therefore, his only choice is the man who was beaten and robbed and left for dead.

So I've been thinking about what it means to identify myself with the man who fell into the hands of robbers and received the mercy of a stranger. That is really not far off from my reality right now. No, I'm not almost dead on the side of a road, but I am quite dependent on people I didn't know two weeks ago and who are at home in a culture that is different from my own. I am dependent on them to eat food. I am at their mercy to learn about this culture. Without them, I would have no place to sleep! Rather than being the one with the power to help, I am in a position of receiving from mi familia. I am learning that that requires a lot of humility. It is often (for me) a lot easier and more comfortable to give than to receive, but God is stretching me and teaching me how to receive well.

Likewise in the following reflection, a student recognizes the need to both receive and give hospitality as part of his time abroad:

In his book The Wounded Healer, *Henri Nouwen says that genuine hospitality is when a person comes to terms with his own loneliness and offers hospitality to others. We are called to make space in our own souls for the souls of others to reside, reflect, rest, and grow; to Nouwen, "hospitality asks for the creation of an empty space where the guest can find his own soul."[3] Tourism is about consumption, but pilgrimage is about hospitality because hospitality desires vulnerability and learning. While I am in Honduras, I will be a pilgrim by both accepting and giving genuine hospitality. I want to make space for mutual indwelling between myself and Hondurans with whom I will share my experience. By accepting the hospitality of others, I can share life with the people surrounding me. I will learn their food, music, language, and friendship as they wish to show me. At the same time, extending my life to others, especially in an uncomfortable and unfamiliar environment, will stretch me to see my experience abroad as more than a class trip or a chance to travel.*[4]

This student's attitude toward hospitality recognizes that one way of practicing hospitality is to honor other people's stories. How are you sharing and listening to stories of those around you?

RECEIVING HOSPITALITY

Receiving hospitality can often be more difficult than extending hospitality because it means you are not in control and must follow the lead of others. In the following excerpt, writer Kathleen Norris describes the hospitality of her own community:

The people of the Great Plains can be hospitable as well, in the fashion of people who have little and are willing to share what they have. The poorest among us, in the Native American community, are exceptional in this regard, with a tradition of hospitality that has deep cultural roots in the giveaway, a sacred event that in application served the purpose of providing for the entire tribe. Hunters brought their surplus meat or buffalo robes, and those too old or infirm to hunt brought handicrafted items like quillwork; and in the exchange everyone received what was needed to survive the winter. Even today the ceremonial giveaway, in the words of Arthur Amiotte, a Lakota artist, remains an important and "reciprocal activity in which we are reminded of sacred principles," an act of giving which "ennobles the human spirit."[5]

In this excerpt, Norris attributes the hospitality of the Great Plains to the severity of the winter. What might be the reasons for the hospitality you have encountered? How does the hospitality you have received compare with that given to strangers in your home culture?

Read the following two stories and think about how both the giving and receiving of hospitality can be viewed differently.

Reflection One

I was attending a barrio fiesta with my host family and spending time with various family friends of my host family. As guests moving from house to house, we would always be asked to partake in the various delicacies that had been prepared for the occasion. I ate sparingly, always aware that each

Hospitality is often the first characteristic we notice when we are new to a host community. Perhaps we see it because we are so anxiously looking for and needing it. Who welcomed you when you arrived and in what ways? How have you responded? Have you trusted the sincerity of their motives, or has the welcome made you somewhat uneasy?

family had so little and that what I didn't eat would be passed on to other members of the family. As we moved from house to house my host mother, a small feisty woman, pulled me aside and asked, "How does it make you feel to give a gift to someone?" Surprised by the question, I answered, "It makes me feel good." She then looked me in the eye and said, "Then stop denying that feeling to others who want to share with you!" In that moment, my host mother had taught me another valuable lesson: the importance of receiving hospitality gracefully, by letting the giver be a blessing to me.[6]

What barriers limited this individual's ability to accept the hospitality of others? What are some barriers that prevent you from experiencing the hospitality of others?

Reflection Two

It is early, and I decide to walk the beach. It is a beautiful morning; the sun is warm on my face; the wind is blowing; there are all kinds of activities taking place. I watch the fisherman coming in on their small fishing boats powered by the wind. The small dots on the horizon become bigger as each fisherman approaches the shore and skillfully maneuvers his craft through the surf and onto the beach. . . .

As I walk further down the beach, I see other fishermen beginning to pull on a large rope. I ask if I can help and join the group. I grab the rope at the surf and slowly walk up the beach about twenty yards, drop the rope, and walk back to the surf and pick up the rope again. Others follow the same routine, and we soon find a rhythm that continues for about a half hour. The nets have been laid the night before and are a long way off shore.

As I start to wonder if there will be anything in the nets, I notice more and more people gather waiting to see what the nets will yield. Slowly the net begins to appear but still no fish . . . and then the last of the nets come out of the water holding all kinds of marine life — small fish, medium sized fish, sea snakes, squid, shrimp, sting rays. As the bounty from the sea emerges, the people who are standing and watching spring into action.

It seems that everyone has a job. Some begin to sort the bounty brought up from the sea. Some animals are thrown back into the surf, while others are thrown on the sand. Other people start to tend to the net itself, while still others take the fish thrown on the beach and make piles in what I assume is dividing up the bounty of the sea for the families who depend on this fishing net for their survival. Everyone seems to get a share; everyone seems to be taken care of. Then as quickly as the commotion started, it is over. The nets

How were these fishermen practicing hospitality with one another? Were these fishermen being hospitable to the writer by allowing him to share in their experience? Why or why not?

are stowed and the piles of fish disappear, and I am left with an incredible sense of gratefulness for the opportunity I had to share in the lives of this fishing community, if only for a few short minutes.[7]

Accepting the hospitality of others allows both the giver and receiver to share equally. It is easy to think of ourselves as the ones who are feeding the people, giving them clothing, taking care of their needs — especially when we are in a country that has obvious financial and material needs. But on your study abroad experience, you may be the one who is hungry or thirsty. You are definitely the stranger who needs welcoming. As a guest, however, you may also offer the gift of curiosity, taking an interest in what other people do and how they do it. A hospitality-focused curiosity gives us an opportunity to live out our Christian faith in concrete ways, whether that means eating foods we wouldn't normally eat, wearing clothes that aren't comfortable, or speaking in a language that doesn't easily roll off our tongue.

GIVING HOSPITALITY

Receiving hospitality opens our hearts to share hospitality with those we meet along our journeys. But this realization does not come without risks and responsibilities. Leonard Biallas reminds us that "historically, some forms of hospitality — such as cities of refuge, the underground railroad, the sanctuary tradition — have actually cost some people their lives. Strangers occasionally take advantage of us, bring unanticipated trouble, or intend harm."

So we must begin the process of seeking out the stranger as Jesus did, but we must also remember that the kind of hospitality that God demands also requires us to challenge our society when and where it is inhospitable. Biallas continues, "This might mean pressing for human rights and economic equality, or being sensitive to social injustices and celebrating racial diversity. It might entail pushing for public policies that affect the poor, the homeless, the neediest, the most vulnerable. It might involve looking after people in extended care facilities, aging parents, or people with disabilities. It might include educating migrants and refugees to become literate in English. . . . Hospitality works toward dismantling the barriers of the world, as problems regarding diversity and inclusion, boundaries and community, challenge us daily."[8]

As we extend this kind of radical hospitality, we catch glimpses of God's vision for our world and experience what the Hebrews call shalom. Although shalom is often referred to as peace, it is so much more. As Cornelius Plantinga shares in his book, *Not the Way It's Supposed to Be,*

The webbing together of God, humans, and all creation in justice, fulfillment, and delight is what the Hebrew prophets call *shalom*. We call it peace, but it means far more than mere peace of mind or a cease-fire between enemies. In the Bible, shalom means *universal flourishing, wholeness and delight* — a rich state of affairs in which natural needs are satisfied and natural gifts fruitfully employed, a state of affairs that inspires joyful wonder as its Creator and Savior opens doors and welcomes the creatures in whom he delights. Shalom, in other words, is the way things ought to be.[9]

Jim Forest in *The Road to Emmaus: Pilgrimage as a Way of Life* invites us to consider how strangers can speak into our own lives when we extend hospitality to them. For Forest, extending hospitality is an invitation to be in relationship with others:

Again and again we meet strangers along our way who speak with unexpected clarity about things that really matter. . . . Perhaps it is only for an hour or a day. A hesitant conversation takes wing. A reluctant tongue becomes fluent. Finally, we eat together. By now the stranger has become a named person — José, Carl, or Ahmad, Maria, Larissa, or Teresa. Sooner or later we part, but we remember that encounter as a shining moment. We didn't literally meet Jesus risen from the dead, and yet, in this brief communion with a stranger, Jesus became present and traveled with us. . . . Ideas about Jesus were replaced with an experience of Jesus.[10]

Thus, being a disciple of Jesus means to be open to contact with others, willing to share stories, willing to talk about the real issues in one's life, willing to listen with undivided attention. Henri Nouwen explores the connection between hospitality and community when he writes,

In our world full of strangers . . . we witness a painful search for a hospitable place where life can be lived without fear and where community can be found. . . . Hospitality is not to change people, but to offer them space where change can take place. . . . Hospitality is not a subtle invitation to adopt the lifestyle of the host, but the gift of a chance for the guest to find his own. . . . That is our vocation: . . . to create the free and fearless space where brotherhood and sisterhood can be formed and fully experienced.[11]

What does it mean to make our lives overflow with hospitality? How do we create places where everyone feels welcome, and all of us can be encouraged and challenged to become what God wants us to be? How can we create communities "where we can

What blessings and lessons have you learned from reaching out to strangers?

Have any strangers spoken into your life since you have been abroad?

In your current experience, what can you do to build community with others through the use of hospitality?

be free to let others enter into the space created for them and allow them to dance their own dance, sing their own song and speak their own language without fear," free also to leave and follow our own vocations and to return and share what we have learned?[12] How can we learn to seek the welfare of others, to be a disciple of Jesus, to remain open to contact with others, willing to share stories, willing to talk about challenges, willing to listen with undivided attention?

HOSPITALITY PRAYER

Lord Jesus Christ,
We believe you welcome us all to your banquet table.
　　May we open our arms to embrace you,
　　May we see you in the face of a stranger,
　　May we welcome you in the love of a friend.
We believe you welcome the abandoned, the misfit, the wretched to your feast.
　　Forgive us for the times we have allowed our prejudices to overrule,
　　　and rejected you because you are different, ostracized or despised.
We believe that there is beauty hidden in each person,
　　Forgive us for the times we have failed to see your face,
　　　because you are disabled, poor, or homeless.
We believe we are all precious in your sight.
　　Forgive us for when we have counted you unworthy of our love,
　　　for when we have been indifferent to your cries.
We believe we are called to share life together as members of one family,
　　Forgive us for when we have been unconcerned for your suffering,
　　　and failed to see others in your worldwide community as you do.
We are all created in God's image,
　　redeemed by Christ,
　　filled with the Holy Spirit.
We are all invited to feast at God's banquet table.
　　We are welcomed into God's eternal kingdom,
　　with all the peoples of the earth.[13]

Chapter Twelve ———————————

Dwelling Well, Traveling Well

Six months anywhere is enough to begin to complicate life.
By that time, if you stay in one place, you are bound to
know people too well for things to be any longer simple.
–Langston Hughes

I mean there is a part of my soul that will always live in Paris whether I'm there
or not. And there's literally not a day that goes by, even three or four years
later, that I don't think about something that happened while living in Paris.
. . . I can't explain it, something in me fundamentally changed because of my
experiences abroad . . . it sort of made me realize how big and yet how small
the world is. It made me realize how diverse it is, but also how accessible it is.
–Student interview, France

This at least seems to me the main problem for philosophers. . . .
How can we contrive to be at once astonished at the world and yet
at home in it? . . . How can this world give us at once the fascination of
a strange town and the comfort and honour of being our own town? . . .
We need this life of practical romance; the combination of something that
is strange with something that is secure. We need so to view the world
as to combine an idea of wonder and an idea of welcome. We need to
be happy in this wonderland without once being merely comfortable.
–G.K. Chesterton

Recently, I heard a former study abroad student speak about a post-graduation adventure: he had biked from Grand Rapids, Michigan to the Pacific Ocean, fulfilling a long-held dream. While he loved the adventure and thrill of travel, he also talked about a tension he constantly feels. He wants to be rooted in his community and develop a deep affection for one particular place, but he also wants to travel.

I can relate to this tension, as I love to travel and to encourage students to do the same. But I also struggle with the importance of helping students connect to their home communities and encouraging them to dwell

well in those places, too. Understanding ourselves as pilgrims is one way of dwelling well both at home and abroad.

SOJOURNERS AND PILGRIMS

In their book *Beyond Homelessness*, Steven Bouma-Prediger and Brian Walsh suggest that, as pilgrims, we learn to see ourselves as inhabitants rather than residents. When we come with a humble heart, being willing to develop relationships with those we meet, seeking the justice that God demands, and being open to the possibilities of this world, we open ourselves to discover God's wonderful plan for our lives. We begin to see our calling and how we can be a part of God's work in his world. We begin to see what it means to not only live deeply but to dwell well as inhabitants, wherever we may find ourselves. They cite David Orr, who says that "A resident is a temporary occupant, putting down few roots and investing little, knowing little, and perhaps caring little for the immediate locale beyond its ability to gratify . . . The inhabitant, by contrast, 'dwells.' . . . Good inhabitance is an art requiring detailed knowledge of a place, the capacity for observation, and a sense of care and rootedness."[1]

Bouma-Prediger and Walsh also explore the tension of being rooted in one place versus the desire to move and be nomadic through the metaphor of a sojourner. This metaphor is similar to the pilgrim metaphor, but they think of the sojourner as a dweller in this world, one who sinks roots in a particular place and makes a home. The sojourner always knows that he or she could be called elsewhere to sink roots there, to make a home and dwell in another place. For the sojourner, what is of utmost importance is being in communion with God and being open to go where he calls, for it is only in God that we find a safe and secure home.

Whether you resonate with the metaphor of the sojourner or that of the pilgrim, it is important to recognize the need to live within the tension of both dwelling and moving as you journey toward God. As you embrace this journey, you are called to be a blessing to the people you meet and the places where you set your feet, to make beautiful, temporary homes and communities by bringing God's presence and strength with you. Part of learning to be a pilgrim is learning how to invest in each place, not living on its surface or merely consuming its resources, but sinking roots into the soil and making the place home, even for a short while. Part of learning to be a sojourner is learning to embrace the journey as you move from place to place.

As Susan Felch has said,

Because our hearts are set on pilgrimage, we recognize that all our homes — our birth homes, the homes we make for ourselves at college, the homes we make in the places we travel — are but shimmering images of the home that God creates for us in his own heart. It is not that God reflects the homes we love here on earth, but that these homes are — and ought to be — mirrors of God's gracious hospitality.[2]

Sharon Daloz Parks also writes about the relationship between home and pilgrimage. She criticizes the tendency in the West to use "the journey" as the controlling metaphor for our spiritual lives, without stressing its companion metaphor: "home." Parks argues that the future of our planet depends upon reconnecting the metaphors of journey and home, detachment and connection, pilgrims and home-makers: "For the primary task before us . . . is not that of becoming a fulfilled *self* (or a fulfilled nation) but rather to become a faithful *people*, members of a whole human family, dwelling together in our small planet home, guests to each other in the household of God."[3]

What does it mean for us to be at home in this world? On the one hand, we as Christians are called to remember that this world is not our home and that we are just passing through, but on the other hand, God calls us to embrace the places that we inhabit. Consider the words of Jeremiah 29:4–7:

> Thus says the Lord of hosts, the God of Israel, to all the exiles whom I have sent into exile from Jerusalem to Babylon: Build houses and live in them; plant gardens and eat their produce. Take wives and have sons and daughters; take wives for your sons, and give your daughters in marriage, that they may bear sons and daughters; multiply there, and do not decrease. But seek the welfare of the city where I have sent you into exile, and pray to the Lord on its behalf, for in its welfare you will find your welfare.

A SENSE OF HOME

Although *home* is a word used frequently in our culture, this is also an age of increasing homelessness. Elie Wiesel once described the twentieth century as "the age of the expatriate, the refugee, the stateless — and the wanderer. Never before have so many human beings fled from so many homes."[4] The desire not to be alone and the desire for home are powerful human impulses.

How are you dwelling well in your current situation? What might it mean for you to "seek the welfare of the city" where you now live?

The sense of home can become even more complicated for students studying abroad as they try to understand a new home, or contend with homesickness, or reflect on where home really is. Read Emily's reflection on what home means to her.

I was born in Winston-Salem, North Carolina. And then my family transitioned to Lafayette, Indiana, and they've been there ever since. But when I was a sophomore in high school, we moved to Lima, Peru, for three months. And after high school, I moved to Grand Rapids to attend school here. But last semester I lived in York, England, for four months. Then back to Indiana for the summer. Then back to Grand Rapids. And here I am.

I'm sure we've all felt this way, like we don't belong anywhere. Sometimes I feel like a conglomeration, a collage, a drawer full of bits and pieces, a batch of random memories. Where do I fit in? How do I reconcile my past experiences to my life right now? How can I relate to other people? I feel as though there is no common thread in my life's narrative. There is no place where I feel that I can truly call home.

When I go out to the grocery store, I say to my housemates, "Okay, I'm running to the store! I'll be home soon!" But then I talk to my family about Thanksgiving break, and I say, "I'll drive home on Wednesday morning." Then I'll reminisce about living in Peru or England, and wish I could go back to those homes. However, the question remains, "Where is my home? Where am I from?"

Studying abroad in York, England, changed my perspective about what constitutes home. I never thought that I would consider York to be a home to me, but as our group spent the days, the weeks, the months walking among cobblestones and bricks, I felt a deep connection to this place that was becoming increasingly familiar and strange to me. "But," I argued with myself, "this place can never be home to me. If this is home, what does that make my childhood house? What does that make college home? But if York isn't home, what is?" When we were traveling, too, I attached myself to many of the locations to which we ventured. The city felt like home. The countryside felt like home. The bus felt like . . . well, never mind.

One of our assignments in York was to find a place in the city at which we would spend at least thirty minutes each week writing, journaling, and meditating. I chose York Minster, a massive Gothic-style cathedral that has been part of York in one form or another for literally a thousand years. Each week as I walked into the Minster, feeling its cool, dry air in my nose and craning my neck to take in the stone columns and stained-glass windows, I was overwhelmed with contentment and joy. I still feel the reverberations of those feelings six months later. But this is a place that I only knew for four months out of the two hundred and fifty-five that I have been alive. How is it that I felt at home here?

I am a theatre major, and I love to act. There is a certain state of consciousness to which all actors strive in a performance, when they are so immersed in a scene that they are fully "in the moment." They are prepared for whatever might happen on the stage, physically, emotionally, psychologically. They have intentionally and voluntarily surrendered to the scene and have become embedded in it. They have created for themselves and the audience another world.

I think that the concept of home might be different for everyone, maybe slightly, maybe drastically. For me, home is not a place. Home is not a person. Home is not a thing, and it is not even an idea. In my life, home is a state of being. It is like that moment on the stage where I create a place for my character. It is a connectedness with other human beings. It is intentionally surrendering oneself to the scene. Home is giving oneself over to being shaped and molded by God and finding rest for the heart. Home can be anywhere with anyone in any circumstance. Home is now. It is up to you to make it.

Why did the Minster feel like home? Why did the slums of Lima, Peru, feel like home? Why does an Indiana sunset feel like home? Why does this moment feel like home? Because I am here. I am fully present. I have chosen to make today a part of who I am. I have chosen to surrender to God's will for me.[5]

How might studying abroad help you feel at home in the world? Read the following scenario adapted from Bouma-Prediger and Walsh. What challenges and issues does it raise for study abroad programs? Do these challenges or issues change for Christians?

Meet Kenneth and Kenny; they are neighbors, although they've never met. Kenny lives in a ravine in the park with his brothers. They have set up a couple of tents and added some furniture they picked out of the garbage. Kenneth lives in the building next to the park on the twentieth floor in a condominium.

Kenny is poor and homeless and panhandles on a busy intersection that Kenneth passes frequently driving his BMW. Kenneth is rich and actually has two other "homes" in other parts of North America. Kenneth's business activities require him to work out of three cities, so his wife, Julie, suggested that they should have three places to live, that way Kenneth would not be stuck in boring hotels, and she could accompany him regardless of which office he was working out of at a particular time.

Kenneth and Kenny both enjoy a drink once in a while. Kenneth drinks better stuff than Kenny does, but the inebriating effects are similar. Of course,

Where do you consider home? Is it one place or multiple places? How do you define the concept of home? Does it revolve around a sense of place or around friends and family, or is it a state of mind?

If you are able, watch Pico Iyer's TED talk on home. In this talk, Iyer examines his sense of home and states, "It's only by stopping movement that you can see where to go."[6] Do you think this semester will help or hinder you seeing where you want to go and where you want to call home?

Kenny is also a crack cocaine addict, which greatly impairs his ability to live a "normal" life.

There are other things that are different about Kenny and Kenneth. Because Kenny lives in a ravine, he knows that white-tail deer and coyotes are becoming plentiful in the city again; some days he notices migrating magnolia warblers and Baltimore orioles flying past his tent. Kenneth and Julie notice little about the natural world living in their condo but they do have a few potted plants to remind them of the natural world.

Kenneth and Julie spend about one week a month in their condo so they have made few friends and they don't know their neighbors. Kenny on the other hand knows lots of folks in the neighborhood. He hangs out at the local street outreach ministry and helps cook for other homeless people. Because of the time he spends observing and hanging out in the community he knows what is going on in the neighborhood and has many people he connects with regularly.

So here's the question: Who is homeless here? Kenneth or Kenny? There is no denying that Kenny is homeless and there is no virtue in esteeming his impoverished, drug addicted life. But again, we need to ask the question: Who is homeless here? Do Kenneth and Julie really experience any place in the world as home to them? In their wealth, their mobility, their power, are they any less homeless than Kenny is? Or perhaps that is the wrong way to put the question. Perhaps we need to ask whether Kenny and Kenneth are both deeply homeless, albeit in different ways? Both Kenneth and Kenny are at home in their respective worlds, and yet they are both, in important respects homeless, because they both experience deep displacement in their lives.[7]

PLACEMAKING

The story of Kenneth and Kenny raises questions about how we live in a particular place. Does our power and affluence allow us to live like global nomads, not connecting to people or places but rather consuming resources that allow us to live in our own personal bubbles? If so, how do we move from being global nomads to global citizens — people who think beyond the boundaries of identity and place and act on their moral responsibilities to other human beings? Studying abroad can be one way to broaden our thinking beyond ourselves if we take the time to understand the places where we are living and studying.

As Wendell Berry once said, "If you don't know where you are, you don't know who you are."[8] Getting to know the place where you are living adds another layer to your study abroad experience. Regardless of the courses you are taking or the program you are pursuing, are you learning about the places where you are living and studying? Are you connecting as deeply to place as you are to the people in that place? Are you learning anything about the ecological principles and challenges of your place? How will this knowledge help you to feel more at home in your host community? Read the following two reflections about feeling at home while studying abroad:

> What have you done to make yourself feel at home in your host community? What would you still like to do to deepen this feeling of being at home while studying abroad?

Reflection One (from Nicole)

I remember the moment I suddenly felt at home in Ghana. It was nothing spectacular; it was just a brief moment about two weeks after arrival. It was a thought in my head and a feeling in my heart that this was home, for now. In the weeks and months after that moment, there were many more moments that reminded me of why I was there and why this felt like home. There were many more moments in which I experienced God's grace, and in which I simply experienced God in Ghana. . . .

We really had to make ourselves at home in Ghana; in a culture so different from our own, that's the only way to make it work. Just do it. Go to the market and buy food you've never tried before, talk with your roommate and their friends who've never met a white person before, wave down a taxi and bargain for what you guess is a good price, and hop on a trotro going to the complete wrong city and just laugh at your mistake when you get there. Throughout our four months, we slowly figured out that if we were going to seize the day and make the most of every opportunity, those are exactly the things we'd have to do. And pray. We asked God to open our eyes and our hearts, to make us strong, to stretch us wide, to show us the beauty of his world, his people, and his church in Ghana, and our prayers were answered well beyond our imagination.[9]

Reflection Two (from Grace)

It happened on the train ride home from a rainy weekend at Lake Balaton, a popular getaway spot about three hours outside Budapest. After two hours of seemingly endless plains dotted with occasional villages and glimpses of the lake, we started to see buildings. And I thought to myself, we must be almost home. That's right — home. Exactly seven days after my departure from the Grand Rapids airport, I called Budapest home.

In these two reflections, what role (if any) does a particular place play in making each student feel at home? In what ways has a sense of place contributed or not contributed to making you feel at home while studying abroad?

The shift was gradual. On our first full day in Budapest, I felt like the quintessential tourist. We took a tram into the city and hit up many of Budapest's most famous landmarks, taking a kazillion pictures along the way. And by the end of that day, I was in love with Budapest, but I was far from at home in it. I felt like I was just on a really good vacation.

Yet little by little, I began mentally moving into the city. I bought groceries and cooked meals. I unpacked my suitcase and bought a new blanket for my bed. And then I packed my backpack and left for that rainy weekend at a small town on Lake Balaton. I spent most of that weekend sitting in cafes to get respite from the rain, and I found myself missing Budapest. By the time I got on that train back to Budapest, I was already dreaming of my comfortable dorm bed and the endless places to go and things to see in Budapest. I couldn't wait to get back to the little life I had begun building there. I felt like I was going home.

Scott Russell Sanders in *Staying Put: Making a Home in a Restless World* makes the case that rootedness in a particular place is vital:

> It has taken me half a lifetime of searching to realize that the likeliest path to the ultimate ground leads through my local ground. I mean the land itself, with its creeks and rivers, its weather, seasons, stone outcroppings, and all the plants and animals that share it. I cannot have a spiritual center without have a geographical one; I cannot live a grounded life without being grounded in a *place*.
>
> [There is an] orthodoxy that I wish to counter: the belief that movement is inherently good, staying put is bad; that uprooting brings tolerance, while rootedness breeds intolerance; that imaginary homelands are preferable to geographical ones; that to be modern, enlightened, fully of our time is to be displaced.[10]

How would you respond to Sanders' argument in light of your study abroad experience? How could you use the concepts in this chapter to explain the connection between home and pilgrimage?

THE ART OF TRAVELING WELL

Perhaps you will feel the tension between rootedness and movement most vividly when you consider how much traveling away from your host communities you will do as you study abroad. After all, a semester anywhere in Europe opens up the continent for weekend travel. Discount airfares contribute to this tension: for instance, if you live in London, you can often travel round trip to Greece for the weekend very reasonably. In addition, most semester programs include a week-long break when you can plan additional traveling.

All of these opportunities for independent travel are amazing, but choosing when and how often you should be gone from your host community is difficult. Typically, these decisions are individual ones based on money, opportunities, and desire; however, there is also value in stepping back and discussing with friends or mentors the decision to stay or go. Just because you can doesn't mean you should.

Given the tension between rootedness and movement, you need to ask yourself, "How can I travel wisely, taking time to deeply invest in the places where I am studying but also taking advantage of the unique opportunities I have to be amazed at God's awesome world?" Just as there is real value in deeply rooting yourself to a particular place, there is also value in exploring and experiencing the joys (and sometimes hassles) of budget travel. As J. R. R. Tolkien remarked, "Not all those who wander are lost."[11] Travel allows us to experience new perspectives, meet interesting people, see beautiful places, and think about the world differently. Consider the following reflection on independent travel from Lindsey:

> *This past week, the majority of students took a raincheck on their midterm exams and headed out to explore different parts of the country and city of Arequipa. Peru is an incredibly diverse country, hosting three distinct regions: the coast, mountains, and jungle. Different groups of students headed to each of these regions, taking in incredible scenery and meeting other travelers from around the world.*
>
> *These voyages put to the test everything that we have learned thus far about the language and culture here in South America, as we traveled independently from our professor and in many cases without our Peruvian families as well. This may have been a week of vacation, but I would dare say that we each learned more about the geography and people of Peru and about ourselves than we could have ever learned sitting in a classroom.*
>
> *Throughout our trips, we prided ourselves in not being your typical tourists. We enjoyed exploring the marketplaces and striking up deals with the vendors with ease, being confident and familiar with the custom of bartering. We cherished the opportunity to act as the facilitator between those who spoke broken Spanish and those who spoke broken English in our lodges and hostels. We rejoiced when a waiter in Cusco asked us if we were from Lima, confused as to why a group of gringos were speaking Spanish in a highly populated tourist café. We praised God when our Spanish-speaking guide asked us what religion we were and when we replied, "Christian" he replied, "I knew there was something different about you guys."*

What benefits did these students experience in their independent travel that went beyond what they could learn in their host communities?

How are you consciously making the effort to connect with your host community? How does spending time in your host community help you to dwell well?

What places have you visited outside of your host community, either individually or with your study abroad group? What benefits have these travels provided? How are you managing the tension between staying and going while you are studying abroad? Where do you still want to explore before you return home? Do you have any guidelines or principles that you are using to make these decisions? Are you actively consulting others in making these decisions?

As you look for ways to balance the tension of staying or going, you might want to consider the concept of micro adventures. Micro adventures encourage individuals to create adventures that are self-propelled, close to home, affordable, easy to organize, and designed to get people moving and learning about their local places. In his book *Microadventures*, Alistair Humphreys calls micro adventures "a refresh button for busy lives."[12] How can you foster a mindset for planning and doing micro adventures that allows you to connect with local people and local places?

In contrast to microadventures, consider the life of James Holman (1786-1857), who went blind in 1811 at the age of 25 but who has been called one of the world's greatest travelers. Holman's adventures have been described by Jason Roberts in *A Sense of the World: How a Blind Man Became History's Greatest Traveler*.[13] As Roberts notes, "When the permanence of his condition became clear, [Holman] found that only one thing could minimize the pain and keep depression at bay: the act of placing himself in entirely unknown surroundings. So he wandered off, traveling entirely alone."[14] Holman took three major trips: traveling around Europe, meandering through Russia, and ultimately circumnavigating the globe from 1827 to 1832.

Roberts says that

[Holman] knew no foreign languages, had almost no money, and carried little more than a primitive writing machine — yet he also had a prodigious memory, hyper-acute remaining senses, and vast amounts of personal charm. He wrote seven volumes of travelogue, became a bestselling author and a fellow of the Royal Society, celebrated and commemorated as "the Blind Traveler." His wanderings left their mark on history. The Holman River in Africa was named in his honor. In China he was one of the first Westerners to warn of the growing class conflict that culminated in the Taiping Rebellion. His accounts of indigenous cultures in Zanzibar, the Seychelles and Madagascar are still prized by modern-day anthropologists.[15]

When asked in an interview what we can learn from Holman's story, Roberts replied, "There will never be another James Holman, but there will always be people who must summon the courage to plunge wholeheartedly into a world complex beyond their illusions of comprehension."[16]

For Holman, dwelling well meant experiencing the world completely (with all his senses) and sharing what he had felt and experienced with others. As you make decisions about upcoming adventures to a variety of places, challenge yourself to explore what it means to dwell well in your travels.

Chapter Thirteen

Experiencing Thin and Dark Places

Travel to thin places . . . does disorient. It confuses.
We lose our bearings, and find new ones. Or not.
Either way, we are jolted out of old ways of seeing the world,
and therein lies the transformative magic of travel.
–Eric Weiner

Wisdom sits in places.
–Apache proverb

One of the best parts of any study abroad professional's job is the opportunity to visit students while they are away. When I travel, I often join students on excursions to important historical or cultural sites, and I get to hike with them in their surrounding region. One of my most memorable experiences occurred on a visit to Santiago, Spain. It was Sunday morning, and we were in the square in front of the Cathedral of Santiago de Compostela, watching travelers arrive as they finished the Camino de Santiago, the pilgrim route to the shrine of the apostle Saint James the Great. There we saw tears of joy, hugs for fellow pilgrims, and prayers of gratitude. It was moving to share in these sacred moments as people of all ages and nationalities finished their personal pilgrimages.

Experiences such as these are not unusual for students studying abroad. Students talk often of program excursions and experiences that bring them face to face with both the beauty and the brokenness of the world. Put another way, students often experience both thin and dark places during their time abroad.

THIN PLACES

The concept of the thin place, which is rooted in Celtic spirituality, acknowledges that there are certain locations where we sense the divine more readily, where we feel a porous boundary between heaven and earth. The separation between heaven and earth seems narrowed, the line between them thin. Christians and non-Christians alike have claimed this idea of thin places. As one secular writer noted,

Given your worldview, how would you define a thin place?

I'm drawn to places that beguile and inspire, sedate and stir, places where, for a few blissful moments I loosen my death grip on life, and can breathe again. It turns out these destinations have a name: thin places. . . . They are locales where the distance between heaven and earth collapses and we're able to catch glimpses of the divine, or the transcendent or, as I like to think of it, the Infinite Whatever.[1]

Nature often plays a prominent role in our experience of thin places, as evidenced in the following excerpt from the book *Listening Point*:

As I sat there on the rock I realized that, in spite of the closeness of civilization and the changes that hemmed it in, this remnant of the old wilderness would speak to me of silence and solitude, of belonging and wonder and beauty. Though the point was only a small part of the vastness reaching far to the arctic, from it I could survey the whole. While it would be mine only for a short time, this glaciated shore with its twisted trees and caribou moss would grow into my life and into the lives of all who shared it with me.

I named this place Listening Point because only when one comes to listen, only when one is aware and still, can things be seen and heard. Everyone has a listening-point somewhere. It does not have to be in the north or close to the wilderness, but some place of quiet where the universe can be contemplated with awe.[2]

Have you ever experienced a thin place? Where was it? What made it a thin place for you?

Yet a natural setting is not the only kind of thin place. A thin place can be anywhere that we are transformed. Author Eric Weiner suggests that "In thin places, we become our more essential selves," and yet he also notes that "You don't plan a trip to a thin place; you stumble upon one. . . . To some extent, thinness, like beauty, is in the eye of the beholder."[3]

While the concept of thin places appeals to me, I am compelled to examine it through the lens of my Christian faith.[4] If a thin place is defined as a place where God's presence is known with particular immediacy, then there are many examples of thin places in both the Old and New Testaments: the burning bush, the pillar of cloud and fire, Mount Sinai, the tabernacle, and the temple. However, these thin places and others in the Bible have less to do with geography than with God's choice to make himself known there. For example, Mount Sinai, where God made himself known to Moses, could be thought of as a thin place, but after the time of revelation had passed, the place retained none of its miraculous thinness. What matters is not where we are when we encounter God, but rather how open we are to God's presence wherever we are.

Another concern about thin places is that if we believe in an omnipresent God, then he is everywhere and the whole world should be considered a thin place. So the idea of thin places takes on another meaning for Christians. Thin places are not certain geographical locations that are special portals to the divine; rather, they are places — and they could be anywhere — where for whatever reason we become more attuned to God's presence. Given this definition, God continues to be everywhere, but our openness to him is often facilitated by a certain place.

Can you see your whole study abroad experience as a thin place? What might this look like for you?

DARK PLACES

If thin places are often focal points of pilgrimage, where ordinary matter seems to shine with God's presence, perhaps we can describe those places that seem forever shadowed with the power of destruction as dark places. For example, battlefields, places of torture or mass execution, areas associated with genocide, slave markets, and concentration camps — all those dark places seem at first to proclaim the absence of God.

Yet if God is everywhere, then we should be able to find him everywhere, even in the dark places. Consider the following blog posts from students who visited dark places. Do you think these students were able to find the presence of God through their experiences?

Reflection One (from Ryan)

On Friday we toured The Cheoung Ek Genocidal Center in Phnom Penh, one of the 20,000 former killing fields in Cambodia. The Khmer Rouge executed about 20,000 people here, burying the bodies in 129 mass graves. In the middle of this now beautiful park, the Memorial Stupa stands tall. This memorial contains only skulls, lots of them. They rest in stacked glass boxes, staring solemnly outward. As I walked around the memorial, trying to understand what 20,000 people gone looks like, one of the skulls caught my eye. This skull had no distinguishing feature, but when I saw it my mind created the living person who once had this skull in their head. I could see this person eating, laughing, and talking to people, experiencing similar hopes and fears that I feel. This person could have been me, a normal law-abiding citizen. My skull could be staring blankly out of a glass box at somber tourists seeing hundreds of skulls just like mine. But I stand on the other side of the glass. This person happened to be at the wrong place at the wrong time while I happened to be born at a better place at a better time. This determined which side of the glass I looked through in the Memorial Stupa. I have done nothing to deserve the life I have and I should always understand how blessed I am.

Reflection Two (from Laura)

History has never felt so real. For our Eastern European culture class, we read a memoir called Castles Burning, *written by Magda Denes, who was a Jewish child in occupied Budapest in 1944. Her family survived Nazi roundups by hiding in attics and safe havens, on streets that, today, are just a few metro stops from where I live. After four months hiding in a basement, Magda's family emerged to find their city a smoldering ruin. The Budapest that I now call home barely existed after the war.*

Learning about the Holocaust in the past, I could always think about it having happened in Other Places. But here I am, and here it was. Last week on a tour of the city's Jewish Quarter, we visited a tiny courtyard, tucked behind a synagogue, where over 2,000 Jews are buried. Most remain unidentified. They are the casualties of Budapest ghetto, which was active during the last three months of the war. A mass grave, hidden in the middle of the city.

In America, war is fought in distant lands, and the Holocaust filters in through books and imported museum artifacts. Here, the memories are real and tangible: in bullet holes on the sides of buildings; in the preserved stones of the ghetto wall; in long-lost names etched on memorial plaques.

Across from the Parliament, near the river's edge, sits a small memorial called Shoes on the Danube. *Sixty pairs of iron shoes, cast in the style of the 1940s, sit on the sidewalk, pointing toward the water. High-heeled shoes, children's shoes, work shoes so real you feel you could step into them and walk away. The memorial is for the hundreds of people who were arrested in 1944 by the occupying Nazis and marched to the Danube. They were ordered to take off their shoes, and they were shot into the water. One of them was Magda Denes' brother.*

Budapest is full of beauty to reveal, but beneath the postcard panoramas simmer the memories of a dark history. That history is becoming more of a reality the longer I'm here, though I've barely scratched its surface. Tomorrow, our group leaves for Poland. We will see castles, cathedrals, and the beautiful city of Krakow. But then we will tour Auschwitz concentration camp, a place that till now has only seemed like a nightmarish story.

In Laura's next blog post, she wrote:

How has history come alive for you during your study abroad experience? What are some insights from seeing history firsthand that you want to remember long after you return home from your study abroad experience?

It was a beautiful day at Auschwitz, and it didn't make sense.

Not a lot of things made sense that day — not the blue sky or the gently warming sun, not the pleasant red brick of the buildings or the green grass or anything about Auschwitz, really. The existence of the place is beyond comprehension, but there it stands, just outside Krakow, Poland. If there's one thing I understand after studying the Holocaust here, it's that I cannot possibly understand the Holocaust. Yet there we all were, touring and trying to make sense of it all. . . .

We walked through barracks that have been converted to multi-floor museum rooms, displaying things like Nazi documents, prisoner uniforms, and maps of Europe showing the far reaches of the continent from which Jews were deported to Auschwitz. We saw photos taken illegally of people who had just arrived on rail cars to the nearby extermination camp, Auschwitz-Birkenau. One photo shows a line of young children, just after the selection process. I realized with a jolt that they are walking toward the gas chamber. "On the way to death," the caption reads.

Part of the museum is devoted to displaying the masses of items stolen from the prisoners by the Nazis. The Jews deported to Auschwitz didn't know where they were going to, and were encouraged to bring their suitcases; now hundreds of those trunks are stacked to the ceiling behind glass display cases. Some have the owner's name painted on: Klara, Franz, Margaret, Sara. I wondered what they were like, these forgotten people, lost in the commas of seven-digit casualty statistics.

The masses of stolen items are breathtaking. There is the famous room of shoes, each of its walls a display case stretching as far as you can see, with mountains of deteriorating shoes behind its glass. Elsewhere is a pile of eyeglasses, some pairs gut-wrenchingly small — toddler-sized. Another huge display holds two tons of hair, shaved from the heads of the prisoners to make cloth and pillows for German soldiers. Standing in that room, I could not cry, but a heaviness pressed on me and it was suddenly hard to breathe. I couldn't look away.

At the conclusion of the first part of our tour, before we took the bus to Auschwitz-Birkenau, we stepped into a small gas chamber. Sunlight streamed in from holes in the ceiling through which poison gas canisters had once been thrown. The walls were concrete, and somebody had left flowers on the floor. We stepped out, boarded the bus, and nobody spoke for half an hour. I guess sometimes there are no words.

At Birkenau I walked the very train platform where hordes of prisoners were dropped off and sorted into two groups: those who would live, and those who would die. The expansive, 600-barrack camp was half-destroyed by fleeing Nazis who tried to burn the evidence of their crimes at the end of the war. But we could

How does your faith help or hinder your understanding of dark places? Does your faith provide reassurances or create doubts or both?

see the rubble of the giant, destroyed crematoria, looking eerie in the afternoon sun. "A million bodies were burned here," our guide reminded us. "You are walking on the ashes of thousands of people."

Visiting Auschwitz was difficult. It was heartbreaking, disturbing, and confusing. There are decades between me and the things that happened there, and it was hard to escape the detachment I felt from everything. The weather was nice, the air was calm. I wondered if I should have been crying, if there was something wrong with me for feeling almost numb to the place. But my friend James said it well when he pointed out, "It's not about what I felt. It's about what happened to them." I didn't go to Auschwitz to feel something; I went to see and learn and try to understand; to connect, in some distant, terribly incomplete way, with the people who suffered there; to give the victims my respect by acknowledging their suffering.

How did these two students process the experience of visiting a dark place differently? Do you think they saw or felt God's presence during the experience? What do you think each student learned from the experience?

Think of a time when you experienced a dark place. Where were you? Did it happen while you were studying abroad? Do you remember what you felt? What helped you come to grips with what happened there?

While the horrors of Auschwitz and even the Killing Fields are well documented, we live in a world where beauty and darkness often coexist. Part of the value of studying abroad is that you are able to experience the world in all its complexity. One of the challenges and blessings of faith is that we can find God everywhere. Through experiencing dark places in person, we can realize, as Jim Forest says, that "each dark place is an encounter with Christ's cross and, like the cross, confronts us with painful questions: Are we among that small circle of faithful disciples standing near the cross as an act of solidarity? Or are we among the many who have fled from it for fear we too might get into trouble?"[5] With a mindset such as this, dark places can become thin places where God speaks to us and offers us the opportunity to confront our own humanity and our response to injustice in this world.

Chapter Fourteen

Living in the Middle

*The test of a first-rate intelligence is the ability to hold
two opposed ideas in the mind at the same time,
and still retain the ability to function.*
—F. Scott Fitzgerald

*Standing in the middle of the road is very dangerous;
you get knocked down by the traffic from both sides.*
—Margaret Thatcher

Throughout this book, we explore a number of tensions inherent in the study abroad experience:

- Striving to be a pilgrim, yet realizing a part of you might always be a tourist (chapter 2).

- Crossing the threshold to studying abroad, yet wanting to stay connected to friends and family at home (chapters 4 and 10).

- Building internal community with your fellow study abroad students, yet reaching out to connect to the people of your host comunity (chapter 7) .

- Being free to shape the person you want to become, yet embracing your responsibilities to be a part of something bigger than yourself (chapter 8).

- Being safe, yet taking appropriate risks as you connect to the people and culture of your host region (chapters 8 and 9).

- Learning how to accept hospitality, yet learning how to offer it to others (chapter 11).

- Staying put, dwelling well, and creating a sense of connection with your host community, yet taking advantage of the opportunities to explore new places (chapter 12).

- Striving to understand a new culture, yet realizing the depths of your own culture (chapter 15).

- Acknowledging your doubts, yet working to grow in your faith (chapter 15).

- Working to embrace justice in this world, yet realizing that you are often a part of the problem (chapter 16).

- Wanting to share your Christian faith with others, yet realizing that to share, you must also be open to listening to the faith journeys of others (chapter 17).

- Learning to serve, yet also embracing the opportunities of serving to learn (chapter 18).

In your time abroad, you may have identified other tensions as well. Rather than resisting or trying to resolve these tensions, remember that studying abroad is a prime opportunity for you to learn how to "live in the middle," as Bethany reminds us in this blog excerpt:

Here in Honduras, I'm living in the middle. In the middle of English and Spanish, in the middle of the comfortable and the uncomfortable. I'm in between loving life here and wishing I could be there for my friends and family back in the U.S. I still don't have a major (no surprises there), and I don't really know where my life is headed. I am caught between cultures and languages and my old ideas and new ideas, and sometimes it can be a bit overwhelming because I have no idea where I stand.

And it is so tempting for me to want to be either here or there. I want to be standing on concrete ground; I want to be able to look around me at this world and say, "This is where I fit." But slowly I'm realizing that there is so much for me to learn in the middle. As much as I want to rush ahead and be comfortable and have my life figured out, there is even more value in right here, right now, embracing every moment and understanding that I don't need to have all the answers. So for now, I'm learning to live where I am. To wake up and be thankful for another day in this beautiful country, surrounded by new family and friends and occasionally huge spiders. To be content and joyful and appreciate every funny and exhilarating and difficult experience, and to realize that right now, I am supposed to simply live in the middle.

It can be difficult to live in the middle and to deal with the tensions that are discussed in this book and that you are experiencing in your study abroad program. But if you begin to embrace these tensions, you will learn how to thrive in the messiness of this world. In this chapter, several students share their struggles to embrace the tensions they experienced as they studied abroad.

What are some of the tensions that have been especially hard for you to embrace while studying abroad? What are some of the tensions that have been easier for you to embrace?

In your life, what are the benefits of being open and willing to live in the middle of tensions that are harder to embrace?

Reflection One (from Bethany)

When I was in kindergarten, I had this vague dream of growing up to become a nurse, a fairy, or some combination of the two. I was convinced, however, that I would never actually become a grown-up. I'm nineteen, and I'm still convinced that I'll never actually become a grown-up; although I no longer dream of being a fairy, so I guess I've made at least a little progress.

But in kindergarten, even though I didn't have the most realistic career goals, I knew I had plenty of time to figure out life. And as elementary school blurred into middle school, and middle into high school, I always looked forward to that vague, distant future in which I would finally know "what I was supposed to do" with my life. As I grew up, I struggled with demanding perfection of myself, and realizing that was a goal I could never achieve. But I looked toward a future in which, despite my brokenness, the circumstances around me would be in perfect order. Ha. Little did I realize that life is not that clean.

I'm a sophomore in college. I kind of need to figure it out. My current plan of staying in college indefinitely and going on a different semester abroad every year is probably not going to fly with the whole financial situation of me not being a millionaire. But if I can't even decide what kind of bagel I want to buy, how in the world am I supposed to pick a major?

But I think I've finally figured out the real problem. I'm afraid to make a decision because I'm afraid I won't be perfect. I'm afraid that whatever I pick will be a real career, and I can't be a fairy. I'm worried that I'll make mistakes and regret some choices. And I've spent a long time believing the lie that if something I accomplish in life isn't perfect, then it isn't worth doing.

I'm coming face-to-face with my unrealistic expectations of perfection. I know I will never be perfect — in fact, I am smacked in the face with all the ways I'm inadequate more times than I'd like to admit. But this past week I've realized that I am still seeking perfection in my circumstances. I want our group in Honduras to be completely unified and patient and loving. I want so badly to fully understand the roots of poverty and corruption, and I want to fix them. I want to pick the perfect career, and I don't want it to be full of the pitfalls, drudgery, and mistakes that it inevitably will be. When I was little, my grandparents had a saying hung over their sink, one that I never actually understood:

> *Ring the bells that still will ring*
> *Forget your perfect offering*
> *There is a crack in everything*
> *That's how the light gets in*

How has your time abroad helped you to learn more about yourself? What have you learned?

How do you respond to messiness in your own life? Are there actions, attitudes, or values that you would like to relinquish in order to better live in the messiness of the middle?

What resources are available for you as you live in the middle of your own tensions? How could you use these resources well?

But maybe I understand it a little bit better now. Everything in this world is a little bit cracked. And when we expect perfection, we will always be disappointed. But we can't be afraid to live and to act simply because we know our actions will be imperfect. So sometimes we have to unclench our hands from this unreachable goal and instead embrace what is right next to us.

What's right next to me? A group of college students who are wonderful, energetic, hilarious, and have blessed me incredibly despite our collective imperfections; a country that is full of beauty and hope in spite of rampant corruption; and my future that will not be filled with perfect choices, but that will be filled with a God of grace who redeems my imperfections each and every day.

Reflection Two (from Johnson)

(At the time he went abroad, the author was an All-American on his college's swim team.)

"You're going to Hungary? What about swimming?"

"I'll swim in Hungary."

"Oh."

So went many of my conversations during the past few months. To be honest, I had no idea if swimming in Hungary would actually happen. Fortunately through contacts in Hungary, I was able to find a suitable placement. After a bit of rerouting, I was directed to a competitive swim club twenty minutes away from my dorm. The first contact I had with the coach was an invitation to an all-night swimming party where I could meet the coaches and swimmers.

"All-night swimming party" is a loaded term. It could mean a lot of swimming, or a lot of pretty much anything else. I had no idea what to expect, but I couldn't pass up an invitation like that.

Turns out it was a lot of swimming — specifically an all-night continuous relay in which each team volunteered four swimmers for thirty minutes, after which the next four took over. I left early because I had an all-day excursion the next day, but in total the team swam 500 kilometers (and we won, apparently). The swimmers were incredibly kind, and I felt at home surprisingly quickly.

Last week, I started my actual training. To say the least, I was a bit worried because I was (and still am) out of shape. I missed the second practice, but these are the distances I know:

1st practice: 2500 m

2nd practice: ????

3rd practice: 5000 m

4th practice: 6000 m

Now, I'm not saying these are inordinately long practices — I just saying that if you graph it out, the trajectory becomes unsustainable very quickly. Anyone who has swum with me knows I can't do anything past a 200. Which brings me to my next Hungarian swimming experience: The five-kilometer swim.

I got invited to an open-water swimming competition in Porec, a sea-side town in Croatia. Obviously, you'd be loony to turn down a weekend in Croatia, but you'd also be loony to swim a 5k. Unfortunately, they were inextricably linked.

Sparing some details, the town was picturesque with terraced houses leading down to rocky beaches and clear blue water. The weather was mild, and most of my time was spent relaxing on the shore. Except for The Swim.

The swim was a huge clockwise circle around the bay. I couldn't see the whole circle from the shore. That was encouraging. I asked the coach if anyone had ever died swimming a 5k. He didn't think so. That did not reassure me.

Instead of staggering the start, all the swimmers started at the same time, which meant a lot of jostling and getting kicked in the face. For the first 1000m, I felt fine. At the turn for the longest stretch, I figured it was time to drop the hammer, which I did for a little while. Then I started getting passed by some guys, then some girls and then a girl in a pink bikini. That was where I drew the line. I was determined to stay with pink bikini girl if it was the last thing I did.

Around the 4000m mark, my left hand fell asleep (I finally understood why you shouldn't breathe to one side only). I tried singing albums in my head to keep track of time, but I kept getting distracted by my hand. The water was so cold that I couldn't feel myself moving anymore; I could have been drowning, and I wouldn't have noticed. At long last, I sighted the finish line. I mustered enough energy to pass pink bikini girl. I thanked her in my mind for the moral support. If I looked half as bad as I felt, I'm sure I was a sight to behold. I finished in 1 hour 25 minutes. I was just glad I finished.

Looking back, I couldn't have imagined all the stuff I've experienced in the last three weeks. I'm very grateful to the team for inviting me into their club for a semester, and for the kindness I've already encountered from so many Hungarians. I also think it's cool that my college's study abroad program makes five-kilometer swims in Croatia possible. This isn't the education I expected, but it's certainly worthwhile.

Reflection Three (from a class blog)

It was another day in Nairobi that included a trek to the Masai Market, through heavy, chaotic traffic. What we didn't know was that the market itself was to be just as chaotic and potentially more traumatic. Our goal was to get long traditional skirts called kangas. As we walked into the market, the vendors flocked to

What experiences have you pursued in your host community in an attempt to make a dream come true? Are there still experiences you would like to attempt prior to leaving your host community? If so, what are they and how could you make them happen?

Have you learned to laugh at yourself while living abroad? What is the role of humor in helping you live in the middle while abroad?

our big group of Americans, pulling people aside to look at their goods. One of the variables in this, though, was that we were deliberately not told how much those skirts should cost. And the bargaining began. Some got away with steals, others did not — I being one of those. When I first decided on a skirt, they said it would be almost $1000 USD. What they didn't realize was that though I was a rich American, I was actually a poor college student. We hassled a bit, seemed to sincerely offend them, and got away with two skirts for about $16 USD each. We then found out that they should have been closer to $8 USD. A cultural experience, yes. But I think this highlights something we've been discovering more and more in the time we've been here, and that is this:

There are so many questions. Where do you draw the line between feeling compassion for these people and wanting to support their goods and livelihoods and just being ripped off? And how do Kenyans view Westerners? How has Western culture impacted Kenya, and where is that good and where is it not? How much can we propose and push changing their traditions to replace it with what is our culture and things we view as right? What about when some of these practices are deeply harmful to the people, and often more specifically, the women?

Yes, there are cool giraffes in Kenya, and delicious mango juice, and perfect warmth with a slight breeze. But there are big questions, things we are wrestling through as a group. We're about to head up to the Northern part of Kenya to spend time in the Samburu community. And there very well may be a huge clash of our culture and theirs. And it's bound to produce more of these questions, and more of a face to the health and water issues we expect to see. We're excited; these questions are good. God is good.[1]

> Throughout this book, questions have been presented to help you explore the challenges, questions, and tensions that you may be experiencing while studying abroad. How have you seen these questions and challenges change over your time abroad?

When you live in the middle, there are no guarantees that everything will work out as you hope or that you will find all the answers that you seek, but you do create the context where deep learning can happen and rich experiences can be had. Living in the middle is an invitation to experience life to its fullest and to grow in unexpected ways. As Ellie notes in her blog:

> Have you been able to answer any of your big life questions while studying abroad? What lessons or insights are you hoping to take from your living in the middle while abroad?

My faith has matured. I no longer need black-and-white answers. Living in this tension, this in-between, like we wait with eager expectation during advent for Christ to come, and as Jeremiah talks about in chapter 29, is what life is about. It is about living in the complexity, thinking, reflecting, and weighing the multiple factors. Life is a myriad of colors with varying shades. Back at school I want to keep embracing this complexity, this tension, with hope. I want to keep service-learning and communing with the Lord, joining him in his great work and joining my brothers and sisters as we seek shalom.

Chapter Fifteen
DEALING WITH ADVERSITY

An adventure is only an inconvenience rightly considered.
–G.K. Chesterton

Nothing in the world is worth having or worth doing unless it means effort, pain, difficulty. . . . I have never in my life envied a human being who led an easy life. I have envied a great many people who led difficult lives and led them well.
–Theodore Roosevelt

Detours and other glitches are dancing lessons from God.
–Kurt Vonnegut

Traveling and study abroad come with both promises and pitfalls. Smooth transitions and trial-free travels and pilgrimages are rare. The very term *travel* originates from the Middle English *travaile* (to labor, toil, suffer, journey).[1] Although traveling today is easier than in the past, when things go wrong — and they always do at some point, no matter how well prepared we are — we are reminded again of its difficulties. When you study abroad, a challenging situation seems even harder because you are in new surroundings and do not yet know how to navigate a different culture. How you respond to adversity makes all the difference between being miserable or thriving as Hannah, who studied in Peru, discovered:

There are times when we struggle, when we just barely survive the daily pressures. There are times when issues in the States, a world away, bring us to tears. Sometimes, we are stressed out by the workload that comes with our Spanish classes. Even the Spanish language or culture itself confuses and discourages us. Other times, spending days in bed, in the clinic, or over the toilet eats away at our energy physically, mentally, and even spiritually. Every one of us has had times in which we felt depressed and helpless, times when we just wanted to be home where everything in our lives is much easier to understand. Yet in all of this, we truly are blessed. We aren't just surviving the days anymore; we are thriving.

SOURCES OF ADVERSITY

As you study abroad, difficulties can come from many directions. Two common sources are culture shock and doubt.

Culture shock

Culture shock is the personal disorientation you may feel as you adjust to living in an unfamiliar culture. The severity and length of this adjustment will depend on a number of factors, including your personality, the amount of time you spend in the new culture, the degree of social and cultural difference between you and individuals in your host community, and the level of support you experience.

Culture shock is frequently described as a cycle of stages. Although the stages below do not describe every instance of culture shock accurately (and many variations have been proposed), they can serve as a reference as you navigate the ups and downs of living cross culturally.[2]

1. *Wonder*: As you leave home and arrive in a new place, everything is new, interesting and exciting. You experience your host community as a tourist. The new sights and sounds are charming and present no challenge to your status or identity. During this phase, you experience people and culture passively and regard it positively.

2. *Disorientation*: Differences become apparent — and irritating — as you experience difficulties in everyday life. You begin to be overwhelmed by the new culture as you are bombarded by stimuli in your new environment. You feel disoriented and inadequate.

3. *Irritability and hostility*: You may feel homesick, depressed, and helpless as you see yourself as an outsider, someone who doesn't belong. You may start to distance yourself from your host community by reading, connecting constantly with friends and family at home, sleeping too much, or sticking with the other members of your group. You may even find yourself beginning to feel angry with, or hostile towards, the host culture.

4. *Adjustment*: You develop strategies to cope with external difficulties and personal feelings, make new friends, and learn to function better in your new culture. During this phase, you may slip back into disorientation and irritability, but slowly you begin to experience a sense of comfort in your

Up to this point in your study abroad experience, what frustrations have you experienced individually? Collectively as a group? How have you responded to these frustrations?

What support do you need or does the group need to respond to these difficulties?

new surroundings. You are now willing, and sometimes even eager, to engage more fully the joys and challenges of living in a new culture.

5. *Integration*: You accept and embrace cultural difference; you increasingly see the good and bad elements in both your host and home cultures. You not only accept the physical discomforts and cultural differences, but you also begin to enjoy them. The environment hasn't changed, but your attitude has. You begin to feel at home in your new community, and as your return date approaches, you feel sad. Preparing to leave can be a time of confusion and pain as close bonds are broken with no promise of renewal in the future. You may also begin to sense how much you have changed as a result of your experience.

6. *Returning home*: The difficulty of leaving your study abroad experience is replaced (at least initially) with the excitement of seeing your family and friends again.

7. *Reverse culture shock*: As you return home, the excitement of seeing family and friends quickly wears off and can be replaced with new challenges. Family and friends are initially excited to hear about your experiences, but this interest quickly wanes, and they want the same person who left to study abroad to be back. In various ways you may experience the pressure to become just one of the crowd again. The problem is, you can't. You may feel frustrated, angry, or lonely because friends and family don't understand what you experienced and how you have changed. Your experiences have challenged you to think and act differently. You need time to process and integrate new values and perspectives into the person you have become. This reintegration can be thought of as reverse cultural shock. For some of you this will be acute; for others the process will go more smoothly.

8. *New normal*: You incorporate what you learned and experienced abroad into your life at home. This often requires a shift in perspective and in the understanding of your home society and your own future growth and development. You explore getting involved in new activities at home and planning a life that is built upon the future rather than the past. As this process plays out, you will be able to integrate your intercultural experiences and learning into a new normal for you, wherever you find yourself.

In what ways have you experienced culture shock as you have been studying abroad? In what ways have you witnessed other classmates experience culture shock? How does your experience and that of your classmates match or differ from the stages described in this chapter? What have you learned from these experiences?

Google the phrase "strategies to respond to culture shock." What resources did you find? As you review these resources, which ones might work for you?

How does the following blog post from Andrew, who was studying in Britain, demonstrate — or not — aspects of culture shock?

> *[This] past week has been challenging for sure. . . . We hit the two month mark, and that made me freak out a little bit. We have been living in England for such a long time, and we still have such a long time to go! I want to be here living in England, but I also want to be experiencing life at home. It was also spring break for all my friends back home, so seeing pictures and knowing that people were traveling or going home was hard to see. The weather was also pretty bad. It was rainy and cloudy every day. I just had no motivation and was just quite homesick. All of these factors made for a week that was full of homesickness, exhaustion and many challenges. I emailed my parents, Skyped and texted friends, and just had to get out of the "funk" (props to my dad for calling it this) and get right back on track.*

You will inevitably deal with the some type of culture shock while you are abroad. Consider it an opportunity for growth rather than a negative experience to avoid or overcome as quickly as possible. Richard Slimbach, who has directed many study abroad programs, writes:

> Some experience of culture shock *always* accompanies productive culture learning. . . . Implicit in the discomfort and disorientation posed by our host culture is the opportunity to see ourselves as cultural beings, perhaps for the first time. At home we are rarely forced to face that part of us that is the product of our cultural conditioning. . . . Our cultural identity only becomes evident by contrast — by encountering another set of values, customs, and habits in which we feel hopelessly lost. At the moment of experiencing the unusual behavior of the foreigner, a mirror is held up to our own.[3]

Doubt

Doubt, the second common source of frustration, often shows up as doubt about God, your beliefs, and your own spiritual life. Encountering religious diversity, blatant disregard for faith, and ways of living that are very different from your own moral code can be challenging, as these students discovered.

Reflection One

[At my college], I took a class called "The Problem of Religious Diversity" that quickly had me believing that just about any belief system could be true and that

no one could prove anything. It never occurred to me until then that people who believed something other than Christianity had the same reason for believing their faith as I did for believing mine.

How about that?

I ran into an old Sunday school teacher sophomore year and told him I'd been thinking that maybe it's not true that everyone who's not a Baptist will go to Hell. He looked me straight in the eye with saintly gravity and said: "The Bible is very clear: if you believe that, you aren't a Christian." . . . The way he said it put me in a state of fear at first, then repentance, then confusion, and lastly anger. I rebelled from the religion that contained all the smallness of my childhood. I cursed my Baptist teacher and God and fled to Russia for a study-abroad semester sponsored by a coalition of Christian colleges.

The first person I talked to there was Dan, a student at Grace College in Michigan. He immediately asked the last question I wanted to hear: "So what's your faith look like?" I went cold. I wanted to bleat my usual Jesus-story and be done with it, but the ice on my ribs wouldn't let me lie. I reluctantly collapsed and told him that honestly, I didn't know anything anymore and nothing was real. Turns out, Dan was in the same place I was.

Together we raved and doubted and yelled and trembled all semester long. We felt the black blood of Dostoevsky and descended the dark stairs of Derrida and Sartre. Some nights, we would just sit across from each other and stare, estranged by the cold of a new, uncertain world. After one of these nights of existential fog, as I got up to go, I turned to Dan and said, "The only meaningful thing left to do in this world, it seems, is to sit quietly with a friend until dark and then say goodnight."

Then, on a snow-gray Russian day, riding a packed bus, a song came on my iPod that froze me in time. In a sense, I'm still there on that bus listening to that song with watering eyes. It was a song called "Clouds" by As Cities Burn that said: "Is your god really God? / Is my god really God? / I think our god isn't God / If he fits inside our heads."

With the terrifying pull of rubber bands, I expanded beyond the length of the bus, grew from the street to the sky. Then I snapped and everything came undone. I resigned entirely. God won't fit inside our heads, and if He does, we're missing something. And I knew all I'd been waiting for was to know that to admit doubt was not to lose faith. A few simple lines of an Indie rock song pushed me to see hope amid uncertainty.

It snowed continually my last two weeks in Russia. I met Dan one morning at a small cafe, Biblioteca, where we drank bottomless black tea and watched the snow

Over the course of your time studying abroad, what spiritual struggles, doubts, or questions have you grappled with? Are you developing any strategies for living into these questions? Is your wrestling moving you further from or closer to God?

If you have struggled with your faith while abroad, how have these struggles helped clarify your values? Have these struggles moved you closer to God in any way?

What role should we take as we see others struggling with God? It can be difficult to let friends wrestle with God without wanting to "solve their problems" or change them. How can we simply walk with others in their life instead of pulling them through our way?

What aspects of your study abroad experience — such as classes, excursions, host family, roommates, worship, and the like — have had the greatest impact on your spiritual growth? Have you gained any new spiritual insights or knowledge that you want to remember as you return home?

pile up on the street. He said he had prayed the night before. I said I was ready to step back into a church.

Our last Sunday in Moscow, we attended Mass, an Orthodox church, then a mosque. Dan said we were a Protestant service away from a monotheistic grand slam. At Mass, I wrote in my journal, "God, see that I'm trying."

It was the first time I had prayed in more than a year.[4]

This reflection shows how study abroad can open up a space in which to doubt honestly and freely. For this writer, his pilgrimage in Russia allowed him to wander closer to God.

Reflection Two

As far as faith goes I haven't changed my mind at all. If anything this semester has shown me more problems that I have with the idea of religion and God. Between Auschwitz and readings on the Civil Rights Movement, I more than ever can't believe in a God that is all powerful and loving who allows terrible things to happen for no reason. Nothing that has been said this semester has convinced me otherwise. I have no advice for development except to try not to be angry all the time. I have been [angry] most of this semester, and it is not sustainable. There was no one I could talk to about it without arguing, and to be honest, it feels better to bottle up the anger than to inflict it on others who would prefer I just "get over myself."[5]

The honesty these students reflect is necessary if we want to cultivate intimacy with God. Henri Nouwen explains the connection:

The [person] who never had any religious doubts during college years probably walked around blindfolded; he who never experimented with his traditional values and ideas was probably more afraid than free. . . . But he who did, took a risk . . . the risk of being alienated from his past and of becoming irritated by everything religious, even the word "God." The risk even of searing loneliness which Jesus Christ suffered when He cried, "God, my God, why have you forsaken me?" . . .

We can discover, with pain and frustration, that a mature religious [person] is very close to the agnostic, and often we have difficulty in deciding which name expresses better our state of mind: agnostic or searching believer. Perhaps they are closer than we tend to think.[6]

DEALING WITH ADVERSITY

Culture shock and doubts about faith are two areas where you may experience adversity while studying abroad. You may also encounter many smaller inconveniences and difficulties, including minor health issues, logistical challenges such as lodging and transportation, and miscommunication, among others. How you respond to these minor irritating difficulties can have a big impact on your overall study abroad experience.

These challenges remind us that the first rule of living abroad is flexibility. There is so much that you can't control when you travel that it is good to take a deep breath and a longer view of the situation. Remind yourself that when something goes wrong, it will probably make a great story later (with a little embellishing). So if it would be funny later, let it be funny now. Humor is a great tool for responding to challenges.

A second strategy for dealing with adversity is to welcome interruptions. Although interruptions are often seen in a negative light — they are something to be dismissed as quickly as possible — surprise is a word full of promise. Jim Forest, in *The Road to Emmaus: Pilgrimage as a Way of Life*, encourages us to consider how we might view unwelcome interruptions as heaven-sent surprises.

> Pilgrimage — whether the sort that involves going long distances in unfamiliar lands or simply being aware of ordinary life as a cradle-to-the-grave pilgrimage — is an invitation to become a person capable of seeing interruptions, most of all those involving the urgent needs of others, as heaven-sent opportunities that have the potential of bringing one closer to the kingdom of God. Whether washing dishes in the kitchen or walking to Jerusalem, life is learning to see interruptions as God's plan for the day rather than one's own plan, and thus to live in God's time rather than clock time.[7]

A third strategy is to learn to look below the surface of those things that seem challenging or irritating. Bethany, studying in Honduras, writes about a snorkeling expedition:

> *We started swimming around the reef. We saw schools of tiny fish that all moved together, and intricate coral formations. We saw the reef, only four feet deep in places, gradually be swallowed up by the deep blue of the ocean. We saw a sea turtle lazily winding its way through the reef, and beautiful yellow and black fish nibbling on seaweed, and it was like having a glimpse into another world. A world*

How do you view difficulties? Can you find the humor in an event that makes you want to cry? Have you learned to see interruptions as surprises?

Have you experienced the joy of looking below the surface of what seems to be merely an ordinary or even annoying circumstance? Do you stay focused on the task at hand, asking for the strength for "one more," or do you worry about what is far in the future?

where taxi fares and language barriers are just (literally) a drop in the ocean. Where I can feel insignificant, and blessed, and amazed at God's creation, and they are all wonderful feelings.

And you know the craziest part? If I lifted my head up and simply watched the horizon instead of looking into the water, I would miss everything that's going on right underneath the surface. Sometimes that uncomfortable snorkel mouthpiece and my lack of coordination can get in the way. Sometimes it's easier to keep my head above water. But I can't be afraid to look deeper — in snorkeling, in friendships, in prayer, in everyday life. It's easy to keep things superficial. It's easy to deal with difficult questions by simply refusing to wrestle with them. And it's not even hard to justify these decisions. But I'm realizing that staring at the horizon and refusing to look underwater is not the answer, because there is so much more to see and to understand if you're willing to simply look beneath the surface. And really, who would pass up the chance to see a sea turtle?

A fourth strategy for dealing with adversity is to take life "one step at a time." During an off campus program, students spent seven days canoeing and kayaking in Everglades National Park. After a difficult twelve-mile crossing in the open ocean, Joey wrote:

Each paddle [stroke] I made for the last half of our trip was prefaced with the phrase "one more." And I prayed for strength not to get to our final destination, not to get to our next resting place, but simply for "one more." It was a silent, repetitive prayer offered every five seconds to acknowledge my failing weakness and God's unfailing strength. Enough strength to paddle once more and enough presence of mind to perform each stroke flawlessly, what a lesson to learn! And what a way to learn it! That I don't have to ask God for the strength and presence of mind and wisdom for every hardship and every decision I have to make. Just the next one; then after the next one and then the one after that. Life is so much simpler that way.

God isn't worried about next week or next year when we are paddling a canoe in the middle of the open ocean. He cares about whether we are walking, running, or paddling while remaining focused on Him. He is most concerned with that next step or paddle we take. And when that one is done, the next one will be the most important. So why not live as if each decision was just as important as the last or as the next one will be? I cannot see how God would want it any differently.[8]

From these four strategies, what insights can you glean about how you would like to respond to adversity while studying abroad?

Chapter Sixteen

Doing Justice

Irresponsibility:
No single raindrop believes it is to blame for the flood.
–Motivational Poster

Thus says the LORD:
Do not let the wise boast in their wisdom,
do not let the mighty boast in their might,
do not let the wealthy boast in their wealth;
but let those who boast boast in this,
that they understand and know me, that I am the LORD;
I act with steadfast love, justice, and righteousness in the earth,
for in these things I delight, says the LORD.
–Jeremiah 9:23-24

suspect that for some of you the phrase "doing justice" resonates strongly with your motivations for studying abroad, while for others justice and study abroad are words that are not obviously connected. In many places, studying abroad provides daily reminders of the need for justice in this world, as the study of poverty, disease, forced immigration, and other difficult realities form a central part of the curriculum. In other places, however, the concept of justice may take a back seat to studying such things as language, art, or history. However, regardless of where you are studying, issues of justice are present, and if you are trying to live in accordance with the Bible, the call to justice is inescapable.

We do justice when we treat all human beings as image-bearers of God, when we work to address inequality among the poor and helpless, when we acknowledge our responsibility to care for the natural world, and when we confront the power of privilege in our own lives. Paying attention to justice leads us to the kind of life that reflects the character of God. Justice flows from God's heart and character, and as we seek to be in relationship with God, it leads us to seek right relationships with one another and with the natural world.

In *Generous Justice*, Tim Keller helps us understand how the Bible calls us all to think deeply and to act justly. Keller notes that the Hebrew word for justice, *mishpat*, occurs more than two hundred times in the Old Testament: "Its most basic meaning is to treat people equitably. . . . *Mishpat* means acquitting or punishing every person on the merits of the case, regardless of race or social status. . . . It also means to give people their rights. . . . *Mishpat* then is giving people what they are due, whether punishment or protection or care. . . . Over and over again, *mishpat* describes taking up the care and cause of widows, orphans, immigrants, and the poor—those who have been called 'the quartet of the vulnerable.'"[1]

The Hebrew language also offers a second word to understand the concept of being just. The word *tzadeqah* means a life of right relationships. As Keller explains, "*Tzadeqah* refers to day-to-day living in which a person conducts *all* relationships in family and society with fairness, generosity, and equity."[2]

Mishpat corresponds to what is sometimes called "rectifying justice," which punishes those who do wrong and cares for victims who are treated unjustly. *Tzadeqah* corresponds to what is sometimes called "primary justice" which refers to a right way of living. Keller puts it this way: "Primary justice, or *tzadeqah*, is behavior that, if it was prevalent in the world, would render rectifying justice unnecessary because everyone would be living in right relationship to everyone else."[3] The terms *misphat* and *tzadeqah* are often tied together in the Bible, and the English expression that best conveys their dual meaning is social justice, the focus of this chapter.

POWER, PRIVILEGE, AND STUDY ABROAD

One aspect of social justice, often overlooked, is to understand one's own power and privilege within the world. Privilege can be thought of as a special right, advantage, or immunity granted or available only to a particular person or group of people.[4] Acknowledging privilege can be difficult, as we like to believe that we've earned our success through hard work and personal merit. It's much harder to accept the notion that our success *also* depends on our society's system of power and privilege, which favors some groups over others.

The idea of privilege is very much evident in the opportunity to study abroad. Your role as a student or your nationality (e.g., as a citizen of the United States) can provide you with certain privileges that you may not even realize. For example, having the time and money to travel and study abroad is already a privilege that few experience. This privilege may be increased by the color of your skin, your gender, or your religion. These privileges don't stop once you leave to study abroad. Once you arrive in your host community, you may have privileges that locals may not have. For example —

- Referring to yourself as an American (for those from the United States).

- Having the resources to travel and explore the region where you are living.

- Having the option of leaving and returning home if things get tough or unbearable.

- Having a passport, which offers the freedom of crossing borders throughout the world.

- Having the freedom to criticize governments without fear of reprisal.

Privilege allows us to feel at home in the world, escape dangers that others may suffer, and choose whether to address certain issues of oppression, or injustice, or identity, or lifestyle. The following reflection offers an example of both power and privilege that might be enjoyed as a student from North America studying abroad.

Talya Zemach-Bersen spent a semester in a Tibetan-studies program in 2005, sure that her experience would turn her into a "global citizen." However, she soon discovered that her home-stay hosts in India refused to treat her as family, but rather as an honored guest. "*Despite my protests,*" she wrote, *I always received five times more food than they served themselves, and I was never allowed to make my bed, step into the kitchen, or even turn on the bathroom light myself.*" During her last week, she was asked to give an envelope of cash to her hosts. Although she was happy to contribute to their family income, she also realized that "*As a first-world student, I had literally purchased a third-world family for my own self-improvement as a global citizen.*"

Later, as she visited Tibet, the home country of her host family who had fled Chinese persecution, she realized that while she could visit freely as a tourist, they would face imprisonment and possible death if they returned. Talya noted, "*As Americans, our national citizenship, passports, skin color, and currency exchange rate all worked in our favor. . . Unlike our host families, we could go wherever we wanted, from family homes to fancy tourist clubs, from private burial ceremonies and temple ruins to Chinese-owned stores selling imitation North Face jackets. We had bought a product, and we expected to consume our experience.*"

These experiences raised many questions for her: "*Why had we not analyzed race, identity, and privilege when those factors were informing every one of our interactions? Why was there never a discussion about commodification when our relationships with host families were built on a commodified relationship? . . . Was there nothing to be said about the power dynamics of claiming global citizenship?*[5]

What makes a global citizen? Do you think that people can become global citizens? Do you think your time living and studying abroad has made you more or less likely to be a global citizen?

🐚 Are you living with a host family while studying abroad? If so what are some of the joys and challenges of living in this relationship?

🐚 What are some of the privileges (and aspects of power) you have enjoyed as a student studying abroad in your host country? Did your program address any of the issues related to the power and privilege of traveling? In what ways could your program have better prepared you for these issues?

🐚 What other ways have you seen privilege affect your experiences? Are there any ways where you observed that people in the local community have privileges that you don't have? What lessons can you learn from these observations?

ENVIRONMENTAL JUSTICE

Another aspect of social justice that is easy to overlook is environmental justice, which expands the idea of justice to the natural world. The act of travel often places many pressures on our natural world, and finding ways to travel sustainably is difficult. For example, did you know that traveling 2,000 miles in an airplane emits one ton of CO_2 per passenger?[6] It is easy to talk about the many benefits of studying off-campus, but it is more difficult to address the environmental costs. As Christopher Hirschler notes, "Study abroad presents academia with a unique problem. It is universally believed to deliver high-impact academic experiences. . . . Because it's valued and popular, it's easy to understand why colleges and universities promote study abroad without critically examining and accounting for its environmental impact. However, failure to engage students in this quandary means colleges are missing an opportunity to promote critical thinking.[7]

You may recognize the environmental cost of your study abroad program and yet be confused about how you should respond. A student participating in an environmental science program in Australia wrote,

> [In this program], students take courses in terrestrial ecology, marine biology, cultural anthropology, and environmental policy throughout the semester; class work includes lectures and workshops but also field trips and research projects in state and national parks. . . .
>
> While our group overall had an amazing time and gained a great deal of knowledge and perspective on an individual level, the irony of a bunch of Chaco-wearing, environmentally-minded college students flying to the other side of the

world to drive around in a giant bus was not lost on us. It led me to wonder: what exactly are the environmental implications of this program? And study abroad in general? [8]

Some study abroad programs are beginning to respond to this tension. Many have encouraged students to think about carbon offsetting — buying carbon credits so that individuals and institutions can say that they are carbon neutral. While this is one strategy, it is not enough for a number of reasons. First, it sends the message that we can buy our way out of a problem, passing on the responsibility for certain behavior to someone else. Responding to the complexity of environmental issues demands that we take a personal stand and become more carbon conscious about the decisions we make.

Second, the environmental impacts of study abroad are not limited to carbon footprints and air travel. A study abroad experience can actually assist you to change behaviors and help you to live more sustainably. As one director notes, "I think that when students are traveling abroad and observing these different ways of living and how other cultures may be living more simply, this has a lasting impact on them." [9]

Your experiences abroad are likely to expose you to people who live greener lives. They — and you — will consume less, bike more, use mass transit more, and eat locally grown foods. When you return home, you can find ways to incorporate these changes into your daily life. You can also encourage your college or university to address the issue of environmental sustainability in its study abroad programs, and you can work with your institution to achieve carbon neutrality. [10]

- How does your environmental footprint abroad compare with your lifestyle back home? Are you walking more, using mass transit, and/or living more simply while abroad? If yes, how can you incorporate these behaviors into life when you return home?

- What environmental issues have you been exposed to while living abroad? Has your time away encouraged you to think about environmental issues differently?

- Did you consider purchasing carbon credits for your study abroad experience? Why or why not? If you were going to purchase carbon credits, what organizations would you use? Does your college have an energy recovery fund? If so, would you consider donating to this fund as a result of your time abroad?

Google "study abroad and sustainability" or "green passport for study abroad." What websites did you find? What suggestions did you find for reducing your carbon footprint and living more sustainably?

Which suggestions would you like to implement in your life now and when you return home?

SOCIAL JUSTICE

As you encounter and confront issues of social justice during your time abroad, you may experience a variety of feelings ranging from guilt, indifference, and depression to empathy. For example, spending more money on airfare alone than most people in the world earn in a year can conjure up feelings of moral guilt. As Ellie studying in Budapest notes:

> *Several times in the past week, I've been overwhelmed with how incredibly blessed I am to be here. . . . Twice last week I relaxed by the base of the Széchenyi Chain Bridge and read while the sun slipped beneath the horizon. If I have ever felt absolute bliss, it was in that moment. However, the bliss left in its wake feelings of guilt and unworthiness. How is it possible that this "dream" is my life? When millions around the world are plagued by war and violence, poverty and disease, slavery and hopelessness? Why do I get to live in such a beautiful city, take fascinating classes, and engage my passions through volunteering? Why am I granted every opportunity I seek and desire?*

Yet these types of tensions and issues can lead to thinking deeply about one's role in the causes and possible solutions to these problems. As Molly wrote:

> *Our last day in Shanghai we had a free day and I unfortunately spent it seeing the worst of human consumerism. Outside of these three buildings of five floors [shopping center] were three or so beggars. I think they were mentally ill, and they just lay in the mud and rain, in nothing but underwear pleading for money. Some were missing limbs, some had no energy even to speak, and they just rolled in the mud getting trampled on by those whose hands clutched a mass of goods. It was the saddest thing that I have seen in China, and I did not know what to do. I regretfully just looked at them and passed, being careful to avoid having my legs grabbed at by their dirty hands. I still do not know what I should have done. And I wonder what Jesus would have thought of their plight, and I am now saddened by my behavior as well. I am accustomed to seeing beggars, but have never been faced with such desperation, and honestly it frightened me. . . . I know that it is not only China where such suffering occurs, but everywhere, and I know that the Lord must grieve for these people.*

When seeing injustice, we all respond differently, from trying to understand the reasons for injustice to looking for how we should personally respond to examining what can be learned from each situation. Read the following student blogs, and note the different ways these students reacted to seeing injustices.

Are there any specific injustices that your host community or country is experiencing? If yes, how are these injustices affecting the community?

What social injustices (if any) have you witnessed firsthand while living abroad? What type of feelings (e.g., guilt, empathy, anger, indifference) have these experiences generated in you? How did you respond to these feelings?

Reflection One (from Jacob)

Today we went to the zoo. It wasn't actually the zoo, it was the floating village of the Tonle Sap lake. I say we went to the zoo because our visit felt like going to a zoo. We got to ride on a boat and see the "exotic poor people" in their natural habitat. We got to peer straight through their floating homes. And, the best part was that we never had to leave the safety of our boat and interact with the people.

All of that is cynicism, of course, but it's how I felt. It disgusts me that tourists come to see the people of the floating village as an attraction, rather than as people. Yes, the people of the floating village rely on tourist income to live. It could be argued that "going to the zoo" helps these people, but I think we could still visit the area, providing them with precious income, without dehumanizing them.

While thinking on this, I realized the answer may lie in my use of a camera. We take pictures of zoo animals. We interact with our friends, using our cameras to record memories of the relationship. Does your camera just take pictures or record relationships? Today I never left the safety of the boat. There was no relationship with the people to record. In some of the schools we visited, I had no chance to develop a relationship with the students. My camera took pictures and didn't record memories. Maybe the next time you go out, use your camera to gauge if you were just going to the zoo. If you don't know the name of someone in your pictures, you may have been treating the situation like a zoo.

Reflection Two (from Katherine)

Before coming to Honduras, one of my friends gave me a very wise piece of advice. She told me to not be afraid to be vulnerable. When she told me this, I didn't really know what that meant. I mean mentally, I understand what being vulnerable is, but how do you put it into practice, especially in a different country where everything's new?

Heading into my fourth month in Honduras, it's feeling like home. I'm accustomed to eating tortillas with every meal and count on the fact that five minutes means anywhere between ten to forty-five. I'm not even surprised anymore when people come on the bus to yell a sermon about giving your life to Jesus at the top of their lungs or to sell magic pills that will heal all types of pain as well as reduce stress. I've grown used to living a little more simply without internet at my house and only using an unbreakable (thankfully) brick phone. I've also learned a lot of things. I've seen a different way of life and a different culture. I've begun to see and understand poverty more as well as the themes of violence, corruption, and justice.

In this reflection, Jacob talks about the importance of building relationships and ultimately memories with people you meet. Do you think this is possible in situations where there is such a power disparity in place? Have you been able to build relationships with others in your host community where a power disparity exists? If so, what has made these relationships successful or challenging?

What relationships would you like to develop that might speak into some of the justice issues you have encountered while living abroad?

But most importantly, I've started to care. These issues are not far away anymore to me, but personal.

And I think this is a piece of what vulnerability is. Allowing yourself to be changed and to care about the lives of other people. Forcing yourself to look hard issues in the face and let yourself feel and be hurt by what you see. The other side of vulnerability is sharing yourself. Sharing who you are and allowing others to see the hard places and stuff in yourself that is not so pretty. It's hard, and I'm still not very good at it, but I think vulnerability is necessary to truly live a life like Christ.

These student reflections raise two additional questions as we all struggle with how to "do justice." First, how will you work to promote social justice not just in your study abroad program, but throughout your life? Second, what is the role of hope as you respond to social issues in your life and community?

Seeing your study abroad experience as a pilgrimage reminds you that life is a marathon, not a sprint. What matters is not simply how you respond to one situation in your host community, but rather how you weave justice into all aspects of your life over the course of your lifetime. Pilgrimages are as much about journeying well as about arriving at a destination, and so they also remind us that while we can't do everything, we can do something. This prayer, written in honor of Archbishop Oscar Romero, helps us acknowledge our limitations and our responsibilities:

It helps, now and then, to step back and take a long view.
The kingdom is not only beyond our efforts, it is even beyond our vision.

We accomplish in our lifetime only a tiny fraction of the magnificent enterprise that is God's work. Nothing we do is complete, which is a way of saying that the Kingdom always lies beyond us.

No statement says all that could be said.
No prayer fully expresses our faith.

No confession brings perfection.
No pastoral visit brings wholeness.

No program accomplishes the Church's mission.
No set of goals and objectives includes everything.

This is what we are about.
We plant the seeds that one day will grow.

We water seeds already planted, knowing that they hold future promise.
We lay foundations that will need further development.

What role does education play for you in responding to injustice? What are you learning about injustice within your host community? Do you feel that learning has led to caring for you? If so, how?

We provide yeast that produces far beyond our capabilities.
We cannot do everything, and there is a sense of liberation in realizing that.

This enables us to do something, and to do it very well.
It may be incomplete, but it is a beginning, a step along the way, an opportunity for the Lord's grace to enter and do the rest.

We may never see the end results, but that is the difference between the master builder and the worker.

We are workers, not master builders; ministers, not messiahs.
We are prophets of a future not our own.[11]

Beyond making justice a lifelong pursuit, this prayer gives us a hope based in faith. In dealing with issues like poverty, corruption, powerlessness, and the lack of health care and education, it is easy to lose hope and to despair over the brokenness of this world. But as humans, we need hope; we can't live without it. Hope is the lifeblood of spiritual survival and can pull us out of the deep trenches of the pain and hurt in life. Can living and studying abroad opportunities offer you this hope? I believe they can. The following blog post from Bethany reflects on ways to respond to social injustices: building relationships, seeing brokenness, trusting in God, learning about root causes of social issues, seeing visions of hope, and committing ourselves to live lives in response to the social issues of our day.

What are the stories of hope you have encountered during your time living abroad? How has your faith helped to sustain these stories of hope?

The hardest part of being in Honduras? Seeing corruption and violence nearly everywhere you look. Walking through a hospital and seeing loud waiting rooms overflowing with patients who probably won't even be able to afford medication. Passing through a grocery store parking lot and having five year olds come up to you and ask for money, and you don't know what to say. It's hearing the story of a woman whose son was killed by police for absolutely no reason. Staring at a mural commemorating the life of a lawyer who was murdered because he was working for justice.

The most difficult part of being in Honduras is asking why, and not having an answer. Seeing the brokenness, and having no way to bring healing. Watching injustice occur and standing by, because I don't know how to fight.

In Honduras, these things punch me in the face. They are impossible to ignore. But there is oppression and inequality and injustice in the United States, and everywhere. What do we do? When we realize that the world we live in is filled with brokenness, where do we turn?

For me, it's becoming clearer. I can't live trapped under the weight of the world's sorrows. I can't spend my life questioning God and His goodness, because I know

How are you offering hope (related to justice issues) to those you meet in your time abroad?

As you think about returning home, what lessons related to justice do you hope to remember and incorporate into your life? How do you hope to do justice moving forward?

injustice grieves Him so much more than it affects me. I shouldn't ever become numb to violence or hatred or suffering, but I can't dwell on it either.

Because whenever I walk staring down at the street, asking these questions, all I have to do is lift my eyes and look at the mountains around me and remember that there is so much beauty. Hatred and injustice don't have the final word — God is redeeming this world, day by day. I need to wrestle with difficult questions, while never doubting the fact that love and peace and justice are overcoming evil.

I see this everywhere. In a nineteen-year-old boy who is organizing all of the teenagers in his dangerous neighborhood to help serve the community. In the smile of an elderly woman who, with the help of Project Global Village, bought fish to raise and sell so she can provide for her family. In people who devote their lives to fighting corruption in the government. In the kindness and concern of our host families here in Santa Lucia, and in the hospitality that we have been shown in nearly every corner of this beautiful country.

Chapter Seventeen

ENGAGING OTHERS FROM DIFFERENT FAITH TRADITIONS

When we travel to the sacred sites of other religions,
we learn how they describe their experiences of the sacred. More than this,
we discover their particular ways to explain their inner experiences of the
sacred and the many distinct ways they describe the sacred itself.
Once we locate the sacred in these religions, we always carry it with us.
We do not necessarily trigger new knowledge, so much as fresh
and exciting ways of regarding what we already know.

–Leonard Biallas

Tolerance implies no lack of commitment to one's own beliefs.
Rather, it condemns the oppression or persecution of others.

–John F. Kennedy

How do we live faithfully as Christians in a world of many religions? As you study abroad, how do you live your faith, letting it permeate all aspects of your experience? How might you build relationships with others from different religions? How might you better understand other faiths? Exploring other faiths or building interfaith relationships may seem daunting. Like anything new, it may require that you learn new skills, and it will involve reaching out to people whose perspectives are different from yours. A little courage is needed, but the curiosity that drove you to study abroad should serve you well as you take the additional steps of engaging those of different faith backgrounds.

The need to build relationships with those from different faith backgrounds has never been greater, and yet interfaith dialogues are sadly lacking in our world today. Extremists on all sides have contributed to this lack of dialogue and to the pervasive mistrust between believers of the major religions of the world. As you study abroad, however, you have an opportunity to contribute to re-establishing dialogue and building trust between believers. That responsibility cannot be taken lightly.

Your study abroad experience may be the first time you have had the opportunity to really connect with others from different faiths. As one student wrote,

Traveling to Sarajevo in Bosnia was eye opening to me. It was fascinating being in a city full of recent traumatic history that I had not heard about until this semester. Sarajevo was the first time I have been surrounded by so many Muslim people. Talking with the lady at the front desk of our hotel gave me a small window into the scars left from the war, like the economic situation. The woman at the front desk had her master's degree, but could not find a better paying job in the city to support her family.[1]

As Christians, how do we respond to these opportunities to connect with believers of other faiths? How do we meet the challenge of Matthew 28:19–20: "Go therefore and make disciples of all nations, baptizing them in the name of the Father and the Son and the Holy Spirit, and teaching them to obey everything that I have commanded you. And remember, I am with you always, to the end of the age." How does this passage speak to your study abroad experience? You are not a missionary or an evangelist, and you likely don't feel called to preach the gospel on a corner in your neighborhood. Yet you do want to live out your faith in appropriate ways during your time abroad.

Our response to this passage should be twofold. The first response is gratitude. As we travel, we see Scripture fulfilled: there are indeed followers of Christ in all nations around the world! One way we can live out our faith is to come together with other Christians, encourage them, and be encouraged in our faith. This is one reason why finding a local church can be such a blessing. The second response is curiosity. As you sincerely explore the faith practices of others, you should be prepared, if given the opportunity, to humbly share your own faith.

Students often struggle with how to share their faith while living abroad. Their concerns are multi-faceted, but can be summarized in the following way:

> Sharing my faith abroad makes me a bit uneasy for several reasons. First, the history of Christianity in places around the world is mixed. There have been missionaries that have done so much good, but there are also examples of Christianity being used to colonize and subvert local cultures in negative ways. Second, culture and religion are tied together. So how do I honor my host culture and be a good guest while also being somewhat confrontational and critical about their faith beliefs and customs? Third, the world has seen so much violence related to religion that I feel we need to create spaces where we can learn from one another and work together to address our shared problems, without fighting over our various faiths.[2]

What are you doing to nurture your faith while you are studying abroad? How can you create the space you need to think and reflect on your faith and to claim it as your own while you are away? Are you finding opportunities to worship with Christians in your host communities?

These concerns are valid and have been raised by thoughtful Christians in the past. One valuable resource is *The Christ of the Indian Road* by E. Stanley Jones, one of the most admired Christian missionaries of the twentieth century. In this book, Jones recounts his decades of experience as a missionary in India and describes the mistakes he saw many Christians make as they tried to impose their culture on Indian culture. In contrast, Jones claimed that the gospel can and should be separated from our own cultural experience of it. As Christians, we can learn from other cultures, respect the truth that is found in them, witness to our own faith, and then let Christ do his work around the world.[3]

When Jones asked Mahatma Gandhi how it might be possible to bring India to Christ, the Indian statesman replied:

> I would suggest, first, that all of you Christians, missionaries and all, must begin to live more like Jesus Christ. . . Second, . . . I would suggest that you must practice your religion without adulterating or toning it down. . . Third, I would suggest that you must put your emphasis upon love, for love is the center and soul of Christianity. . . Fourth, I would suggest that you study the non-Christian religions and culture more sympathetically in order to find the good that is in them, so that you might have a more sympathetic approach to the people.[4]

CREATING SPACE FOR INTERFAITH DIALOGUE

As you interact with people of different faiths, you may think about creating a space for dialogue that moves you toward goals related to the common good. This is a difficult endeavor and tensions remain if we take religions and their differences seriously. How can you share who you are and what you believe with someone from another faith without viewing that person only as a potential convert? How can you listen to their criticisms of Christianity without feeling defensive?

Your time abroad can provide you with the space needed to think and reflect on this tension as you explore your faith and claim it as your own. This openness can be seen in the following reflection from Kate's blog as she returned from her semester in Honduras:

> *Seeing something new, meeting new people in a new culture, seeing the wonderful and hard things in Honduras helped me to understand who God is, what he has given us, and what we can do to be a part of what God is doing.*

What other faith traditions (beyond Christianity) are prevalent in your host community? In your host country? How can you learn more about these faith traditions? How can you do a better job of studying non-Christian religions more sympathetically in order to find the good that is in them?

What concrete things could you do to express your faith in a culturally sensitive way, if you had the opportunity?

Kate's reflection demonstrates how a study abroad experience can help deepen your faith, but it also offers some hints about sharing your faith with others. First, God is in control, and we are called to be a part of what he is doing in the world by bearing witness to his faithfulness in our own lives. Second, we are called to connect to people from other cultures and faiths. As we build relationships with others, we must be willing to learn who they are, what their faith journey looks like, and how their religious practices deepen their faith. When we honor their stories, we are often given opportunities to share our own faith journey with them.

It is hard to say how this openness may play out in your study abroad experience; no doubt it will be different for each of you. Yet if we are serious about living out our faith in a complex world, we must work toward certain values or virtues:

- Developing the courage and diligence to appreciate diversity and learn the stories of others. Where courage signifies the willingness to take risks to meet others, share in their lives, and ask and answer hard questions, diligence can be thought of as the willingness to commit to these tasks for the long haul, not just for a quick conversation.
- Being faithfully present with others from different cultures.
- Practicing cultural humility.
- Sharing hospitality with others, both giving and receiving, in ways that nurture the virtues of humility, charity, empathy, and patience.

The complexity of today's world demands that we have the knowledge, skills, and virtues to live, work, and worship in a diverse world. We need to practice the cultural competence that will enable us to communicate and behave appropriately in intercultural situations. As one example, consider the following story (told by a study abroad program director) of how relationship building can lead to opportunities to acquire the knowledge, build the skills, and practice the virtues needed to listen to the story of others and to share deeply about our own lives and faith.

Megan is sick and in the hospital. It happened quite quickly as her Ghanaian roommate Khadija brought her to the campus health clinic last night. This morning she was far more comfortable than yesterday, and her temperature has been normal all day. She is still very weak, but that's always the case when malaria strikes. Megan is in no danger and is receiving good medical care. She's also being very closely attended by other students and Khadija. One of the students actually slept in her room last night, and another will take a turn tonight. In addition, Khadija continues to spend a lot of time with her.

Khadija and Megan have become close friends, and the religious difference — Khadija is Muslim — has only made them more eager to understand each other. When I returned to Megan's room last night, I found Khadija sitting at Megan's bedside reading to her from the Bible. Khadija also bowed her head and prayed with us before I left.[5]

What a wonderful picture of what God can do when we open ourselves up to others. In some ways this story is an especially good anecdote because Megan is the recipient, rather than the giver, of care and attention. It also provides a glimpse of the virtues discussed above.

One of the gifts you experience while studying abroad is the people you live with, whether host families or other international students. One of the gifts you can give back to these people is to honor where they are in their faith journey. If their faith practices are more conservative than yours, how can you respect and support them? If they are very unsure about Christianity and don't want to talk about faith, how do you honor this request? If you have a chance to tell someone about your faith journey and the good news of Jesus Christ, how can you do so with cultural humility?

The World Council of Churches has developed recommendations for promoting interfaith dialogue. They include the following:

1. Build relationships of respect and trust with people of all religions. . . .

2. Encourage Christians to strengthen their own religious identity and faith while deepening their knowledge and understanding of different religions. Christians should avoid misrepresenting the beliefs and practices of people of different religions. . . .

3. Pray for [your] neighbors and their well-being, recognizing that prayer is integral to who we are and what we do, as well as to Christ's mission.[6]

SEEING GOD IN OTHERS

As you learn to engage well with people from different faith backgrounds, you will begin to see and understand how God manifests himself in your host culture. The following reflection by Grant describes a series of incidents that helped him seize the opportunity to search for God in all people. This story takes place in Honduras

Have you been in any situations where you were the first Christian that the people you met had ever talked with? If so, what did you learn in those situations?

As you read through these recommendations from the World Counsil of Churches, how might they relate to your study abroad experience? Although you are not a missionary, how can these recommendations help you integrate your faith into your relationships with host country nationals?

How have you seen God in the people you have met while studying abroad? Have any of these individuals been people of other faith traditions or people of no faith?

Is there anyone with whom you would like to share your faith or from whom you would like to learn about his or her faith in your remaining time studying abroad?

during a long weekend as a group of students traveled together to a beach in El Salvador, about an eight-hour trip by bus. While there, the group met up with a number of other travelers from all over the world and had a great time sharing, surfing, and getting to know one another.

As they were preparing to leave El Salvador, two members of the group realized that their passports had been stolen. So while the rest of the group got ready to return to Honduras, these two students had to file a police report and figure out how to get new passports. While they were saying good-bye to the group at the bus station and feeling sorry for themselves, they were again reminded that God was in control. Grant writes:

> As we were at the bus station, I recognized an El Salvadorian woman who was standing in line for a bus ticket. I'm not going to lie; I didn't think I knew anyone in El Salvador, but here was this young woman from a class at my college in the States. I walked up to her and asked if she had gone to my college and taken an interim class entitled "Called to Serve, Called to Lead." It was amazing to hear her say yes. Is our God amazing or what? She was from El Salvador but was now working in Honduras. She, along with her family, took us in and helped get our passports the next day so we could get back to Honduras and our classes.
>
> This crazy, unfortunate experience actually taught me so much more than I could have ever thought. I stand in awe of God's providence and how he cares for us, but this experience and my time in Honduras has also helped me to see that I want to recognize God not only in the big events of my life but also in the everyday, the normal, not the amazing. I was so blessed by this young woman and her family and God's providing hand in this situation, but I want to continue to search for God in all his people. I can find God in strangers, atheists, gang members, new friends, in anyone. Some may not know God is working in their lives, although he is. Throughout my time in Honduras I have seen what awesome people God has created and put into my life. I have had the chance to meet such great people from all over the globe, and each person has a different story worth listening to and worth taking notes.

As you consider how to foster more interfaith dialogue in your interactions with others, there are definitely no easy answers. You should pray for wisdom and also talk about hard questions with your classmates and others you meet. Being open to faith questions reaffirms that your travels are a pilgrimage as you move from certainty to dependence, discovering God's involvement in human history while being challenged to become more like our Lord in thought, word, and deed.

Chapter Eighteen

LEARNING TO SERVE, SERVING TO LEARN

The challenge of dealing with difference will be the greatest challenge confronting our society – greater than issues of environmental integrity, greater than the broad issues of war and peace, greater than the problems of poverty and want. It will be the greatest challenge because none of the others can be adequately confronted if we do not learn how to deal with, and cooperate with, one another.
–Humphrey Tonkin

[We need an education that] enlightens the mind and inspires the heart so that the hands can serve.
–Richard Felix

If you have come to help me, you are wasting your time. But if you have come because your liberation is bound up with mine, then let us work together.
–Aboriginal Activist Group, Queensland

Engaging with the people and culture of your host community is one of the great pleasures and benefits of studying abroad. Host families, conversation partners, study groups, and structured excursions are all possible means to deepen your connections to the people and places where you are living. Another important component, however, is service-learning, which can help to foster connections and prepare you to be an active global citizen.

The call for international service-learning opportunities is not new. Over twenty years ago, Ernest Boyer wrote that

there used to be a big debate that we needed to study western cultures in order to understand our past. But I'm convinced that we must start to study non-western cultures in order to understand our future. Somehow we must find a way to interact and interconnect the two. I would [also] like to see all colleges and universities make community service a core requirement of liberal learning. When all is said and done, the quality of liberal learning must be measured by the willingness of graduates to be socially and civically engaged, and to begin to develop a perspective that's global.[1]

Boyer reiterated this theme in his famous opinion piece "Creating the New American College," where he challenged colleges to return to their historic commitment to civic service and to recover a sense of moral purpose. He highlighted the fact that higher education in the United States has drifted from its early commitments to reality, practicality, and service toward "a place where professors get tenured and students get credentialed . . . a *private* benefit, *not* a public good."[2] Boyer challenged North American institutions of higher education to think about their role in addressing the most urgent issues facing our global world.

This "private benefit" criticism can be directed at study abroad programs as well. Many of these programs center on the individual benefits of studying abroad. Less attention, however, is paid to the importance of study abroad as it relates to promoting civic engagement and connecting the global and local. In light of this criticism, some study abroad programs now include international service-learning opportunities to foster a deeper understanding of host communities and the challenges they face.

Service-learning was first coined in the late 1960s to describe the efforts to link educational goals for students with their active participation in the local community. The term reflects the desire of educators to move students toward a richer understanding of themselves, their communities, and their academic courses. Service-learning provides a context for connecting feeling (heart), thinking (head), and acting (hands), and international service learning simply broadens these concepts to an international setting.

The combination of service-learning and study abroad can strengthen your overall experience. An effective service-learning component provides you with opportunities to be involved in experiences that "(a) complement and augment [your] classroom learning, (b) contribute to the community in the host country in a number of ways (c) support face-to-face interaction with others, (d) increase cross-cultural understanding of others, and (e) challenge [you] to clarify and reconsider [your] role as a citizen."[3]

DESIGNING SERVICE-LEARNING PLACEMENTS

Designing effective service-learning experiences during a study abroad program is complex, especially in developing countries where the socio-economic gap between

What volunteer opportunities have you had while studying abroad? Does your program offer opportunities for service-learning in your host community? If so, how do these opportunities differ from simply volunteering in your home community?

study abroad participants and people in the local communities is so pronounced. As Kurt Ver Beek, a study abroad director in Honduras, notes,

> The vast majority of the service-learning experiences, which I have witnessed in my fifteen years in Central America, neither understand nor address the true dilemmas of poverty and consequently provide little or no long-term benefit to the poor. They therefore result in learning that is mediocre at best. Students and professors are intruding into poor people's lives, often trying to fix things they do not understand. This service often causes them to think better of themselves, worse of the poor, and makes them too busy to take full advantage of their learning opportunities. More importantly, this service based on superficial understanding seldom empowers the poor or builds up their capacity. It is often neither equitable nor sustainable.[4]

Despite these concerns, Ver Beek still envisions a place for international service-learning and believes that it can be done well. He provides the following two case studies in Honduras after Hurricane Mitch in 1998 as examples of the challenges but also the promise of international service-learning. "The hurricane was followed by a flood," he notes, "not of water, but of very well-intentioned groups who came to Honduras to help. Many of these groups were college students and their professors."[5]

Group One: "We Came to Serve"

After the hurricane, an engineering professor from a Christian university asked one of his classes to design a house for hurricane victims in Honduras. At the end of the semester, those who were able would fly down to Honduras and build their house for a family. A simple $4,000 house was designed, and a group of twenty students had some orientation meetings to discuss what to bring, what the country was like, learn a little Spanish, and so forth. The group also raised the $30,000 from family and friends to cover their expenses and the cost of the house they would build.

The professor contacted a friend who was a missionary in Honduras and who agreed to select an appropriate area and family to receive the house. In their two-week stay in the south of Honduras, the group almost finished the house, working with the assistance of three Hondurans who had lost their jobs because of the hurricane. A local church was paying them $3 a day to rebuild and repair houses. When the group returned home, they told us that they were overwhelmed by the immensity of the destruction, impressed by the hard-working Hondurans, and a little frustrated by how little they had accomplished. They all agreed with the woman who said, "I have so many questions. I wished we would have seen and learned a little more about the rest of Honduras."

When I later visited the family who had received the house, they were extremely grateful to the group for such a wonderful gift. The house was well-built and larger than that of most of their neighbors. Their only complaint was that they would have rather had fewer but bigger bedrooms since the children usually all slept together. However, while I was talking to their pastor, he said that two of the family's neighbors were not speaking with them because they felt they had been more deserving of the house. Some in the community were also upset because the group had mostly stuck to themselves, had brought down all their own food, and usually would not take the food or drinks they offered them. In addition, the students' seeming amusement at the Hondurans' more simple building techniques had offended two of their Honduran coworkers.[6]

Group Two: "We Came to Learn"

A second group of twenty college students from a Christian college planned to go to Honduras for a three-week class to try to better understand why Honduras was poor and what responsibility they held as Christians and global citizens in the face of that poverty. After they arrived, several of them shared that they felt embarrassed when people in the United States, who assumed they were coming to help, looked at them disapprovingly when they found out they were coming "*just* to learn." While in Honduras, the group did spend a day alongside a group of Hondurans, digging out a house in the south of Honduras — and their aching muscles convinced them of the enormity of the task. They also lived with Honduran families — learning firsthand about daily life, the culture, and the struggle to seek true development. These students were also able to learn about Honduran history and culture and about development theories that seek to explain Honduran poverty and possible solutions. They met Honduran leaders, including the president of the Honduran Congress and leading activists for the poor, and could ask for their perspectives on the hurricane and how to best help Honduras. Finally, they were able to visit almost a dozen communities that were devastated by the hurricane, and they were able to see and hear what the *community members* were doing, sometimes with the help of development organizations. At the end of their time, they were encouraged to continue learning and sharing with others what they had learned about Honduras, poverty, and development and to begin to act and support the development work of at least one of the organizations they visited.

After one of the one-day visits to a rural development project, the coordinator said he felt very blessed by their visit. He said it was the first time that a group had come to humbly listen to the people, visit their farms and houses, and see how their lives were changing, without some other agenda. He said he felt very encouraged by the fact that they cared enough to be willing to come "just to learn" from the people.

While these students also lamented that they had only been able to stay for three weeks, they seemed less frustrated with how they had used their time and what they had accomplished. One of the students wrote in her final evaluation, "I learned that in order to really help the poor we need to learn more — to understand the causes of the problems before we try to solve them. I also saw that there is hope — that God works through us and we can support and help organizations that are changing the lives of the poor. I'm excited to go home and learn and do more."[7]

Ver Beek concludes with three principles that should serve as the foundation for well-designed service-learning experiences: "evaluating the impact on the poor, evaluating what students are learning, and . . . concentrating on learning before serving."[8] Here are some questions that he raises:

- *Empowerment:* Are we relatively certain that those we serve will be empowered by this intervention? Are they the ones making the decisions, controlling the process? Are the economic and human resources from the outside being given in a manner that contributes to rather than overwhelms a local process? Are we building on the strengths of the local community?

- *Capacity building:* Are we relatively certain that those we serve will improve their capacity as a result of this intervention? Will they be learning new skills and gaining new energy and motivations? Finally, will their existing skills, ideas, and motivation be respected and encouraged?

- *Equity:* Will the benefits of this intervention be distributed equitably or at least be focused on the most needy in the population? Can we design

Has your service-learning experience helped you question your stereotypes, form new understandings of the problems facing the poor, and begin to develop new alternatives for addressing them?

the intervention in a way that the community benefits, rather than individuals, and if not, can we make sure that the beneficiaries are chosen in a way that prioritizes the most needy?

- *Sustainability:* Will this project be sustainable given the human, environmental, and economic resources available locally?[9]

Ver Beek also asks whether true learning is taking place. He notes that

an overemphasis on doing . . . means that service-learners may often consciously or unconsciously pass up opportunities to learn more about their context and those they are serving. In Honduras, we regularly hear of groups who were too busy to take a break when Hondurans arrived offering coffee and cookies at work sites. As a result, they do not listen to Hondurans — to their joys, needs, accomplishments, and daily struggles. Other groups have turned down opportunities to visit historical sites such as Copan or complain of wasting their time in orientation or talks about Honduras' history. The groups' focus on finishing their project is especially disconcerting when we analyze the costs. The $4,000 house [built by service-learners] could have been built by much-in-need-of-work Hondurans for an extra $500. The $25,000 the group raised to come down and do the work could have built five more houses.[10]

Ver Beek concludes that "service-learners who want to help the poor need to *learn* much more before they *serve*." This focus, he argues, will change their attitude "toward non-doing activities such as having coffee with a poor neighbor woman, visiting historical sites, or having a lecture on the United States' role in Honduran poverty."[11]

- As you think about the context of your own opportunities for service-learning, how is your situation similar to or different from the two case studies presented here?

- Successful service-learning experiences are a result of strong partnerships with local organizations that can provide both context and support for you. Who is your community partner, and what do you know about the history of this organization? What do you know about the issues they are addressing in the local community?

- Daniela Papi Thornton, a social entrepreneur who has spent many years in Cambodia and who founded an educational development organization called PEPY, states that "action without learning is ignorance. Learning without action is selfishness."[12] Through her work in Cambodia, she has become a strong advocate for learning-service and believes that learning must precede serving. Google her online presentation, "What's Wrong with Volunteer Tourism?" How is she addressing concerns about learning and serving in her organization PEPY?

RELATIONSHIP BUILDING AND SERVICE-LEARNING

In any service-learning opportunity, the importance of building relationships with those you meet cannot be overstated. John McKnight in *The Careless Society: Community and Its Counterfeits* argues that we have a "professional problem" in the United States today. Too often we concentrate on finding needs or deficits to fix in our communities. Each newly discovered unmet need creates a demand for a new profession, which in turn focuses our attention on deficiencies and problems in our communities rather than on assets. In his last chapter, McKnight paints a different vision, one based on relationship building for strengthening our communities. Taking as his model Christ's words to his disciples at the Last Supper, "I do not call you servants any longer . . . but I have called you friends" (John 15:15), McKnight suggests that

friends are people who understand that it is not servants—the professors, lawyers, doctors, and teachers—who make God's world. Rather, friends are people who understand that it is through their mutual action that they become Christians. . . . Why friends rather than servants? Perhaps it is because [Christ] knew that servants could always become lords but that friends could not. Servants are people who *know the mysteries* that can control those to whom they give "help." Friends are people who *know each other*. They are free to give *and* receive help. In our time, professionalized servants are people who are limited by the unknowing friendlessness of their help. Friends, on the other hand, are people liberated by the possibilities of knowing how to help each other.[13]

- Do you agree with McKnight's argument that professionals need to be more focused on building relationships with those they serve? What are some examples of how you have been caught up in identifying deficits rather than assets of your host community?

- What might be some limitations (if any) of becoming friends rather than servants in your current international service-learning placement?

Read an excerpt from Ellie's blog below. How was she able to put into practice some of the principles discussed in this chapter? What other challenges existed for her as she participated in this service-learning experience?

The highlight of my semester abroad was participating in service-learning. I volunteered with a ministry (RMK) that assists refugees and immigrants to successfully adjust to their new lives in Hungary. Not only do they practically help them, but they also provide newcomers with a community and familial atmosphere. At RMK, I met with three teenage girls, Lina, Luna, and Mish, weekly for one-on-one English tutoring sessions, and babysat two little girls, Maya and Mitra, once a week while their mom had Hungarian language tutoring. I loved volunteering at RMK so much because I was able to build relationships with the girls I tutored. I had the privilege of hearing their stories as well as their thoughts on various issues and their aspirations for the future. I was able to get a glimpse into the diverse cultures they come from through the lens of their life experiences. I became their friend and helped them become friends with one another, too. It was a deeply impactful experience and shaped my time and me in Budapest greatly.

RMK had their annual Christmas party on the Wednesday before we left, and it was an absolute blast. . . . As we held sweaty hands and danced in a circle and laughed as we stumbled, trying to learn the steps, I realized that this is what beloved community looks like. It is the image of unity in the midst of diversity. It is choosing to build bridges and come together, not allowing differences to divide us and destroy the potential of authentic love and community. There was an openness, a freedom, and a spirit of acceptance and love in the atmosphere. It was a privilege to simply witness it and to be a part of the RMK community for a few short months; the people I met there will never know how much they blessed me.

Although the term *service-learning* is relatively recent, the concept is much older. Jane Addams, an early twentieth-century social reformer, opened the Hull House in Chicago in order to bring together new immigrants and young middle-class people such as herself who had the advantages of higher education. Hull House was to be an experiment in mutual aid and mutual education, with each group benefiting, though in different ways, from the association. In explaining some of her hopes for starting the Hull House Addams wrote,

I gradually became convinced that it would be a good thing to rent a house in a part of the city where many primitive and actual needs are found, in which young women who had been given over too exclusively to study, might restore a balance of activity along traditional lines and learn of life from life itself; where they might try out some of the things they had been taught and put truth to "the ultimate test of the conduct it dictates or inspires."[14]

Jane Addams' settlement house movement is similar to service-learning today. What benefits has a service-learning experience brought to you? What benefits has your presence and service provided to those among whom you have lived and worked?

SERVICE LIVING

Students and faculty together must be thoughtful as we think about how best to engage others while studying abroad. International service-learning can be helpful in this process, but we must ensure that the experience benefits everyone involved, that learning and serving are deeply intertwined, and that relationship building is an integral part of the process.

This focus on service-learning should not end with your study abroad experience. Rather, it must be brought back and applied in your home community so that the goal of fostering active global citizens can be realized.

One resource that may help you is the book *Service Living*, which focuses on what it means to live a life distinguished by lifelong action that contributes to the health and well-being of all living things. Through the life stories of Frederick Law Olmsted, Jane Addams, Benton MacKaye, and Marjorie Stonewall Douglas, the authors explore what it means to be a citizen in a democracy: "Democracy demands that individual citizens take personal responsibility for its proper functioning by getting involved in it. The work is too important to be left to the politicians and their designees. We cannot sit back and allow someone else to do for us what we should be doing for ourselves."[15] As Christians, we are also called to take personal responsibility, to act locally with a global perspective, and to work to bring about God's kingdom in small ways wherever and whenever God calls.

This call for responsible service and responsible learning are reflected in Kate's blog, written during her service-learning placement in Honduras.

I gripped the motorcycle with my knees as it sputtered like a balky horse. It was the second day of my two-week internship for "Growers First," an organization that works with coffee farmers in Honduras, and we were spending most of our day checking on coffee projects and interviewing farmers and their families. All these families lived up in the mountains, and the roads to get there rivaled any dirt bike course.

We were late getting back, and I only just had time to pull off my sweatshirt and muddy rubber boots and run a hand through my motorcycle-whipped hair before my host family here took me to a Thanksgiving dinner.

At one farmer's house in the morning, we had sat in plastic chairs on his concrete floor, looking out a window with no glass at a pit latrine screened by tattered sheets. He had given us dark coffee with so much sugar it stung at the back of my throat.

This taste was still in my mouth when I sat down at a table laden with every kind of good food. We had two forks each, I remember, and two spoons. With turkey, mashed potatoes, stuffing, cranberry sauce, and three kinds of pie, it was a Thanksgiving meal to rival any. So what was I supposed to do? I gave thanks.

I have so much to be thankful for. I could start with great parents, and siblings who are some of my best friends. I love my school. I love what I'm studying. I have enough food to eat, more clothes than I can wear. I'm safe and healthy. I have incredible friends and an amazing boyfriend. But I'm starting to realize that the question isn't what I'm grateful for, but maybe what is grateful for.

What does being grateful matter if I don't do anything about it?

If you ever wonder what upper-middle class Hondurans talk about at Thanksgiving dinner — it's probably exactly what your family talked about. Politics. How good their kids are at technology. Whether or not they should buy an iPad.

And I sat, smiling at the jokes, stuffing my face. The house where we ate had more Christmas lights than Bronner's Christmas store, and all I could think of was the bicycle at that one house in the mountains that had been turned into a generator. By pumping the pedals by hand, a single light bulb in the house would flicker on.

What does it mean that so many people don't have the things I'm grateful for, let alone the things I take for granted? As my attention span dozed in and out of a conversation about children's grades and a new proposed tax, I thought about what it means to be grateful. I think, in the end, it's —

1.The recognition that something is good, and
2.The recognition that it was not you who made it so.

*So, **Gratefulness isn't Self-Congratulation.** If I come back from Honduras remembering the poverty I saw and thanking God that it's not me who uses a squat latrine, then my time here will have been wasted. If my takeaway is, "I'm glad I'm not them," then I have everything backwards. Because that brings with it the ludicrous assumption that it was me who put me in my position. I did very little to be where I am. I owe a God who made me, and parents and teachers who helped shape me. However, I need to be careful not to go to the opposite side and loathe myself for what I have . . .*

*Because **Gratefulness isn't Guilt.** After spending three months taking cold showers, am I ready to give up warm showers forever? Heck no! I can't wait to get back to a warm bath. See, part of recognizing that something is good means enjoying it. Are you eating a sumptuous dinner surrounded by loved ones? Don't begrudge yourself the happiness! This is a good thing. But . . .*

*If these are really good things, then gratitude goes beyond simply acknowledging them. **Gratefulness does.** Do I recognize that my family is a good thing? Then how am I caring for them, showing my appreciation for them, supporting them? Am I thankful for warm food, a comfortable bed, or entertainment? If these things are good, then how can I share them with others?*

I can't say it's easy to accept the reeling proximity that allows me to see subsistence in the morning and feasting in the afternoon. But giving based on guilt is only charity. It is to soothe the giver's conscience.

Giving based in gratefulness comes closer to the needs of another's heart. What is it you most cherish? What is it you most miss? How can you share this with others so that they'll know the same joy? As you count your blessings and I count mine, let's think of what to do with all of them. Let's not leave our thankfulness as a list recited one day a year, but let's make our gratefulness do.

Kate is considering how the lessons she is learning in Honduras will have an impact on her life as she returns to the United States. What are you learning from your own service-learning experience? How will these lessons affect your life as you return from studying abroad?

Chapter Nineteen

ENDING WELL

Every experience God gives us, every person He puts in our lives
is the perfect preparation for the future that only He can see.
—Corrie ten Boom

I have never felt more alive than while I have been abroad.
More than I ever have, I'm living for the moment here. I know I won't be
able to do that when I get home. I'll have responsibilities to think about,
so I'm doing my best to enjoy it while it lasts.
—Student reflection, France

Loving a culture involves more than just enjoying it while you're there.
It includes having a desire to share it. . . . I know now that I have a desire,
and a kind of obligation, to help erase stereotypes and bring
respect to Mexicans and their culture in the United States.
—Student reflection, Mexico

With the end of your study abroad experience rapidly approaching, I suspect that you are excited to be going home but also sad to be leaving newfound friends and a place you have grown to love. Lori reflected on this bittersweet time in her blog:

Just a few weeks stand between us and our return to the States. This is a fact that we try not to dwell on these days, as it causes us a flurry of conflicting emotions. We are blessed to have many great things to look forward to upon stepping foot back home, being greeted by family or friends, going home to celebrate Christmas, starting life back up again at college, and (most importantly?) eating peanut butter to our heart's content. However, the heartache caused by leaving behind our Peruvian families and friends, this city that has become our own, this enchanting country, and this once-in-a-lifetime experience is already beginning to taunt us.

Leaving and returning home can be an emotional time, and you want to get it right, to be intentional with your goodbyes. At the end of the book *Life of Pi*, the narrator arrives on a beach in a small boat with a tiger, named Robert Parker, with whom he has shared a 227-day journey. The tiger jumps from the boat and runs off into the jungle. In reflecting on this moment, the narrator notes:

How might you plan to say goodbye? How can you say "thank you" to the people and places you've come to love during your study abroad experience? What might it mean to say "God be with you?"

I wept like a child. It was not because I was overcome at having survived my ordeal, though I was. . . . I was weeping because Richard Parker had left me so unceremoniously. What a terrible thing to botch a farewell. I am a person who believes in form, in the harmony of order. Where we can, we must give things a meaningful shape. . . . It's important in life to conclude things properly. Only then can you let go. Otherwise you are left with words you should have said but never did, and your heart is heavy with remorse. That bungled goodbye hurts me to this day. I wish so much that I'd had one last look at him in the lifeboat, that I'd provoked him a little, so that I was on his mind. I wish I had said to him then — yes, I know, to a tiger, but still — I wish I had said, "Richard Parker, it's over. We have survived. Can you believe it? I owe you more gratitude than I can express. I couldn't have done it without you. I would like to say formally: Richard Parker, thank you. Thank you for saving my life. And now go where you must. . . . I hope you remember me as a friend. I will never forget you, that is certain. You will always be with me, in my heart. What is that hiss? Ah, our boat has touched sand. So farewell, Richard Parker, farewell. God be with you."[1]

REFLECTING ON YOUR TIME ABROAD

T.S. Eliot once said, "we had the experience but missed the meaning."[2] It is easy in our fast-paced lives to take in lots of experiences but miss their meaning. As you prepare to leave your host community, it is important to reflect on what you have seen, and done, and learned.

In addition, if you have studied abroad in a group, you've developed shared meaning as a result of your collective experience. Exploring this sense of shared meaning is helpful as you transfer the lessons learned during your time abroad to your life when you return home. Making this transfer is an integral part of the experiential learning process described in chapter two. You've been thinking, both formally and informally, about connections between your study abroad and your life at home throughout the semester. Now, making space to process your experience is essential to ending well.

As a group studying abroad, you have experienced a lot together. You have had highs and lows. Perhaps, at times, you have fought like brothers and sisters. Perhaps there has been a traumatic event that has brought the group together. Whatever your experience, it is important to claim it together. Some possible questions to start this collective reflection include these:

» When did your study abroad group (collectively) laugh the hardest?
» What was your favorite excursion? What was the group's favorite excursion?
» What was the low point of the semester for the group?
» What were some of the high points of the experience for the group?
» What collective lessons did the group learn that should not be forgotten? What individual lessons do you want to remember?
» Did your group set any group goals or create any type of group contract at the start of the experience? If so, review these goals and commitments. How did the group do in terms of achieving these group goals?
» What are two or three questions (if any) that the group struggled with over the course of your experience?

Beyond processing your overall experience as a group, there are a number of things you can do individually to reflect on your experience abroad, including the following:

Answer the group questions above for yourself as an individual. How do your individual answers compare to the answers of the group? In addition, review your own journal or blog. Are there any themes that emerge?

Look again at the goals you set for yourself prior to departure. What goals were realized, and what goals were not? Why or why not? Did your goals change over the course of the experience? What is one thing you know now that you wish you would have known then? What have you learned about yourself?

As you read the student reflection below, think about what you don't know now that you thought you knew when you arrived:

I've grown a lot throughout my time here. Most of the time, I couldn't see myself growing while it was happening. In the beginning of the semester I thought I knew everything. I was overconfident (arrogant) about community life, cross-cultural engagement, and justice. I thought I knew who I was and what I wanted to do. I thought I wouldn't be in as much of a learning position as the other people in the group. But I realized that I was wrong about that.

I'm still learning, even after I've spent four months in Europe. This realization has opened me up even more for personal development and learning.[3]

In what ways do you see the world differently as a result of your time abroad? Has your worldview changed? Often students report that their time away also affected how they see their home culture. Has this happened for you? If so, how?

As one student reflected:

I'm starting the long process of reflecting on and integrating all the things I've seen and learned this semester into my worldview. I definitely came to Hungary with an idealized view of Europe. It seemed so much more sophisticated and beautiful than America to me. Architecturally, I can now confirm that much of Europe is more beautiful than the United States. But beyond that, my perception of Europe hasn't held up at all. Now I'm not saying I don't like Europe, or that I think the United States is superior. I guess I've just realized that, cliché as it is, "the grass is never as green as it looks." Dysfunctional governments, corruption, and racism are problems in Europe, too. In fact, sometimes they are even bigger problems here. Furthermore, Europe has some problems the United States doesn't.

Partially because the United States is built on a forward-thinking mentality, and partially because we haven't had time to make all that much history, Americans aren't especially attached to the past. By contrast, many Europeans seem to be defined by it. I used to think that remembering history was a good thing, so in the past, I might have commended them for this. However, now, I think it's a good thing to remember what we learned from history, but a bad thing to remember the feelings associated with our history.

My shift in view regarding history and Europe and America in general really surprised me. While I've also noticed many things that Europeans do better than the United States, I expected to see those things when I came to Hungary. I didn't expect to come out of this appreciating anything about the United States more. I feel very self-conscious saying this. I don't want to sound like I think we're better than everyone else. I really, really don't. I just see the global field much more evenly now. Every country has its problems. None of us are perfect. The United States could learn from some of the European countries, just like it could learn from countries in Asia, Africa and South America. Likewise, Europe could learn from the United States.[4]

In what ways have the people and places of your study abroad experience changed you?

As you read the following reflection of Anneke who studied in Budapest for a semester, think about what part of your heart you are leaving behind in your host community and what parts of your study abroad experience you are taking with you.

It doesn't seem like it's been four months since I left America for the beautiful Magyarorszag. And yet, in just four days, I'll be once again boarding a plane that will take me across the Atlantic, take me home to the great white mitten, where snow and family and the promise of two weeks of English await. And then I'll be off again to Haiti. I don't want this time in Eastern Europe to end, but I'm ready for familiar faces and a language that is not only familiar to me, but also understandable. As this semester comes to an end, I'm struck by how much I've learned and how much I've seen this fall. I will miss being surrounded by such history. I'll miss being surrounded by this city.

But this city will go on without me. The cashiers at Spar will no longer be overwhelmed with a mad rush of Americans after Monday night class. There will be more seats on the 47 for the elderly passengers on their way to the markets. My professors will teach more new students; the Christmas markets will be twenty people short; and I'm sure our Hungarian guards will welcome our departure. The green bridge, connecting my Buda to bustling Pest, will not mark my absence; the Hungarian bartenders, baristas, and waiters will no longer have to handle the Americans from our group. This city will go on without me.

In a sense, though, I will not go on without this city. It's become a part of me. I've grown accustomed to the forty minute tram rides, the awkward encounters with basically everyone in this country, even the disgusting dorm in which we live. And when we touch down in GRR, when I leave this family for my own back home, I think I'll finally start to realize how much I really do love this place and its people . . . and, yes, even its language.

Sziastok, Budapest. It's been a great semester!

BRINGING CLOSURE

As you prepare to leave your host community, it is important to think about bringing closure to this chapter in your life. What things do you still want to do in your community before you leave? How can you make some of these things happen? What people do you want to connect with? Take the time (and energy) to say goodbye to the people who made your experience what it was. Don't limit yourself to friends, but think also about saying goodbye to teachers, the cafeteria lady, the security guard, a memorable bus driver, or favorite server at a restaurant. Make sure you let others know how much you have appreciated them.

For closer friends, like fellow students or even close host country friends, exchange contact information so that you have ways of maintaining communication, even if it's just through social media. You never know when you will see them again, but having the ability to call on them if you're nearby, or even just to reminisce, is invaluable.

Don't be afraid to continue reflecting on your study abroad experience and the ways in which it changed you and how you view the world. Appreciate the fact that you did something very few people in the world get to do. Treasure that experience and the new insights you possess because of it.

As you reflect on your experience abroad, you may want to write an open letter or prayer to your host community, expressing your feelings and reflections. An example of such a prayer is presented below. As you read through this prayer, think about what you would write in summarizing your overall experience.

> *Kenya, you have had the power to simultaneously turn the past four months into an eternity and a heartbeat at the same time. I sit here in your soft green grass not knowing if I will ever condense all that you have taught me into a comprehensive lump. So I guess I will start by saying "Thank You."*
>
> *Thank you for embracing me in your soft colorful hands, and taking me to the mountains and the valleys of your country. For sending your wind whispering through the courtyard at night, and sunsets and rainbows to punctuate just the right moments. For conversations on the rocks under your brilliant starry sky, and the silver smile of your moon.*
>
> *Thank you for the flowers and the hills in the Athi River, that created an escape when I needed it and for the layers of your dust I accumulated while running away from and toward myself.*
>
> *Thanks for using my fears and the brevity of lives like little Joe, Emma and Carol [at Mother Teresa's home] to teach me to value whatever space of life I'm granted. For showing me, time and again, that nothing in life is guaranteed.*
>
> *For making me painfully aware of my own blindness, weakness and insecurities, and teaching me that I am not invincible or fearless. For allowing me to sit with the paradoxes of this work and not demanding answers. I thank you. For allowing me to cry again and teaching me to rely on others instead of myself . . . and for, at times, breaking my stubborn independence, I reluctantly say thanks.*

For teaching me to value my family and showing me that I matter to them . . . even if their way of showing it is broken and awkward and takes five weeks (by mail) to get here.

Thank you for loving me through so many people and places and experiences. For allowing my life to cross paths with people like Joy, and using her charred feet to teach me about love, joy, and true perseverance. For Habtu in his little green running suit, for Anna and her brave beautiful smile, for humble prayers in dry riverbeds and tiny roofless churches.

Thank you for holding tightly to the wheels of muddy vehicles threatening to tip over, for sleepless nights, bomb threats, jam with bees, the satisfaction of clean laundry.

Thank you for allowing me to see the face of Christ in the smile of a broken child, the touch of abandoned scabby fingers and the cartwheels of a little boy in a garbage heap. For teaching me there aren't a whole lot of things in this world worth worrying about . . . but that there is a whole lot worth living for.

Kenya, you have scarred my legs and my life forever . . . and taught me what it truly means to say, "I live in grace."

May God Bless you Kenya, and the hundreds of lives that embraced me here. May he keep you and your people safe. May his face shine upon you and give you peace. Asante Sana and Kwaheri.[5]

As you close this chapter of your life, think about any other unfinished business you may have before you leave. What will you miss after your departure? Remember that you may continue to "live in the middle" for a while as you look forward to what is coming, yet lament what you left behind. Bethany, who studied in Peru, expresses these very emotions:

Well, WE MADE IT. All of us are safely back, tucked cozily into our homes with our families, dispersed throughout the States. We're filled to the brim with home cooked food and a multitude of emotions. On one hand we're incredibly ecstatic to finally be back, running to hug our families, squealing with delight upon reuniting with dear friends, receiving a happy lick from our excited dogs. But on the other hand, melancholy thoughts often drift into our minds when we're reminded of life in Peru. It seems for every happy thing we re-encounter in our lives here, there's something we miss equally as much in Peru.

We're happy to reunite with friends and family here,
But we miss our friends and family there.

Beyond writing an open letter or prayer to your host community, what advice or wisdom would you like to pass on to students who might study abroad in your host community in the future?

We're happy to eat peanut butter and jelly, and drink tap water,
But we miss manjar and jugo de fresa.

We're happy to speak in English guilt free,
But we miss Spanish words and phrases that are sometimes the best/only
descriptions we can find.

We're happy to walk in winter wonderlands,
But we miss our Arequipean sunshine.

We're so very happy here,
But we truly miss it there.

It seems that we've allowed Peru to nestle itself deep into our hearts. That
country, with its sunny weather and even sunnier people, has become home
to twenty-two college students, whether we realized it or not. Home is an
interesting concept. More than a house, home is where we're completely com-
fortable. Home is where we're embraced and accepted by family and friends.
Home is where our hearts warm up. Home is here, and home is there.

And that is a beautiful thing.

WHAT'S NEXT

So many things had to fall into place for you to study abroad: you had to apply and be accepted, you had to get a passport, you had to travel safely, you needed a host family or a place to stay, you needed good leaders and teachers. Isn't it amazing how everything has come together? Looking back on my own life, I am always amazed to see how God has used my past experiences to bring me to where I am now. Although I may not know what is to come, I can trust God to take me where he wants me to go. As you reflect on your experience abroad, think about all the good things that God has brought into your life during this time. He has expanded your horizons and has shown you that he is a big God who will provide for you wherever you are.

🐚 Now that your time abroad is almost over, it is time to think about what is next. So give thanks for all that has happened and look ahead with confidence, because God will continue to work in you to do great things! That said, it is still natural to worry about what is next. What anxieties do you have about returning home? How do you want to see God in the transition from this experience to whatever is the next step in your life?

Let's face it. You are leaving your experience abroad as a different person than you were when you started it. Although the change may not be drastic, something has happened. You have studied in a different culture, you have had to budget for a different country, and you most likely have had to be flexible when adjusting to a new culture. You have seen many beautiful places. You have met many people. You had the chance to find yourself away from the comforts of home. You have learned to embrace the challenges and opportunities that came your way. All these experiences are now a part of you and will shape your life moving forward. In the coming weeks, months, and even years ahead, your job is to explore how God will use these experiences in your life, as Bethany, who studied in Honduras, notes in her blog:

> *I'm back. To be exact, I'm sitting on the same couch where I typed the "About" section of this blog, more than four months ago, wondering who exactly I would be when this whole adventure was over.*
>
> *This semester was more than I could have ever imagined. I swam in the Atlantic Ocean and the Pacific Ocean, galloped on horseback, and saw Mayan ruins. I climbed a dead volcano and went surfing and had smoothies in three countries. I became part of a family in Honduras, and I learned what it means to be intentional about friendship, and I saw God work in unexpected and incredible ways.*
>
> *I realized what it feels like to be a stranger. I had to come to terms with the violence and poverty that had never been part of my reality before. I had to ask questions and seek answers about God and about justice and mercy. I learned to find hope in the midst of darkness.*
>
> *I learned that in four months, a different country can become somewhere you belong. And there is always part of me that will remember the bright yellow house at the top of the cobblestone hill, with the rusty gate and the puppy nipping at my ankles, as home. And I know that every time I gaze at a mountain range, a small voice inside my head will say, "Remember? Remember the mountains that go on forever into the distance in Honduras? Remember the laguna and the park with the stone benches and the mirador? Remember your Honduran family and the other students and butchered Spanish conversations and beans and smoothies and everything else that made the semester so incredible?"*
>
> *And I will remember. Because even though this chapter may be finished, it is one that will never really be closed. My experiences these past four months, both the adventurous and the challenging, have made me grow and think and become who I am today. They are not contained in Honduras — I see them starting to spill over into my life in the United States, shaping my decisions regarding my present and my future. And I keep reminding myself that this isn't really an end. It is a beginning.*

How do you hope your study abroad experience will spill out into other aspects of your life upon your return? As memories fade, what do you need to do in the coming months to keep the lessons learned abroad fresh? As you leave your study abroad experience, how is this a beginning rather than an end?

Do you think you will ever return to your host community? If so, what would motivate you to make this return? What would you hope to accomplish with such a return trip?

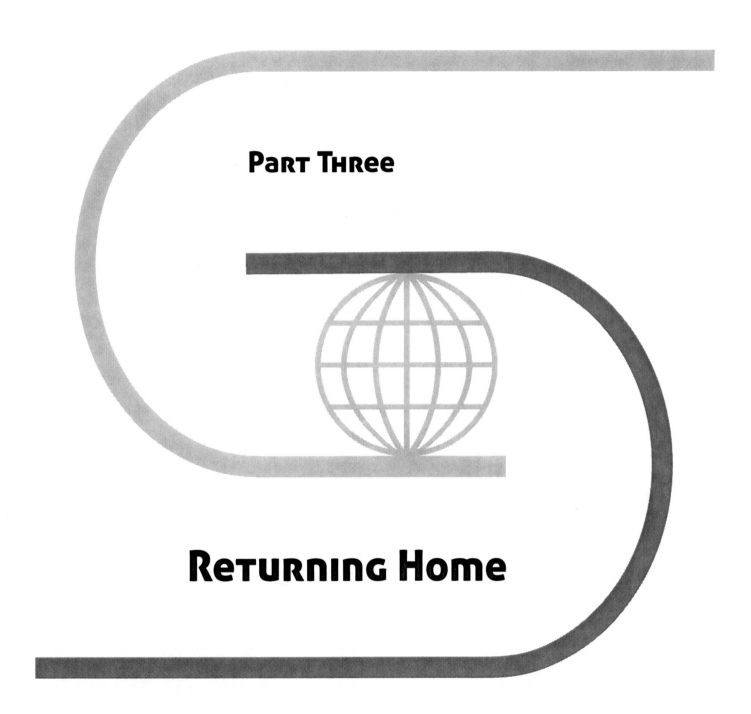

PART THREE

RETURNING Home

Chapter Twenty ——————

Re-crossing the Threshold

The highs and lows of pilgrimage require a time for contemplation,
a time for digesting the lessons and the memories.
It is a time to cement in our consciousness what Christ has taught us.
For me, going home is one of the best parts of the journey.
–Christian George

If a man set out from home on a journey,
and kept right on going,
he would come back to his own front door.
–John Mandeville

And now it is officially over. You are returning or have returned home from a life-changing experience. You probably have mixed emotions, excited to see family and friends but sad to leave the new friends and places you have grown to love. But return you must, for returning home is key to any pilgrimage experience: "The true destination of pilgrimage is not the holy site [or the study abroad location], but home. One passes through the holy site to return home in a new way."[1]

Yet returning home is not simply about arriving at the airport; it is a process. In many ways you need to re-cross the threshold that leads back home. Perhaps the best place to start in re-crossing this threshold is to acknowledge that the home you left is not the same as the one to which you are returning. Likewise, the "you" who left is not the same as the "you" who is returning.

Re-crossing this threshold is not easy. It often entails experiencing some type of reverse culture shock as you navigate both your own emotions and the emotions of the family and friends welcoming you home. Many of these challenges can be seen in Jerry's blog post as he returned home from Ghana:

I am back in the good ole USofA . . . except for the fact that even though "old" is fitting, "good" may not be. Reverse culture shock has hit me a bit harder than culture shock did . . . okay, I admit, much harder. You would think that I would feel more shock going to a culture that I did not grow up in, and feel welcome and comfortable

Look online for suggestions to deal with reverse culture shock. What suggestions are presented? What tips do you think might work for you?

Have you witnessed any of your friends who studied abroad wrestling with reverse culture shock? In what ways are they responding positively to reverse cultural shock? Negatively?

coming back to the one I have lived my whole life in. That seems logical, but sometimes logic needs to be thrown out the window temporarily to open and gain a little perspective . . . and that's exactly what I plan to do and in fact am doing.

I find myself a little lost, not sure how to navigate, both physically and socially. I spent four months in a culture that felt more like home to me than home does. It is hard to capture the full extent and reach of the ramifications of the effects of this paradox. . . . Perhaps part of it is that I am not truly in my own physical home yet, nor am I with my family (my emotional home), but there is the chance that this, even, is wishful thinking. Everything about this life just seems so foreign to me, yet I can't seem to pinpoint any major differences.

This is starting to make me wonder whether or not America is a good fit for me and my future. I feel an overbearing pressure and looming cloud of complacency that squeezes in and chokes me when I think of my future, and all I hear are thoughts about planning for grad school and getting a secure job and finding a way to fulfill my passions while still building up a life for myself . . . and it all sounds nice and grand. But also tiring, over-complicated, non-committal, and stagnant. . . .

Ghana changed me . . . and I'll never be the same . . . and I don't want to be. I don't know what this means for me, but I do know that it means this story has continued and is continuing past this semester, and perhaps will continue past this period of re-entrance. . . . Any semester program or, to broaden the scope, extended period of stay in another country and culture (and continent in this case), not only affects one's life while abroad, but continues to do so, deeply and measurably for a period afterwards, and will continue to do so to a lesser extent for the rest of one's life. . . . I firmly believe that my time in Ghana changed my life immeasurably; I'm curious as to what my time back holds in store for me.

🐚 What are the issues this student was wrestling with as he returned home from Ghana? Are you struggling with any similar issues? Can you name these issues?

🐚 Have you experienced any reverse culture shock? Remember from chapter fifteen that reverse culture shock can be thought of as having difficulty adjusting back to your life at home after living in a different culture for several months. How has the idea of reverse culture shock manifested itself in your life? How did reverse culture shock manifest itself in Jerry's journal as he returned from Ghana?

Read the following email response to a student returning home from a semester of studying in Honduras. The student emailed the professor with some real concerns about reintegrating back into the United States. She asks, "How can I remember all the things that I learned in Honduras? How can I return to my normal life but not go back to how I lived before?" Her faculty mentor responds:

> Thanks for the window into your concerns as you return to the United States. The biggest short-term danger, I think, is in thinking that if you can't change all of your life at once, you'll never really change any of it, so you might as well not try — it's too hard, and you'll lose way too many friends in the process. The more realistic outlook to take, and the much harder road, is to simply put one foot in front of the other and do your best. In this process you will fail, but God also forgives and encourages you to find a community of like-minded fellow travelers who will hold you accountable and encourage you in this journey as you return.[2]

YOUR NEW NORMAL

As you return home, you will undoubtedly try to incorporate what you have learned and experienced abroad into your life at home. This often requires self-reflection and a shift in how to understand your home culture and how you want to continue to grow and develop. This shift in perspective happens as you integrate your experiences abroad into your life at home in an effort to create a "new normal." As this process plays out, you need to think about how your relationships with your family might have changed or will change. Consider the following reflections from students struggling with how their relationships with family and friends have changed or will change.

Reflection One

Throughout my time abroad, I truly felt like my parents learned to let go and allowed me to experience Europe for myself. Yet, upon returning home in December, I felt them reeling me back into the same expectations they had before I left.[3]

What can you do to seek out and find a supportive community who will encourage you to live out (albeit imperfectly) the lessons you have learned while studying abroad?

Reflection Two

The hug from my mom and dad was what I had been missing for months. The smile and the inside joke shared with my brother made me feel welcomed. But after the initial reuniting, I realized that my relationship had changed with my family. . . . My life ran parallel to theirs, as time did not stop in the United States. Family and friends were having their own adventures, shared moments, and transitions.[4]

After reading these student reflections, reflect on the ways in which your relationships with your family and friends have changed. How can you navigate these changes with truth and grace?

As you navigate these changes, what advice would you give yourself as you reintegrate into your home community?

Consider the advice this student gave to herself about returning home:

Give people in the United States grace. They do not understand what you have gone through nor may they care to know. They will want you to be the old Jane: the Jane who did not concentrate on what is wrong with the world, the Jane who did not see the negative in situations. I'm slowly becoming a more well-rounded person, seeing the world for what it is but still loving it. Make sure you do not tend towards oblivion or cynicism. Along with that, do not try to make yourself appear so different.[As has been said,] "Explaining one's personal transformation is not nearly as important as living it."[5]

What advice would you give to your family and friends as you return home?

Kate, on the other hand, gave advice to her family and friends as she re-crossed the threshold and returned home:

Five days left! I can count them on one hand, or one foot if I'm feeling creative. Five days until I walk back into that airport, fly over that ocean, and emerge in weather that will be so shockingly, unforgivably cold. . . .

I'm already preparing myself for the shock of being back in the Midwest USA; for the jolt of leaving a place that's become home and people who have become close. It's going to be a great, but rough, few days; and if anyone wants to give me a hand, here are a few things you can do when you see me soon:

1. **Be Patient.** *Maybe I'll come off the plane so excited that I can't stop talking. Please be patient while I settle into normal human conversation! Be patient when Honduras comes up again and again. Be patient enough to sit through unending photo slide shows.*

   On the other hand, maybe I'll step off the plane quiet. All this takes time to process, so please be patient while I think of the right words to say — or any words at all. Please be patient if I don't have my stories polished yet. Or when I just need to be alone.

   I love Honduras, in a complicated, comfortable way. It's hard to leave my host family, my friends here, my beautiful city, food and music that's becoming more and more familiar. Please be patient when I'm backwards-homesick. Because I'm going to miss this place.

2. **Ask Questions.** *Whenever I'd go anywhere as a kid, my dad would ask me about it this way: "So you got out of the car . . . and then what happened?" Please don't do this. Four months is a long time, so you're going to have to be a little more specific. I'll start practicing a little spiel for the hundreds of casual "how was Honduras" questions I know I'll get, but I can't fit much depth into a spiel. So give me a little more to go off of: "Tell me about living with a Honduran family." "What did you do on vacation?" "What is Development Studies anyway?" I want to share so much with all of you. But I don't want to bore those who'd rather not hear. So if you're curious, ask! One of the best ways to love is to listen.*

3. **Hold Me Accountable.** *I'm coming in with an aching conscience and a thousand new ideas. I want to start putting these ideas I have to work. But I can't do this alone. So will you please help me? Tell me when a plan is silly or overly ambitious. Call me out when my behavior doesn't match my goals. Keep me humble. Help me keep on learning.*

   This is maybe the most important way you can be nice to me when I come home. Don't let me get carried away on the high of my study abroad experience, but don't let me forget it either. This also means . . . expect me to be nice to you too! No matter where you've been, you have your own four months of experiences, ideas, stories, and growth. So make sure I ask you about that. Make sure I'm patient with you; make sure I know what I can do for you too. . . .

   Five more days.

What are some of the ways you want to stretch yourself moving forward? How can you meet new people at home who might help you grow? What experiences do you want to seek out as you continue to connect to your world both locally and globally?

RE-CROSSING THE THRESHOLD

As you left for your study abroad experience weeks or months ago, a blessing was offered for your journey. As you return and re-cross the same threshold, here is another blessing for your continued journey in the weeks and months ahead:

> Our small pilgrimage ends with this large promise. "See, the home of God is among mortals." See. May you continue to walk slowly now and then, with the vision of those who have eyes to see God at work and at rest, broken and healed, dying and rising, in the places and people that surround you.[6]

Chapter Twenty-One

BRINGING THE WORLD HOME

UNLESS someone like you cares a whole awful lot,
nothing is going to get better. It's not.
–Dr. Seuss

Do what you can,
with what you've got, where you are.
–Theodore Roosevelt

After four months of helplessness – of people feeding me and guiding me
and translating for me; giving me deadlines and asking me questions –
it's up to me to keep on going. The things I've learned have to
become the things I do, and that's a tricky process.
–Student reflection, Honduras

Y ou are back home. You had a fantastic time living and learning abroad. But your pilgrimage has ended, and the question "now what?" starts to take center stage. How will your study abroad experience affect your life moving forward? How do you make the moments last and not simply re-enter the life you previously knew? How do you see your coming home as a new beginning?

You may be tempted to see your return home as the end of a once-in-a-lifetime opportunity. Although this approach is understandable, it ignores the challenge of integrating the lessons you learned abroad into your life at home. As Kate's blog illustrates, there is a lot more to come.

Now what?

In some ways, my life isn't as exciting anymore. There won't be volcanoes or trips across borders in my near future. But in another way, my life is just getting exciting. Anyone can have an experience, but it all depends on what you do with it. Now my life, more than ever, is in my hands.

What I'm going to do with the things I learned will fill its own chapter. I'm not going to stop asking questions and exploring ideas. I have three more semesters of college, and who knows what comes next. So stay with me! The story (I hope) is just starting to get good.

The United States Peace Corps understands the importance of helping volunteers see the end of their service not as an ending but as a beginning. The three goals of the Peace Corps are 1) to help the people of interested countries in meeting their need for trained men and women; 2) to help promote a better understanding of Americans on the part of the peoples served; and 3) to help promote a better understanding of other peoples on the part of Americans.[1] While the first two goals relate to a volunteer's experience abroad, the third speaks to new beginnings, challenging volunteers to do something positive with their experiences.

As you settle back into your life at home, one of the best ways to honor your time away is to internalize it, living your life with the knowledge you gained abroad while also seeking to share your new insights with others.

The following poem by Rudyard Kipling humorously summarizes the learning that may occur when you travel there and back with your eyes open.

> All good people agree
>   And all good people say
> All nice people like Us are We
>   And every one else is They
> But if you cross over the sea
>   Instead of over the way
> You may end by (think of it!) looking on We
>   As only a sort of They![2]

COMING HOME WITH NEW EYES

An important part of any pilgrimage is coming home, returning to family and friends and everyday lives. Yet as we have seen throughout this book, pilgrimages have the power to transform us and provide a new lens through which to see familiar places. What do you see at home now that you did not see before? Consider the following reflection from Nora Gallagher as she describes how home changed for her:

> When I returned to Santa Barbara [from Nicaragua], everywhere I looked, the people who had been either invisible to me or a quaint backdrop to this tourist town were suddenly real: the Latino gardener on the street with his leaf blower, the dishwasher in the back room of a restaurant, the old man sitting at the bus stop.

Did your study abroad experience help you to see others differently? How has your time abroad helped you to see and feel firsthand the ways in which the interests of your host community connect to the interests of your home community?

I was shaken. I no longer wished to live as I had been living — working, eating, tending my marriage, dropping in on church. I wanted to have something to do with what I had seen in Nicaragua because I knew that it was a glimpse of something else. . . . What I yearned for was to embody my shaky faith, to feel my faith in my flesh, acted out, incarnate.[3]

VERTICAL AND HORIZONTAL ROOTS

In chapter twelve, we explored the importance of being rooted both to your home and to the places you visit in order to dwell and travel well. As you move on after your study abroad experience, rootedness will continue to present a challenge as you find ways to be an active and engaged citizen of your local community and the world. One way to think about this challenge is to examine how you can develop both a vertical and a horizontal root system.

Jim Citron and Vija Mendelson note that

We think of people who spend a long time living in one place as being "vertically-rooted."

When you go abroad, you deliberately "uproot" yourself from the environment where you have always lived and, in the process, lose a lot of familiar reference points and distance yourself from your familiar support networks. At first your host country may present some challenges, but ideally you learn to adapt as you adjust to a new way of life. You meet new people, from many different backgrounds, and you form new relationships that act as your support network abroad. You become comfortable with this new environment, find your place in it, and develop something akin to what David Pollack, an expert on "Third Culture Kids," has called an extended root system of perhaps less entrenched, but more far-reaching roots that now provide your support.

We think of people who have lived in more than one place as being more "horizontally-rooted," a trait that may be accompanied by a feeling of wanderlust as you realize how eager you are to explore new places. People who have had the experience of adapting to different ways of living develop skills that can enable them to adjust — plant their roots, if you will — in other new environments with increasing ease. This ability to feel almost at home anywhere — but not quite as totally rooted anywhere as you once did — can be at once exhilarating and frustrating.[4]

The challenge is to develop both a deep and a wide root system: cultivating the vertical roots needed to dwell well in a local community while also nurturing a horizontal root system that enables connection to, and concern for, the wider world. As you embrace this challenge, you will explore what it means to be a citizen of the world.

In ancient Greece, the idea of a global citizen was articulated through the notion of a *kosmou polite* or "world citizen," a person who was endowed with membership in both his or her community of birth and in a larger community of humans who shared a fundamental capacity to engage in rational, enlightened thinking. This understanding of citizenship does not reject local identifications; rather, it views humans as surrounded by concentric circles in which local identifications widen to an outermost circle that includes all of humanity.[5]

🐚 Now that you have returned home, how do you hope to plant your roots? What issues and challenges exist in your home community that were also present in your host community abroad? How can you become more actively involved in your home community with the knowledge that you have gained while studying abroad? How can you blend your home and host cultural perspectives and experiences to explore the ever-widening concentric circles that are rippling out from your study abroad experience?

🐚 Answering these questions can lead to further questions about how you want to live in practical terms as a result of your time away. For example, in what kind of neighborhood do you want to live? In what kind of church do you want to worship? How will you pursue justice? Can you use mass transit more? Can you walk more? Will you change your daily diet? How will you stay connected to issues you now care about? Your study abroad experience gives you all kinds of opportunities to be intentional about who you want to become moving forward.

REMEMBER THE MEMORIES

How are you making connections between your past study abroad experience and your present and future life? As Martin Luther reminds us, "We are not now what we shall be, but we are on the way. The process is not yet finished, but it is actively going on."[6] As you return from your time abroad and resettle into your life at home, continue to challenge yourself to grow into the person that God wants you to be, sinking deep vertical roots in your home community but also remembering the importance of horizontal roots reaching out to our world.

Also, consider the advice of Alice, who studied abroad multiple times and wrote a letter to students returning from abroad as a way to keep the memories alive for her and to challenge others to do the same.

Welcome home. As you begin to adapt to life in the United States again, it's normal to feel your international experiences begin to fade. The places and faces that were once your vivid reality now appear only in treasured photos. Your reality is now wherever you find yourself in the United States. . . .

I've only been back in the States for a month now, and I continually fight to cling to the moments, the memories, the experiences which now refuse to grant me permission to look at my surroundings the same way. Yet they're beginning to drift away from me.

After a study abroad experience how does one "make the moments last" and not simply re-enter the life previously known?

It's a question I ask myself daily. How do I live now while paying homage to those who have touched my life in ways I struggle to understand?

I once was just a small town girl. I'd left the country twice before college to go on short-term mission trips and was determined to make that change in college. I wanted to travel the world. And I did. [I participated] in two semesters and one summer abroad. During a four-year span I spent time in Hong Kong, South Korea, Honduras, Guatemala, El Salvador, Uganda, and Rwanda. Each place brought different lessons to me personally, and while I'll always remember swimming in the South China Sea, rafting the Nile, and eating shark, it is the moments I hide deep down inside which altered me.

Those memories are tucked away because they're painful. They're sharp and unappealing like glass shards. Yes, in Uganda I rafted the Nile, but I also spent 30+ hours a week in hundreds of Ugandans' homes who were losing their battle with cancer and/or HIV/AIDS. When I talk about Uganda, take a guess what people often sound more interested in? You guessed it, the fact that I rafted the Nile. You see, as people we tend to shy away from anything that hurts or seems hard. I think it's simply part of our nature and is an act of self-preservation. However, it also means we often don't fully delve into the richness those experiences have to offer us.

In your head flip through the moments which make up your time abroad. Which ones made you laugh with abandon or cringe in horror or cry instantaneously or take a good hard look at your own life? Just try to focus in on one. It may hurt internally, but from that fact alone you can draw great insight. What is it about that moment which causes you to react so strongly?

Cling to those moments. Work to humbly receive the lessons they hold. . . .

Prayerfully consider [those] lessons you've learned during your time abroad. Let the severe edges of memory not be a permanent deterrent. Just like glass in the ocean, roll those memories over and over in your mind. Choose to integrate what you've learned into your life. Share what you've learned, and above all continue to process the experience.

All the best to you as you continue on in this life's journey.[7]

A CLOSING NOTE

As I finish writing this book, I am sitting in the Hanoi airport after a five-week pilgrimage of my own. This pilgrimage had its roots in the Philippines over thirty years ago when I first fell in love with Southeast Asia as a U.S. Peace Corps volunteer. Over the last thirty years, I have lived and worked in South Korea, Hong Kong, and the Netherlands, while also trying to dwell well in a number of different communities in the United States. My initial Peace Corps experience wasn't an ending but rather the beginning of a lifelong journey of exploring what it means to engage fully with the people and places where I have found myself. As my own personal pilgrimage continues, I am excited to see what God has in store for me. Likewise, as you continue your own pilgrimage, I hope you will be excited for the people and places that God will bring into your life in the months and years ahead. May you live and learn wherever you find yourself, and may you continue to move there and back.

Acknowledgments

The writing of this book about pilgrimage has seemed like a long journey — complete with all the ups and downs that any pilgrimage entails. The people that have gone before me, the people who have walked beside me, and the people I have met along the way have all been an important part of this pilgrimage.

Thanks to mentors, including Larry Neal, Christopher Edginton, and Glen Van Andel, who have gone before me, encouraging me to learn, to travel, and to seek God along the way. Thanks to the students whose voices I have tried to highlight throughout this book. Your experiences and reflections continue to inspire me to learn and grow in my own travels.

Thanks to family members, my parents, my wife Kathy, and my wonderful grown children, Isaac and Rochelle, for their constant love and support. Thanks, too, to dear friends Nick and June DeBoer and colleagues Jeff Bouman and Gail Heffner, all of whom have offered me constant encouragement and support. To fellow staff members Mwenda Ntarangwi, Dave Ellens, and Julia Smilde, thank you for taking on extra work to create the space needed for me to complete this project.

I would also like to express my appreciation to the Calvin Center for Christian Scholarship and the Kuyers International Programs Fund for providing the funding needed for key components of this overall project. Finally, thanks to the Provost's Office at Calvin College for allowing me to take a sabbatical in the Spring of 2015 to start and work on this project.

STUDENT BLOGS:

I wish to thank the following students for sharing their student blogs, written while studying off-campus at Calvin College.

- Sara Ball, semester in Spain, 2013.
- Hannah Berridge, semester in Peru, 2012.
- Grant Bouwer, semester in Honduras, 2011.
- Katherine Byl, semester in Honduras, 2014.
- Jerry Chen, semester in Ghana, 2013.
- Johnson Cochran, semester in Hungary, 2014.
- Bethany Cok, semester in Honduras, 2013.
- Lydia Cupery, semester in China, 2014.
- Ryan DeGroot, interim in Cambodia, January 2014.
- Jacob De Rooy, interim in Cambodia, January 2014.
- Lori Dykstra, semester in Peru, 2013.
- Bethany Fennema, semester in Peru, 2013.
- Leesha Gennick, semester in Peru, 2013.
- Kathryn Gerber, semester in Ghana, 2013
- Emily Harrell, semester in Peru, 2013
- Jennifer Hartstein, semester in Spain, 2013.
- Maddie Hartwig, semester in Ghana, 2014.
- Ellie Hutchinson, semester in Hungary, 2014.
- Andrew Kollen, semester in Britain, 2014.
- Hannah Kwekel, semester in Peru, 2013.
- Kate Parsons, semester in Honduras, 2013.
- Grace Ruiter, semester in Hungary, 2013.
- Lindsey Ryskamp, semester in Peru, 2013.
- Laura Sheppard, semester in Hungary, 2013.
- Ben Stark, unpublished journal of a post-graduate bicycle trip from Grand Rapids, MI to the Pacific Coast, 2013.
- Katie Van Zanen, semester at the Oregon Extension, 2012.
- Anneke Walhout, semester in Hungary, 2013.
- Molly Walton, semester in China, 2008.

STUDENT REFLECTIONS

I also wish to thank the unnamed students who contributed their reflections to this book. All have given permission for their work to be quoted.

PERMISSIONS

The following authors and publishers have generously given permission to use extended quotations from copyrighted works. If any rights have been inadvertently infringed upon, the publisher asks that the omission be excused.

Leonard J. Biallas, *Pilgrim: A Spirituality of Travel* (Quincy, IL: Franciscan Press, 2002).

Steven Bouma-Prediger and Brian Walsh, *Beyond Homelessness: Christian Faith in a Culture of Displacement* (Grand Rapids: Eerdmans, 2008).

Phil Cousineau, *The Art of Pilgrimage: The Seeker's Guide to Making Travel Sacred* (New York: MJF Books, 1998).

Jim Forest, *The Road to Emmaus: Pilgrimage as a Way of Life,* (Maryknoll, NY: Orbis, 2007).

Dustin Junker, "What My Faith in God Looks Like," from *The New York Times* July 26 © 2009 The New York Times. All rights reserved. Used by Permission and prtected by the Copyright Laws of the United States. The printing, copying, redistribution, or retransmission of this Content without express written permission is prohibited.

Richard Slimbach, *People and Places: First Steps in World Learning* (Monrovia, CA: World Wise Books, 2003).

Phoenix Sojourners, *Desks to Destinations: 25 students, 49 countries, 175 pages of reflection* (Elon, NC: Carpe Diem Press, 2014).

Kurt Ver Beek, "International Service-Learning: A Call to Caution," in *Commitment and Connection: Service-learning and Christian Higher Education*, ed. Gail Gunst Heffner and Claudia DeVries Beversluis (Latham, MD: University Press of America, 2002), 55-69.

Notes

INTRODUCTION: There is Treasure Everywhere

The epigram is taken from Rudyard Kipling, "The Explorer" in *Rudyard Kipling's Verse, Inclusive Edition, 1885-1918* (Garden City: Doubleday, Page & Co, 1922), accessed October 29, 2015, http://www.bartleby.com/364/. Public Domain.

1. Ken Bussema, Foreword to *Transformations at the Edge of the World: Forming Global Christians through the Study Abroad Experience*, ed. Ronald J. Morgan and Cynthia Toms Smedley (Abilene, TX: Abilene Christian University Press, 2010), 16.
2. The challenge of thinking deeply, acting justly, and living wholeheartedly is a part of the mission of Calvin College.

CHAPTER ONE: Why Study Abroad?

The epigrams are taken from Pico Iyer, "Why We Travel" (2000). Those interested in going deeper can find Iyer's full article online at http://picoiyerjourneys.com/index.php/category/the-inner-world/why-we-travel/. Accessed November 6, 2015; *The Art of Flight*, dir. Curt Morgan (2011), quoted in Phoenix Sojourners, *Desks to Destinations: 25 students, 49 countries, 175 pages of reflection* (Elon, NC: Carpe Diem Press, 2014), 21; *Forrest Gump*, dir. Robert Zemeckis (1994).

1. Michael McCarthy, "Follow Your Bliss: Travel with Purpose and Awareness," *Transitions Abroad Magazine* (January/February, 2008), accessed November 13, 2015, http://www.transitionsabroad.com/publications/magazine/0801/travel_abroad_with_a_purpose.shtml.
2. Pico Iyer, "Why We Travel."
3. Phoenix Sojourners ((Janet Kozlowski), *Desks to Destinations: 25 Students, 49 Countries, 175 Pages of Reflection* (Elon, NC: Carpe Viam Press, 2014), 17.
4. George Lakoff and Mark Johnson, *Metaphors We Live By* (Chicago: University of Chicago Press, 1980), 4.
5. Lakoff and Johnson, *Metaphors We Live By*, 4.
6. David I. Smith and Susan M. Felch, *Teaching and Christian Imagination* (Grand Rapids: Eerdmans, 2015), 6; citing Etienne Wenger, *Communities of Practice: Learning, Meaning, and Identity* (Cambridge: Cambridge University Press, 1996), 176.
7. Philip Barker, *Using Metaphors in Psychotherapy* (New York: Brunner/Mazel, 1985).
8. Smith and Felch, *Teaching and Christian Imagination*, 13.
9. Robert Lewis Stevenson, "El Dorado, An Essay," 1880, accessed November 13, 2015, http://www.readbookonline.net/readOnLine/8384/.
10. Donald Miller, *A Million Miles in a Thousand Years: What I Learned While Editing My Life* (Nashville: Thomas Nelson, 2009), 177-178; 247 (emphasis by the author).
11. David I. Smith, *Learning from the Stranger: Christian Faith and Cultural Diversity* (Grand Rapids: Eerdmans, 2009), 66.
12. Ross Morley as quoted by Rolf Potts in *Vagabonding: An Uncommon Guide to the Art of Long-Term World Travel* (New York: Random House, 2003), 103.
13. David James Duncan, *River Teeth: Stories and Writings* (New York: Dial Press, 1996), 2–3.

CHAPTER TWO: Seeing Study Abroad as a Pilgrimage

The epigrams are taken from Christian George, *Sacred Travels: Recovering the Ancient Practice of Pilgrimage* (Downers Grove, IL: IVP, 2006), 15; Leonard J. Biallas, *Pilgrim: A Spirituality of Travel* (Quincy, IL: Franciscan Press, 2002), x.

1. Sheryl A. Kujawa-Holbrook, *Pilgrimage, the Sacred Art: Journey to the Center of the Heart* (Woodstock, VT: Skylight Press, 2013), 3-4.
2. Biallas, *Pilgrim*.
3. Biallas, *Pilgrim*, 23.
4. Joseph Sax, *Mountains without Handrails: Reflections on the National Parks* (Ann Arbor: University of Michigan Press, 1980), 112.
5. Jim Forest, *The Road to Emmaus: Pilgrimage as a Way of Life*, (Maryknoll, NY: Orbis, 2007), xvi.
6. David I. Smith and Susan M. Felch, *Teaching and Christian Imagination* (Grand Rapids: Eerdmans, 2015), 27–28.
7. Phyllis Tickle, "Foreword" to *The Sacred Journey: The Ancient Practices*, by Charles Foster (Nashville: Thomas Nelson, 2010), x.
8. Foster, *Sacred Journey*, xvii-xviii.
9. Terry Kottman, Jeffrey S. Ashby, and Donald D. DeGraaf, *Adventure in Guidance: How to Integrate Fun into Your Guidance Program* (Alexandria, VA: American Counseling Association, 2001), 13.
10. John L. Luckner and Reldan S. Nadler, *Processing the Experience: Enhancing and Generalizing Learning* (Dubuque, IA: Kendall/Hunt, 1997), 4.
11. David Kolb, *Experiential Learning: Experience as the Source of Learning and Development* (Upper Saddle River, NJ: Prentice Hall, 1983).
12. George, *Sacred Travels*, 15.
13. Michael Yaconelli, *Dangerous Wonder: The Adventure of Childlike Faith* (Carol Stream, IL: NavPress, 2003), 25.
14. Brian Orme, "Ruined," *Relevant* (October 5, 2005), accessed November 13, 2015. http://www.relevantmagazine.com/god/church/blog/957-ruined.
15. Forrest, *Road to Emmaus*, xvii.
16. Mary Oliver, "The Summer Day" from *New and Selected Poems* (Boston: Beacon Press, 1992).

CHAPTER THREE: *Preparing the Way*

All three epigrams are taken from Phil Cousineau, *The Art of Pilgrimage: The Seeker's Guide to Making Travel Sacred* (New York: MJF Books, 1998), 23, 71 (emphasis by the author).

1. Sheryl A. Kujawa-Holbrook, *Pilgrimage, the Sacred Art: Journey to the Center of the Heart* (Woodstock, VT: Skylight Press, 2013), 185.
2. Jim Wallis, *Faith Works: Lessons from the Life of an Activist Preacher* (New York: Random House, 2000), 3.
3. Henri Nouwen quoted by Charles Ringma, *Dare to Journey — with Henri Nouwen* (Carol Stream, IL: NavPress, 2000), 46.
4. Student application, Calvin College's Spain semester, 2015.
5. Langston Hughes, *The Big Sea: An Autobiography* (1940, reprint New York: Thunder Mouth Press, 1986), 5, quoted in Linda A. Chisholm, *Charting A Hero's Journey* (New York: The International Partnership for Service-Learning and Leadership, 2000), 28-29.
6. Cousineau, *The Art of Pilgrimage*, 126.
7. Cousineau, *The Art of Pilgrimage*, 25.
8. Rick Steves quoted by Allison Vesterfelt, *Packing Light: Thoughts on Living Life with Less Baggage* (Chicago: Moody Press, 2013), 12.
9. Steve Hanna, "Why You Should Pack Your Bags Half-full: How to Pack Your Bags (and Yourself) Before You Study Abroad" University Studies Abroad Consortium (blog, n.d.), accessed November 13, 2015, http://usac.unr.edu/travel/packing/pack-half-full.

10. Vesterfelt, *Packing Light,* 252 (emphasis by the author).

11. Richard Slimbach, *People and Places: First Steps in World Learning* (Monrovia, CA: World Wise Books, 2003), 8 (emphasis by the author).

CHAPTER FOUR: *Crossing the Threshold*

The epigrams are taken from Phil Cousineau, *The Art of Pilgrimage: The Seeker's Guide to Making Travel Sacred* (New York: MJF Books, 1998), xvii; Rainer Maria Rilke, *Letters to a Young Poet,* trans. Stephen Mitchell, letter #4 (July 16, 1903), accessed November 14, 2015, http://www.carrothers.com/rilke4.htm.

1. Frederick Buechner, The *Sacred Journey* (San Francisco: Harper Books, 1982), 69.

2. Anne Hillman, "We Look with Uncertainty," quoted in Parker Palmer, "Five Questions for Crossing the Threshold," accessed November 14, 2015, http://www.onbeing.org/blog/five-questions-for-crossing-the-threshold/7167.

3. Palmer, "Five Questions."

4. Amy Patterson, "A Letter to My Students," *Spark* (Summer 2011), accessed November 14, 2015, http://www.calvin.edu/spark/past-issues/dear-patterson-students-from-past-present-and-future- .

5. Joseph Dispenza, *The Way of the Traveler: Making Every Trip a Journey of Self- Discovery,* 2nd edition (Berkeley: Avalon Travel Publishing, 2002), 40.

6. Quoted by Richard Slimbach, *People and Places: First Steps in World Learning* (Monrovia, CA: World Wise Books, (2003), 61–62.

7. Phil Cousineau, *The Art of Pilgrimage: The Seeker's Guide to Making Travel Sacred* (New York: MJF Books, 1998), 63-64.

8. "A Prayer for Pilgrims," accessed November 13, 2015, https://www.caminodesantiago.me/community/threads/on-the-feast-of-st-james-a-pilgrims-prayer.28163/.

CHAPTER FIVE: *Embracing the Journey*

The epigrams are taken from the Hong Kong Outward Bound School; Donald Miller, *A Million Miles in a Thousand Years: What I Learned While Editing My Life* (Nashville: Thomas Nelson, 2009), 59.

1. Frederick Buechner, *The Sacred Journey: A Memoir of Early Days* (New York: Harper Press, 1991), 64.

2. Alexandra Horowitz, *On Looking: Eleven Walks with Expert Eyes* (New York: Scribner, 2013).

3. Nicholas Wolterstorff, "It Takes Two Eyes," commencement address at Calvin College College (May, 2008), accessed November 14, 2015, https://www.calvin.edu/dotAsset/4c400d13-9b9d-4c91-9289-b0591c3bb17a.pdf.

4. Bella DePaulo, "Most Can't Stand to be Alone with Their Thoughts. Can You?" (July 7, 2014), accessed November 13, 2015, https://www.psychologytoday.com/blog/living-single/201407/most-can-t-stand-be-alone-their-thoughts-can-you.

5. Pico Iyer quoted by Maria Popova, "Pico Iyer on What Leonard Cohen Taught Us About Presence and the Art of Stillness" (November 10, 2014), accessed November 13, 2015, http://www.brainpickings.org/2014/11/10/pico-iyer-the-art-of-stillness/

6. John V. Taylor, *The Primal Vision: Christian Presence Amid African Religion* (London: SCM Press, 1963), 188-189.

7. James D. Hunter, *To Change the World: The Irony, Tragedy, and Possibility of Christianity in the Late Modern World* (Oxford: Oxford University Press, 2010).

8. Vincent Harding, *Hope and History: Why We Must Share the Story of the Movement* (Maryknoll, NY: Orbis Books, 2010).

9. Student Reflection, "Final Essay: What Do You Want to Remember from This Semester?", semester in Hungary, Calvin College, 2014.

10. Joseph Dispenza, *The Way of the Traveler: Making Every Trip a Journey of Self- Discovery,* 2nd edition (Berkeley: Avalon Travel Publishing, 2002), 20.

11. Shawn Wong, "The Craft of Good Travel Writing," (unpublished syllabus, University of Washington, n.d.).

CHAPTER SIX: Cultivating Your Intellectual Curiosity

The epigrams are taken from Albert Einstein, Letter to Carl Seelig (11 March 1952), Einstein Archives 39-013, as quoted on Wikiquote, accessed November 14, 2015, https://en.wikiquote.org/wiki/Albert_Einstein; Leonard J. Biallas, *Pilgrim: A Spirituality of Travel* (Quincy, IL: Franciscan Press, 2002), 40.

1. Thomas Aquinas College (n.d.), founding documents, http://thomasaquinas.edu/about/founding-document-7.
2. Student reflection, January interim entitled "Environmental Issues and Urban Sprawl," Calvin College, 2005.
3. Albert Einstein quoted by Donald Latumahina, "Why Curiosity is Important and How to Develop It," n.d., accessed November 13, 2015, http://www.lifehack.org/articles/productivity/4-reasons-why-curiosity-is-important-and-how-to -develop-it.html.
4. Robert Gordon, *Going Abroad: Traveling Like an Anthropologist* (Boulder, CO: Paradigm, 2010), 5.
5. Richard Slimbach, *People and Places: First Steps in World Learning* (Monrovia, CA: World Wise Books, 2003), 90-96.

CHAPTER SEVEN: Building Cultural Competence

The epigrams are taken from Kelly Larsen, Don DeGraaf, Elisa Ditta, and Cynthia Slagter, "The Long-term Personal and Professional Benefits of Participating in Off-Campus Programs," *Frontiers Journal* (Fall/Winter, 2013), accessed November 14, 2015, http://www.frontiersjournal.com/documents/Frontiers-XXIII-Fall2013DeGraafSlagterLarsenDitta.pdf; Peace Corps Volunteer, Guatemala, *Culture Matters: The Peace Corps Cross-Cultural Workbook* (Peace Corps Information and Collection Exchange, 2009), 114, accessed November 14, 2015, http://www.peacecorps.gov; Anais Nin quoted in Kate Berardo and Darla K. Deardorff, *Building Cultural Competence: Innovative Activities and Models* (Sterling, VA: Stylus, 2012), 62.

1. Larsen, DeGraaf, Ditta, and Slagter, "The Long-term."
2. David I. Smith, *Learning from the Stranger: Christian Faith and Cultural Diversity* (Grand Rapids: Eerdmans, 2009), 6.
3. Staff, "Are You Practicing Cultural Humility? The Key to Success in Cultural Competence," April, 2007, *California Health Advocates*, accessed November 13, 2015, http://www.cahealthadvocates.org/news/disparities/2007/are-you.html.
4. National Center for Cultural Competence, Georgetown University, "Definitions of Cultural Competence," accessed May 1, 2015, http://www.ncccurricula.info/culturalcompetence.html.
5. Staff. (n.d.). Sunglasses fable from a training manual of Global Perspective in Education (unpublished paper).
6. Ruth G. Dean, "The Myth of Cross-cultural Competence," *Families in Society: The Journal of Contemporary Human Service* 82, no. 6 (2001): 623-30, quote at 624.
7. Linda Hunt as cited on "Are You Practicing Cultural Humility?"
8. Craig Moncho, "Cultural Humility Part 1: What is 'Cultural Humility'?" *The Social Work Practitioner* (August 19, 2013), accessed November 13, 2015, http://thesocialworkpractitioner.com/2013/08/19/cultural-humility-part-i-what-is-cultural-humility/ (emphasis by the author).
9. Craig Moncho, "Cultural Humility, Part II — Promoting Cultural Humility in the Workplace," *The Social Work Practitioner* (August 26, 2013), accessed November 13, 2015, http://thesocialworkpractitioner.com/2013/08/26/cultural-humility -part-ii-promoting-cultural-humility-in-the-workplace/ (emphasis by the author).

10. Robert Gordon, *Going Abroad: Traveling Like an Anthropologist* (Boulder, CO: Paradigm, 2010), 9.
11. Smith, *Learning from the Stranger*, 94.

CHAPTER EIGHT: *Being Free*

The first epigram is taken from St. Augustine, *The Confessions of St. Augustine*, trans. Maria Boulding (New York: Vintage, 1998), 10(15), p. 206.

1. Cynthia Slagter and Mary Hulst, "Off-Campus Programs Devotions," (unpublished manuscript, Calvin College, 2010).
2. Timothy Ferris, interview transcripts for the documentary *Thomas Jefferson*, dir. Ken Burns (1997), accessed November 14, 2015, https://www.pbs.org/jefferson/archives/interviews/Ferris.htm.
3. Stephen Mitchell, interview transcripts for the documentary *Thomas Jefferson*, dir. Ken Burns (1997), accessed November 14, 2015, https://www.pbs.org/jefferson/archives/interviews/Mitchell.htm
4. Phoenix Sojourners (Caroline Anderson), *Desks to Destinations: 25 Students, 49 Countries, 175 Pages of Reflection* (Elon, NC: Carpe Viam Press, 2014), 36-37.
5. Phoenix Sojourners (Jordan Joshua), *Desks to Destinations*, 40.
6. E. Pedersen, J. LaBrie, J. Hummer, M. Larimer, and C. Lee, "Heavier Drinking American College Students May Self-select into Study Abroad Programs: An Examination of Sex and Ethnic Differences within a High-risk Group," *Addictive Behaviors* 35 (2010): 844–47.
7. Staff, "Administrator Guide: Alcohol Awareness in Study Abroad, " The Center for Global Education, Graduate School of Education and Information Studies, University of California at Los Angeles (unpublished paper, n.d.).
8. Nancy Newport, "Sexual Harassment and Prevention in College Students Studying Abroad," Spring/Summer, 2000. Accessed November 13, 2015. http://globaled.us/safeti/v1n22000ed_sexual_harassment_and_prevention.asp .
9. Tara Isabella Burton, "The Dangers of Traveling while Female," (August 27, 2013), accessed November 13, 2015 http://www.salon.com/2013/08/27/dangers_of_traveling_while_female/
10. Pennylyn Dykstra-Pruim, Cambodian journal, (unpublished manuscript, interim term class to Cambodia, Calvin College, 2014).
11. Student Reflection, "Final Essay: What Do You Want to Remember from This Semester?", semester in Hungary, Calvin College, 2014.
12. Ben Dixon, "How I Encountered Calvinism in Africa," *Perspectives* (November, 2010): 14–17, quote at page 14, accessed November 13, 2015, http://perspectivesjournal.org/blog/2010/11/01/how-i-encountered-calvinism-in-africa/.
13. Edwin Hays, "A Prayer for Pilgrims and Journeyers," World Youth Day, Sydney, Australia, (July, 2008), accessed November 13, 2015 http://www.cbmidwest.org/documents/worldyouthday.pdf.

CHAPTER NINE: *Taking Risks*

The first and third epigrams are taken from Harry Crosby, *Transit of Venus* (Paris: Black Sun Press, 1931), ix; Daniel L. Dustin, *The Wilderness Within: Reflections on Leisure and Life*, 2nd edition (Champaign, IL: Sagamore, 1999), 5.

1. Peter Gwin, "The Mystery of Risk: Why Do We Do It? What Makes an Explorer Face Danger and Yet Press on When Others Would Turn Back," *National Geographic* (June, 2013), accessed November 13, 2015, http://ngm.nationalgeographic.com/2013/06/125-risk-takers/gwin-text.
2. Donald G. DeGraaf (unpublished reflection, Philippines, 1983).

3. Emily Sussell, "Six Risks to Take that Will Improve Your Travels (and Your Life)," *BootsnAll* (December 10, 2013), accessed November 13, 2015, http://www.bootsnall.com/articles/12-11/six-risks-to-take-on-your-round-the-world-trip.html.

CHAPTER TEN: *Using Technology Wisely*

The epigrams are taken from Daniel L. Dustin, *The Wilderness Within: Reflections on Leisure and Life*, 3rd edition (Champaign, IL: Sagamore, 2006), 112; Pico Iyer, "The Joy of Quiet," *New York Times* (December 29, 2011*)*, accessed November 13, 2015, http://www.nytimes.com/2012/01/01/opinion/sunday/the-joy-of-quiet.html?_r=0; Sherry Turkle, *Reclaiming Conversation: The power of talk in a digital age* (New York: Penguin Press, 2015), 16.

1. Thornton Wilder quoted by Don Postema, *Space for God: Study and Practice of Spirituality and Prayer* (Grand Rapids: Faith Alive Christian Resources, 1997), 16.
2. Sarah Woolley, "Constantly Connected: The Impact of Social Media and the Advancement of Technology on the Study Abroad Experience," *Elon Journal of Undergraduate Research in Communications* 4, no. 2 (Fall, 2013): 36–46.
3. Justin Pope, "American Students Abroad Pushed Out of Bubbles," *USA Today* (October 2, 2011), accessed November 14, 2015, http://usatoday30.usatoday.com/news/education/story/2011-09-25/study-abroad/50550430/1.
4. Pope, "American Students Abroad."
5. Sherry Turkle, "Connected, But Alone?" TED talk transcript (February, 2012), accessed November 13, 2015, https://www.ted.com/talks/sherry_turkle_alone_together/transcript?language=en.
6. Turkle, "Connected, But Alone?"
7. Sherry Turkle, *Alone Together: Why We Expect More from Technology and Less from Each Other* (New York: Basic Books, 2012), 278.
8. Pope, "American Students Abroad,"
9. Daniele Quercia, "Happy Maps," TED talk transcript (November, 2014), accessed November 13, 2015, http://www.ted.com/talks/daniele_quercia_happy_maps#t-15530.
10. Craig Detweiler, "Smiling for Auschwitz Selfies, and Crying into the Digital Wilderness," CNN Opinion (July 22, 2014), accessed November 13, 2015, http://religion.blogs.cnn.com/2014/07/22/defending-the-auschwitz-selfie/?hpt=hp_c3—.
11. Melibee Global, "Personal and Pop Culture: Practical Pre-Departure Planning for the Global Sojourner," 2015. This excellent resource is available at melibeeglobal.com.
12. Iyer, "The Joy of Quiet."

CHAPTER ELEVEN: *Practicing Hospitality*

The epigrams are taken from an unpublished student reflection, semester in Honduras, Calvin College, 2014; Ken Kraybill, "Hospitality — Creating Space for the Stranger," (unpublished reflection, n.d).

1. St. Benedict, *The Holy Rule of St. Benedict,* Chapter 53, "Of the Reception of Guests," trans. B. Verheyen, 1949, accessed November 13, 2015, https://web.archive.org/web/20140221065459/http://www.ccel.org/ccel/benedict/rule2/files/rule2.html#ch53.
2. Leonard J. Biallas, *Pilgrim: A Spirituality of Travel* (Quincy, IL: Franciscan Press, 2002), 313–14.
3. Henri J. M. Nouwen, *The Wounded Healer: Ministry in Contemporary Society* (New York: Doubleday, 1979), 92.
4. Student reflection, semester in Honduras, Calvin College, 2014.
5. Kathleen Norris, *Dakota: A Spiritual Geography,* (Boston: Ticknor and Fields, 1993), 112, quoted by Linda A., *Charting the Hero's Journey* (New York: International Partnership for Service-Learning and Leadership, 2000), 88–89.

6. Donald DeGraaf (unpublished reflection, Philippines, 1983).

7. Donald DeGraaf (unpublished reflection, Ghana, 2012).

8. Biallas, *Pilgrim*, 314.

9. Cornelius Plantinga, *Not the Way It's Supposed to Be: A Breviary of Sin* (Grand Rapids: Eerdmans, 1995), 10.

10. Jim Forest, *The Road to Emmaus: Pilgrimage as a Way of Life* (Maryknoll, NY: Orbis, 2007), 174-175.

11. Henri J. M. Nouwen, *Reaching Out: The Three Movements of the Spirit* (1975; reprint New York: Doubleday, 1986), 49, 55-56, 66.

12. Nouwen, *The Wounded Healer*, 91.

13. Christine Sine, "A Litany of Hospitality" (2013), accessed November 13, 2015, re-worship.blogspot.com/2013/07 /litany-of-hospitality.html.

CHAPTER TWELVE: Dwelling Well, Traveling Well

The epigrams are taken from Langston Hughes, *The Big Sea: An Autobiography* (1940, reprint, New York: Thunder Mouth Press, 1986), 67, quoted in Linda A. Chisholm, *Charting A Hero's Journey* (New York: International Partnership for Service-Learning and Leadership, 2000), 119; Student reflection, in research study by Kelly Larsen, Don De Graaf, Elisa Ditta, and Cynthia Slagter, "The Long-term Personal and Professional Benefits of Participating in Off-Campus Programs," *Frontiers Journal* (Fall/Winter, 2013), accessed November 14, 2015, http://www.frontiersjournal.com/documents/Frontiers-XXIII-Fall2013DeGraafSlagter-LarsenDitta.pdf;. G. K. Chesterton, *Orthodoxy* in *The Collected Works of G.K. Chesterton*, Vol. 1 (San Francisco: Ignatius Press, 1986), 212-213.

1. Steven Bouma-Prediger and Brian Walsh, *Beyond Homelessness: Christian Faith in a Culture of Displacement* (Grand Rapids: Eerdmans, 2008), 61.

2. Susan M. Felch, "Home: Psalm 84" (unpublished chapel talk, International Education Week, Calvin College, November 17, 2014).

3. Sharon Daloz Parks, "Home and Pilgrimage: Companion Metaphors or Personal and Social Transformation," *Soundings* 72 (1989): 297-315, quote at page 303 (emphasis by author).

4. Elie Wiesel, "Longing for Home" in *The Longing for Home*, ed. Leroy S. Rouner (Notre Dame, IN: University of Notre Dame Press, 1996), 19.

5. Emily Wetzel, "Home: A State of Being," (unpublished chapel talk, International Education Week, Calvin College, November 17, 2014).

6. Pico Iyer, "Where is Home?" June, 2013, accessed November 14, 2015, http://www.ted.com/talks/ pico_iyer_where_is_home

7. Bouma-Prediger and Walsh, *Beyond Homelessness*, 1–7 (excerpts).

8. Wendell Berry quoted by Brian Wattchow and Mike Brown, *A Pedagogy of Place: Outdoor Education for a Changing World* (Clayton, Victoria: Monash University, 2011), ix.

9. Nicole Vedder, "The Moment I Felt at Home in Ghana" (unpublished chapel reflection, Calvin College, February 8, 2012).

10. Scott Russell Sanders, *Staying Put: Making a Home in a Restless World* (Boston: Beacon, 1993), 120-121, 106.

11. J. R. R. Tolkien, *The Fellowship of the Ring* (1954, reprint New York: Ballantine, 1965), 231.

12. Alistair Humphreys, *Microadventures: Local Discoveries, Great Escapes* (London: William Collins, 2015).

13. Jason Roberts, *A Sense of the World: How a Blind Man Became the World's Greatest Traveler* (San Francisco: Harper, 2006).

14. Jason Roberts, "About the Blind Traveler," accessed November 14, 2015, http://jasonroberts.net/a-sense-of-the-worl /about-the-blind-traveler/.

15. Roberts, "About the Blind Traveler."

16. "The World's Greatest Traveler: A Conversation with Jason Roberts," National Public Radio (2006), accessed November 14, 2015, http://www.npr.org/templates/transcript/transcript.php?storyId=5675082.

CHAPTER THIRTEEN: Experiencing Thin and Dark Places

The epigrams are taken from Eric Weiner, "Where Heaven and Earth Come Closer," *New York Times* (March 9, 2012), accessed November 2015, http://www.nytimes.com/2012/03/11/travel/thin-places-where-we-are-jolted-out-of-old-ways-of-seeing-the-world.html.

1. Weiner, "Where Heaven."

2. Sigurd F. Olsen, *Listening Point* (1958, reprint Minneapolis: University of Minnesota Press, 1997), 5.

3. Weiner, "Where Heaven.

4. The following summary is indebted to Mark D. Roberts, "What are Thin Places? How Should We Think about Them in Light of Scripture" (2012), accessed November 14, 2015, www.patheos.com/blogs/markdroberts/series/thin-places/#ixzz3VAjeg9hK.

5. Jim Forest, *The Road to Emmaus: Pilgrimage as a Way of Life* (Maryknoll, NY: Orbis, 2007), 100.

CHAPTER FOURTEEN: Living in the Middle

The epigrams are taken from F. Scott Fitzgerald, "The Crack Up," *Esquire Magazine* (February, 1936), accessed November 14, 2015, http://www.esquire.com/news-politics/a4310/the-crack-up/; Michael Hurd, "Margaret Thatcher: in Her Own Words," Capitalism Magazine (10 April 2013), accessed November 15, 2015, http://capitalismmagazine.com/2013/04/thatcher-the-lady-who-was-not-for-turning/.

1. Class blog, "Some Fun, Some Hard Questions, All Good," January interim, "In Search of Clean Water in Kenya," Calvin College, January 9, 2014.

CHAPTER FIFTEEN: Dealing with Adversity

The epigrams are taken from G. K. Chesterton, "On Running After One's Hat," in *On Running After One's Hat and Other Whimsies* (New York: Robert M. McBride & Co., 1935), accessed November 14, 2015, https://archive.org/stream/onrunningafteron027309mbp/onrunningafteron027309mbp_djvu.txt; Theodore Roosevelt (November 4, 1910), quoted in "The Sayings of Theodore Roosevelt," accessed November 14, 2015, http://www.frfrogspad.com/trsaid.htm; Kurt Vonnegut quoted in Leonard J. Biallas, "Traveling with a Sense of Passion and Wonder," *National Catholic Reporter Online,* accessed November 14, 2015, http://natcath.org/NCR_Online/archives2/2002b/041202/041202t.htm.

1. "travel, n." *The Oxford English Dictionary.*

2. Material presented on culture shock is taken from Susan C. Schneider and Jean-Louis Barsoux, *Managing across Cultures, 2nd edition* (Upper Saddle River: NJ: Prentice Hall, 2003), 188; Richard Slimbach, *People and Places: First Steps in World Learning* (Monrovia, CA: World Wise Books, 2003), 64–66; Gert Jan Hofstede, Paul B. Pedersen and Geert Hofstede, *Exploring Culture: Exercises, Stories, and Synthetic Cultures* (Boston: Intercultural Press, 2002), 23.

3. Slimbach, *People and Places,* 66 (emphasis by author).

4. Dustin Junker, "What My Faith in God Looks Like," *New York Times* (July 20, 2009), accessed May 5, 2015, http://www.nytimes.com/2009/07/26/education/edlife/26god.html?ref=edlife&_r=0 (). Printed by permission.

5. Student reflection, "Final Essay: What Do You Want to Remember from This Semester?", semester in Hungary, Calvin College, 2014.

6. Henri Nouwen quoted by Phileena Heuertz, *Pilgrimage of the Soul: Contemplative Spirituality for the Active Life* (Downers Grove, IL: IVP, 2007), 156-157.

7. Jim Forest, *The Road to Emmaus: Pilgrimage as a Way of Life* (Maryknoll, NY: Orbis, 2007), 135, 144.

8. Joey DeYoung, journal written during the January interim "Experiential Education: Facilitating Personal Growth," Calvin College, 2008.

CHAPTER SIXTEEN: Doing Justice

The first epigram is taken from "Irresponsibility" motivational poster, accessed May 12, 2015, www.despair.com;

1. Timothy Keller, *Generous Justice: How God's Grace Makes Us Just* (New York: Riverhead Books, 2012), 3-4.

2. Keller, *Generous Justice*, 10 (emphasis by the author).

3. Keller, *Generous Justice*, 10-11.

4. *The Oxford English Dictionary* defines "privilege" as "a right, advantage, or immunity granted to or enjoyed by an individual, corporation of individuals, etc., beyond the usual rights or advantages of others; spec. (a) an exemption from a normal duty, liability, etc.; (b) enjoyment of some benefit (as wealth, education, standard of living, etc.) above the average or that deemed usual or necessary for a particular group (in pl. sometimes contrasted with rights)."

5. Talya Zemach-Bersen, "American Students Abroad Can't be 'Global Citizens,'" *The Chronicle of Higher Education* (March 7, 2008), 34A, accessed November 14, 2015, http://www.yale.edu/yalecol/international/predeparture/pdf/GlobalCitizens.pdf.

6. Wellesley College, "Responsible travel report," 2015, accessed November 14, 2015, https://www.wellesley.edu/ois/handbook/sustainable-study-abroad.

7. Christopher Hirschler, "How 'Sustainable' Universities Can Decrease the Carbon Footprint of Study Abroad Programs" *One Green Planet* (May 11, 2015), accessed November 14, 2015, http://www.onegreenplanet.org/environment/universities-carbon-footprint-of-study-abroad-programs/.

8. Rebecca Spurr, "Student Project: Environmental Science in Australia: An Environmental Analysis," semester in Australia, St. Olaf College (2010), accessed November 14, 2015, http://wp.stolaf.edu/environmental-studies/files/2013/10/Spurr_ESAustralia_footprints.pdf (emphasis by the author).

9. Elizabeth Redden, "Sustaining Study Abroad," *Inside Higher Education* (March 12, 2009), accessed November 14, 2015, https://www.insidehighered.com/news/2009/03/12/studyabroad.

10. Hirschler, "How 'Sustainable' Universities."

11. Bishop Ken Untener, "Archbishop Oscar Romero Prayer: A Step along the Way," November, 1979, Saginaw, MI. Drafted for a homily by Cardinal John Dearden for a celebration of departed priests as a reflection on the anniversary of the martyrdom of Bishop Romero, accessed November 14, 2015, http://www.usccb.org/prayer-and-worship/prayers-and-devotions/prayers/archbishop_romero_prayer.cfm.

CHAPTER SEVENTEEN: Engaging Others from Different Faith Traditions

The epigrams are taken from Leonard J. Biallas, *Pilgrim: A Spirituality of Travel* (Quincy, IL: Franciscan Press, 2002), 325; John F. Kennedy, "Letter to the National Conference of Christians and Jews Conference" (October 26, 1960), accessed November 16, 2015, http://www.jfklink.com/speeches/joint/app24_christiansandjews.html.

1. Student Reflection, "Final Essay: What Do You Want to Remember from This Semester?", semester in Hungary, Calvin College, 2014.

2. Donald DeGraaf (unpublished reflection, Philippines, 1983).

3. E. Stanley Jones, *The Christ of the Indian Road* (New York: Abington Press, 1925).

4. Jones, *The Christ of the Indian Road*, 118-120.

5. David Hoekema, (unpublished newsletter, semester in Ghana, Calvin College, 2010).

6. World Council of Churches, "Christian Witness in a Multi-religious World," (June 28, 2011), accessed November 14, 2015, http://www.pcusa.org/resource/christian-witness-multi-religious-world-recommenda/.

CHAPTER EIGHTEEN: *Learning to Serve, Serving to Learn*

The epigrams are taken from Humphrey Tonkin, "Service-learning: Making Education more Meaningful," *International Educator* (Fall/Winter, 1999), quoted by Richard Slimbach, *People and Places: First Steps in World Learning* (Monrovia, CA: World Wise Books, 2003), 130; Richard Felix quoted by Slimbach, *People and Places*, 133; Aboriginal Activist Group, Queensland, 1970s. This quote is often attributed to Lila Watson, who said she was "not comfortable being credited for something that had been born of a collective process" — but the attribution here is one she accepted, accessed November 14, 2015, http://invisiblechildren.com/blog/2012/04/04/the-origin-of-our-liberty-is-bound-together/.

1. Ernest Boyer, address at Azusa Pacific University (1991), quoted by Slimbach, *People and Places*, 128.

2. Ernest Boyer, "Creating the New American College," *Chronicle of Higher Education* (March 9, 1994): A48 (emphasis by the author).

3. Robert G. Bringle and Julie A. Hatcher, "International Service Learning," in *International Service Learning: Conceptual Frameworks and Research*, ed. Robert G. Bringle, Julie A. Hatcher, and Steven G. Jones (Sterling, VA: Stylus, 2011), 3–29, quote at page 11.

4. Kurt Ver Beek, "International Service-Learning: A Call to Caution," in *Commitment and Connection: Service-learning and Christian Higher Education*, ed. Gail Gunst Heffner and Claudia DeVries Beversluis (Latham, MD: University Press of America, 2002), 55-69, quote at pages 55-56.

5. Ver Beek, "International Service-Learning," 60.

6. Ver Beek, "International Service-Learning," 60-61.

7. Ver Beek, "International Service-Learning," 62-63 (emphasis by author).

8. Ver Beek, "International Service-Learning," 63.

9. Ver Beek, "International Service-Learning," 64.

10. Ver Beek, "International Service-Learning," 66.

11. Ver Beek, "International Service-Learning," 67 (emphasis by the author).

12. Daniela Papi Thornton quoted in Abbey Murphy, "Daniela Papi Thornton on Making International Service more Meaningful," *Her Campus Notre Dame* (April 3, 2015), accessed November 14, 2015, , http://www.hercampus.com/school/notre-dame/daniela-papi-thornton-making-international-service-more-meaningful.

13. John McKnight, *The Careless Society: Community and Its Counterfeits* (New York: Basic Books, 1996), 178–79.

14. Jane Addams, *Twenty Years at Hull-House* (1910, reprint New York: Signet Classics, 1999), 55.

15. Doug Wellman, Dan Dustin, Karla Henderson, and Roger Moore, *Service Living: Building Community Through Public Parks and Recreation* (State College, PA: Venture Publishing, 2008), 89.

CHAPTER NINETEEN: *Ending Well*

The epigrams are taken from Corrie ten Boom, *The Hiding Place* (New York: Bantam Books, 1984), viii. Student reflection from France in Kelly Larsen, Don De Graaf, Elisa Ditta, and Cynthia Slagter, "The Long-term Personal and Professional Benefits of Participating in Off-Campus Programs," *Frontiers Journal* (Fall/Winter, 2013), accessed November 14, 2015, http://www.frontiersjournal.com/documents/Frontiers-XXIII-Fall2013DeGraafSlagterLarsenDitta.pdf; Student Reflection from Mexico from

Laura Montgomery and Mary Docter, "'With Open Eyes': Cultivating World Christians through Intercultural Awareness," in *Transformations at the Edge of the World: Forming Global Christians through the Study Abroad Experience*, ed. Ronald J. Morgan and Cynthia Toms Smedley (Abilene, TX: Abilene Christian University Press, 2010), 130.

1. Yann Martel, *Life of Pi* (Orlando: Harcourt, 2001), 285-286.
2. T.S. Eliot, *The Four Quartets* (New York: Mariner Books, 1968), 27.
3. Student reflection, "Final Essay: What Do You Want to Remember from This Semester?" semester in Hungary, Calvin College, 2014.
4. Student reflection. "Journal: On Going Home," semester in Hungary, Calvin College, 2013.
5. Sarah Dornbos, "A Consortium Student's Prayer of Blessing for Kenya," consortium program at Daystar University Kenya, Coalition of Christian Colleges and Universities, unpublished, n.d.

CHAPTER TWENTY: *Re-crossing the Threshold*

The epigrams are taken from Christian George, *Sacred Travels: Recovering the Ancient Practice of Pilgrimage* (Downers Grove, IL: IVP, 2006), 164; John Mandeville as quoted in Phil Cousineau, *The Art of Pilgrimage: The Seeker's Guide to Making Travel Sacred* (New York: MJF Books, 1998), 226.

1. Brother John of Taizé quoted in Paul H. W. Rohde, *And Grace Will Lead Me Home: A Guide for Pilgrim Journals* (Eugene, OR: Resource Publications, 2012), xiii.
2. Personal email correspondence, student/faculty exchange on returning home from abroad, 2012.
3. Phoenix Sojourners (Whitney Ballbach), *Desks to Destinations: 25 Students, 49 Countries, 175 Pages of Reflection* (Elon, NC: Carpe Viam Press, 2014), 84.
4. Phoenix Sojourners (Maggie Achey), *Desks to Destinations*, 113.
5. Student reflections, "Final Essay: What Do You Want to Remember from This Semester?", semester in Hungary, Calvin College, 2014.
6. Dorothy Bass, "Pilgrimage Guide," Holden Village, quoted in Rohde, *And Grace Will Lead Me Home*, 132.

CHAPTER TWENTY-ONE: *Bringing the World Home*

The first two epigrams are taken from Dr. Seuss, *The Lorax* (New York: Random House, (1971), n.p; Theodore Roosevelt, *Autobiography*, in *The Works of Theodore Roosevelt National Edition*, Vol. 20 (New York: Charles Scribner's Sons, 1926), 327.

1. Peace Corp staff, "Bring the World Home," Promoting the Third Goal, n.d., http://www.peacecorps.gov/resources/returned/thirdgoal/.
2. Rudyard Kipling, "We and They" in *Debits and Credits* (New York: Doubleday, 1926), *Project Gutenberg Australia*, accessed November 14, 2015, http://gutenberg.net.au/ebooks06/0603771h.html#28. Public Domain.
3. Nora Gallagher, *Things Seen and Unseen: A Year Lived in Faith* (New York: Vintage Books, 1998), 72.
4. James L. Citron and Vija G. Mendelson, "Coming Home: Relationships, Roots, and Unpacking," *Transitions Abroad Magazine* (July/August 2005), accessed November 14, 2015, http://www.transitionsabroad.com/publications/magazine/0507/coming_home_from_study_abroad.shtml.
5. Martha Nussbaum, "Patriotism and Cosmopolitanism," in *For Love of Country?* ed. Joshua Cohen (Boston: Beacon Press, 1996), 7-9.
6. Martin Luther, *Career of the Reformer II*, Luther's Works, Vol. 32, ed. George W. Forell and Helmut T. Lehman (Philadelphia: Muhlenberg Press, 1958), 24.
7. Alice Keys, "A Letter to Those Returning Home" (unpublished reflection, 2014).

Index

CPSIA information can be obtained
at www.ICGtesting.com
Printed in the USA
LVOW09s1555171017
552750LV00009B/536/P